HowExp to Jol Careers

Discover 101+ Popular Jobs and Careers Across Various Industries, Maximize Your Potential, and Achieve Your Dream Career

HowExpert

For more tips related to this topic, visit HowExpert.com/jobscareers.

Recommended Resources

- HowExpert.com – How To Guides on All Topics from A to Z by Everyday Experts.
- HowExpert.com/free – Free HowExpert Email Newsletter.
- HowExpert.com/books – HowExpert Books
- HowExpert.com/courses – HowExpert Courses
- HowExpert.com/clothing – HowExpert Clothing
- HowExpert.com/membership – HowExpert Membership Site
- HowExpert.com/affiliates – HowExpert Affiliate Program
- HowExpert.com/jobs – HowExpert Jobs
- HowExpert.com/writers – Write About Your #1 Passion/Knowledge/Expertise & Become a HowExpert Author.
- HowExpert.com/resources – Additional HowExpert Recommended Resources
- YouTube.com/HowExpert – Subscribe to HowExpert YouTube.
- Instagram.com/HowExpert – Follow HowExpert on Instagram.
- Facebook.com/HowExpert – Follow HowExpert on Facebook.
- TikTok.com/@HowExpert – Follow HowExpert on TikTok.

Publisher's Foreword

Dear HowExpert Reader,

HowExpert publishes quick 'how to' guides on all topics from A to Z by everyday experts.

At HowExpert, our mission is to discover, empower, and maximize everyday people's talents to ultimately make a positive impact in the world for all topics from A to Z...one everyday expert at a time!

HowExpert guides are written by everyday people just like you and me, who have a passion, knowledge, and expertise for a specific topic.

We take great pride in selecting everyday experts who have a passion, real-life experience in a topic, and excellent writing skills to teach you about the topic you are also passionate about and eager to learn.

We hope you get a lot of value from our HowExpert guides, and it can make a positive impact on your life in some way. All of our readers, including you, help us continue living our mission of positively impacting the world for all spheres of influences from A to Z.

If you enjoyed one of our HowExpert guides, then please take a moment to send us your feedback from wherever you got this book.

Thank you, and I wish you all the best in all aspects of life.

To your success,

Byungjoon "BJ" Min 민병준
Founder & Publisher of HowExpert
HowExpert.com

PS...If you are also interested in becoming a HowExpert author, then please visit our website at HowExpert.com/writers. Thank you & again, all the best! John 3:16

Table of Contents

Book Overview

If you're ready to discover your dream career, unlock the pathway with HowExpert Guide to Jobs and Careers! This comprehensive guide is meticulously crafted to help you explore 101 popular jobs and careers across a wide array of industries, equipping you with the knowledge to maximize your potential and achieve your ultimate career goals.

Introduction

Welcome to the world of careers, where the possibilities are vast and the opportunities are endless. This guide begins with an engaging introduction that underscores the significance of career exploration and the benefits of finding the right career fit. Learn how to effectively utilize this guide to navigate your career journey with confidence.

Chapter 1: STEM Careers

Begin your exploration with the dynamic field of STEM. Discover the exciting roles of a Software Developer, Data Scientist, Mechanical Engineer, and more. Each career profile offers an in-depth look into the responsibilities, required skills, educational pathways, work environments, career trajectories, and expert tips for success.

Chapter 2: Medical and Healthcare Careers

Delve into the rewarding world of medical and healthcare professions. Explore the paths of a Registered Nurse, Physician Assistant, Pharmacist, and others. Gain comprehensive insights into what each role entails, the skills and education needed, typical work settings, career growth opportunities, and practical advice to excel.

Chapter 3: Business and Finance Careers

Uncover the opportunities within business and finance. From Financial Analysts and Marketing Managers to Entrepreneurs, this chapter provides detailed descriptions of each role, outlining the necessary skills and qualifications, work environments, potential for career advancement, and strategies for achieving success.

Chapter 4: Education Careers

Shape the future by pursuing a career in education. Learn about the vital roles of Elementary School Teachers, College Professors, School Counselors, and more. Understand the requirements, work conditions, career paths, and essential tips to thrive in the education sector.

Chapter 5: Creative and Media Careers

Harness your creativity and explore careers in media and design. Whether you aspire to be a Graphic Designer, Journalist, Film Director, or Social Media Manager, this chapter provides a thorough overview of each role, including required competencies, educational backgrounds, typical work environments, career growth potential, and practical advice.

Chapter 6: Legal Careers

Step into the legal arena with careers such as Lawyer, Paralegal, and Judge. This chapter offers a detailed look at each profession, covering job responsibilities, necessary skills and education, work settings, career progression, and professional tips to excel in the legal field.

Chapter 7: Trades and Technical Careers

Explore hands-on and technical careers like Electrician, Plumber, and HVAC Technician. Each career profile details the role, skills and training required, work environments, opportunities for advancement, and practical advice for success in the trades and technical sectors.

Chapter 8: Hospitality and Service Careers

Enter the world of hospitality and service. Discover the roles of a Chef, Hotel Manager, Event Planner, and others. This chapter provides insights into what each career entails, the skills and education needed, typical work settings, career growth opportunities, and tips for excelling in the hospitality and service industries.

Chapter 9: Retail and Sales Careers

Learn about dynamic careers in retail and sales. From Retail Managers and Sales Representatives to Real Estate Agents, this chapter offers detailed career profiles, outlining job responsibilities, necessary skills and qualifications, work environments, potential for career advancement, and success strategies.

Chapter 10: Public Service and Government Careers

Serve the public with careers in government and public service. Explore the roles of Police Officer, Firefighter, Diplomat, and others. Gain a comprehensive understanding of each profession, including job responsibilities, required skills and education, typical work settings, career growth opportunities, and professional tips.

Chapter 11: Emerging and Future Careers

Prepare for the future with emerging careers like Artificial Intelligence Specialist and E-Commerce Entrepreneur. This chapter provides insights into the expectations, skills and education needed, work environments, growth potential, and tips for future success in these cutting-edge fields.

Conclusion

If you're serious about finding and thriving in your perfect career, HowExpert Guide to Jobs and Careers is your ultimate resource for discovering, exploring, and achieving success. Whether you're just starting out or looking to make a career change, this guide provides the practical and actionable information you need to maximize your potential and achieve your dream career. Get your copy today and take the first step towards your future!

HowExpert publishes how to guides on all topics from A to Z. Visit HowExpert.com to learn more.

Introduction

Welcome to the World of Careers

Welcome to the HowExpert Guide to Jobs and Careers. This guide is designed to be your comprehensive resource for exploring a wide variety of career options across numerous industries. Whether you are a student considering your future, a professional looking to change paths, or someone seeking more fulfillment in your work life, this guide will provide you with the essential information you need to make informed decisions.

Importance of Career Exploration

Career exploration is a crucial step in finding a fulfilling and sustainable career path. It involves researching different professions, understanding what they entail, and reflecting on your own interests, strengths, and values. Career exploration allows you to:

- Discover Your Passions: Identifying what you love to do can lead you to careers that align with your interests.

- Understand Your Strengths: Recognizing your skills and abilities can help you find careers where you can excel.

- Make Informed Decisions: By exploring various options, you can make well-informed choices about your career path.

- Avoid Dead-End Jobs: Proper exploration helps you steer clear of jobs with limited growth potential and satisfaction.

- Increase Job Satisfaction: Finding a career that fits your interests and strengths can lead to higher job satisfaction and personal fulfillment.

Benefits of Finding the Right Career

Finding the right career can significantly impact your life in several positive ways:

- Enhanced Job Satisfaction: When you enjoy your work, it doesn't feel like a chore. You are more likely to be happy and content with your daily routine.

- Increased Productivity: Passion for your job can lead to higher levels of motivation and productivity.

- Professional Growth: The right career offers opportunities for learning, development, and advancement.

- Work-Life Balance: A fulfilling career can contribute to a better balance between work and personal life.

- Financial Stability: Choosing a career that aligns with your strengths and market demands can lead to better job security and financial rewards.

- Long-Term Fulfillment: A career that matches your interests and values can provide long-term personal and professional fulfillment.

How to Use This Guide

This guide is structured to provide a systematic approach to exploring various careers. Here's how to make the most of it:

1. Start with Self-Assessment: Reflect on your interests, skills, values, and personality. This will help you narrow down potential career paths.

2. Explore Career Options: Browse through the different industries and professions covered in this guide. Each section provides detailed information about specific careers, including job descriptions, required skills, education, and potential career paths.

3. Research Further: Use the resources and references provided to conduct deeper research into the careers that interest you.

4. Set Goals and Plan: Once you've identified potential careers, set short-term and long-term goals. Create a plan to acquire the necessary skills and experience.

5. Network and Gain Experience: Seek out opportunities to gain experience through internships, volunteer work, or part-time jobs. Networking can also provide valuable insights and opportunities in your chosen field.

6. Evaluate and Adjust: Regularly evaluate your progress and make adjustments as needed. Career exploration is an ongoing process, and your interests and goals may evolve over time.

By following this guide, you will gain a comprehensive understanding of various career options and be equipped with the knowledge to make informed decisions about your professional future. Let's embark on this journey to find a career that not only meets your professional aspirations but also brings you personal satisfaction and fulfillment.

Chapter 1: STEM Careers

1. Software Developer

1.1 Overview of the Role

Software developers are responsible for designing, coding, testing, and maintaining software applications. They create solutions that meet user needs and solve various problems, working on projects ranging from mobile applications to complex system software. Software developers are key players in the tech industry, ensuring that software products are reliable, efficient, and user-friendly.

1.2 Required Skills and Education

To thrive as a software developer, a mix of technical proficiency, formal education, and essential soft skills is required. Key requirements include:

Technical Skills:

- Programming Languages: Expertise in languages such as Java, Python, C++, and JavaScript.

- Development Tools: Proficiency with Integrated Development Environments (IDEs) like Visual Studio, Eclipse, or IntelliJ.

- Version Control Systems: Familiarity with Git and platforms like GitHub or Bitbucket.

- Database Management: Knowledge of SQL and NoSQL databases.

- Software Development Methodologies: Understanding of Agile, Scrum, or Waterfall methodologies.

Educational Background:

- Degree: A bachelor's degree in computer science, software engineering, or a related field is typically required.

- Certifications: Certifications like Microsoft Certified: Azure Developer, Oracle Certified Professional can be beneficial.

- Continued Learning: Engaging in coding bootcamps, online courses (e.g., Coursera, Udacity), and workshops to stay updated with new technologies.

Soft Skills:

- Problem-Solving: Ability to diagnose issues and develop effective solutions.

- Communication: Clear communication with team members and stakeholders.

- Attention to Detail: Precision in coding and testing to ensure quality.

- Time Management: Efficiently managing time to meet deadlines.

1.3 Typical Work Environment

Software developers usually work in office environments, although remote work has become increasingly common. They collaborate with other developers, project managers, and stakeholders to build software solutions. Work environments can range from large corporations to small startups, and even freelance projects. Full-time work is typical, with occasional overtime to meet project deadlines.

1.4 Career Path and Growth Opportunities

The career path for software developers is highly dynamic, offering numerous opportunities for advancement and specialization:

- Entry-Level Positions: Junior Developer, QA Tester, or Technical Support. These roles focus on building foundational skills and gaining practical experience.

- Mid-Level Positions: Software Developer, Front-End/Back-End Developer, or Systems Analyst. At this stage, developers handle more complex projects and contribute to software architecture.

- Senior-Level Positions: Senior Developer, Lead Developer, or Software Architect. These roles involve leading projects, making critical technical decisions, and mentoring junior developers.

- Specialization Areas: Mobile App Development, Web Development, Data Science, AI and Machine Learning, DevOps, and Cybersecurity. Specializing in these areas allows developers to focus on specific technologies and industries.

- Management Roles: Project Manager, IT Manager, or Chief Technology Officer (CTO). These positions involve overseeing projects, coordinating teams, and aligning development efforts with business objectives.

- Continued Education: Pursuing advanced degrees or specialized certifications can open doors to more advanced roles and higher salaries.

1.5 Tips for Success

To excel as a software developer, consider the following strategies:

- Stay Updated with Technology: Continuously learn about the latest programming languages, tools, and technologies through online courses, tutorials, and industry news.

- Build a Strong Portfolio: Create a portfolio that showcases your projects, demonstrating your skills and versatility. Include a variety of applications and code samples.

- Engage in Coding Practice: Regularly participate in coding challenges and contribute to open-source projects to hone your skills and stay sharp.

- Focus on User Experience: Design software with the end-user in mind, ensuring applications are intuitive, efficient, and accessible.

- Develop Soft Skills: Work on your communication, teamwork, and problem-solving abilities to collaborate effectively with diverse teams.

- Seek Feedback and Mentorship: Actively seek feedback on your work and find mentors who can provide guidance and support for your career development.

- Balance Work and Life: Maintain a healthy work-life balance to avoid burnout and ensure long-term productivity and satisfaction in your career.

By following these tips, you can build a successful and fulfilling career as a software developer, contributing to innovative projects and advancements in technology.

2. Data Scientist

2.1 Overview of the Role

Data scientists are experts who analyze vast amounts of data to extract valuable insights that aid organizations in making strategic decisions. They employ statistical techniques, machine learning algorithms, and data mining processes to uncover patterns and trends. Data scientists play a crucial role in various sectors, including healthcare, finance, marketing, and technology.

2.2 Required Skills and Education

Excelling as a data scientist requires a robust foundation in mathematics, statistics, and computer science. Key skills and educational requirements include:

Technical Skills:

- Programming Languages: Proficiency in Python, R, SQL, and sometimes Java or C++.

- Data Analysis Tools: Familiarity with tools such as Pandas, NumPy, and SciPy.

- Machine Learning Frameworks: Experience with TensorFlow, Keras, or PyTorch.

- Data Visualization: Skills in using Tableau, Power BI, or Matplotlib.

- Big Data Technologies: Understanding of Hadoop, Spark, and NoSQL databases.

Educational Background:

- Degree: A bachelor's degree in data science, computer science, statistics, or a related field. Advanced degrees (Master's or Ph.D.) are highly beneficial.

- Certifications: Relevant certifications like Certified Analytics Professional (CAP) or Google Data Engineer can enhance career prospects.

- Continued Learning: Participation in online courses, workshops, and data science competitions (e.g., Kaggle) is advantageous.

Soft Skills:

- Analytical Thinking: Strong ability to interpret and derive insights from complex data.

- Communication: Skill in presenting findings clearly to non-technical stakeholders.

- Curiosity: A natural drive to explore data and uncover hidden patterns.

- Problem-Solving: Expertise in developing solutions based on data-driven insights.

2.3 Typical Work Environment

Data scientists typically work in collaborative settings with other data professionals, analysts, and business stakeholders. They may be employed by large corporations, consulting firms, or operate as independent consultants. The work environment often involves full-time hours with flexibility around project deadlines. Interaction with data engineers, business analysts, and IT teams is common, and remote work options offer flexibility.

2.4 Career Path and Growth Opportunities

The career trajectory for a data scientist offers various pathways for specialization and advancement:

- Entry-Level Positions: Data Analyst, Junior Data Scientist, or Business Analyst. These roles focus on foundational data analysis and interpretation skills.

- Mid-Level Positions: Data Scientist, Data Engineer, or Machine Learning Engineer. Responsibilities expand to complex data projects and model building.

- Senior-Level Positions: Senior Data Scientist, Lead Data Scientist, or Principal Data Scientist. These roles involve leadership, strategy, and guiding data initiatives.

- Specialization Areas: AI Researcher, Data Architect, Quantitative Analyst, or BI Developer. Specializing in these areas can lead to expertise in specific technologies or industries.

- Management Roles: Data Science Manager, Analytics Director, or Chief Data Officer (CDO). These positions require overseeing data strategies and aligning them with business goals.

- Continued Education: Advanced degrees and specialized certifications can open doors to higher-level roles and increased salaries.

2.5 Tips for Success

To thrive as a data scientist, consider these recommendations:

- Develop Domain Knowledge: Understand the specific industry you are working in, whether it's healthcare, finance, or marketing, to provide more relevant and impactful insights.

- Master Data Storytelling: Learn how to effectively communicate your findings through compelling stories and visualizations that non-technical stakeholders can understand.

- Stay Curious: Always ask questions and explore data with an inquisitive mindset to discover hidden patterns and trends.

- Collaborate with Cross-Functional Teams: Work closely with business stakeholders, engineers, and other departments to ensure your data solutions align with organizational goals.

- Participate in Data Challenges: Engage in competitions like Kaggle to sharpen your skills and stay competitive in the field.

- Focus on Ethical Data Use: Ensure that your data practices comply with legal standards and ethical guidelines to maintain data integrity and trust.

By adhering to these practices, you can build a successful and impactful career as a data scientist, contributing valuable insights and solutions to diverse industries.

3. Mechanical Engineer

3.1 Overview of the Role

Mechanical engineers design, develop, and test mechanical devices and systems, including engines, machines, and tools. They apply principles of physics, mathematics, and material science to create efficient and reliable solutions that meet industry standards and user needs. Mechanical engineers work across various sectors such as automotive, aerospace, manufacturing, and energy.

3.2 Required Skills and Education

To excel as a mechanical engineer, a strong foundation in engineering principles, technical skills, and practical experience is essential. Key requirements include:

Technical Skills:

- CAD Software: Proficiency in tools such as AutoCAD, SolidWorks, or CATIA for designing mechanical systems.

- Engineering Analysis: Understanding of Finite Element Analysis (FEA) and Computational Fluid Dynamics (CFD).

- Material Science: Knowledge of materials and their properties to select the appropriate materials for different applications.

- Mechanical Design: Ability to design mechanical components and systems that meet specifications.

- Project Management: Skills in managing projects from conception to completion, including budgeting and scheduling.

Educational Background:

- Degree: A bachelor's degree in mechanical engineering or a related field is typically required. Advanced degrees (Master's or Ph.D.) can be advantageous for specialized roles.

- Certifications: Professional Engineer (PE) license or certifications such as Certified Manufacturing Engineer (CMfgE) can enhance career prospects.

- Continued Learning: Engaging in workshops, online courses, and industry seminars to stay updated with technological advancements.

Soft Skills:

- Problem-Solving: Strong analytical and troubleshooting abilities to address engineering challenges.

- Communication: Effective communication with team members, stakeholders, and clients.

- Creativity: Innovative thinking to design and improve mechanical systems.

- Attention to Detail: Precision in calculations and design work to ensure safety and efficiency.

3.3 Typical Work Environment

Mechanical engineers can work in various settings, including offices, laboratories, and manufacturing plants. They often collaborate with other engineers, technicians, and project managers. Work environments may vary based on the industry and project requirements, but typically involve full-time hours with potential overtime during project deadlines.

3.4 Career Path and Growth Opportunities

The career path for mechanical engineers is diverse, with numerous opportunities for advancement and specialization:

- Entry-Level Positions: Mechanical Engineer, Design Engineer, or Product Engineer. These roles focus on developing foundational skills and gaining hands-on experience.

- Mid-Level Positions: Senior Mechanical Engineer, Project Engineer, or Manufacturing Engineer. Responsibilities expand to managing projects and overseeing the design and development process.

- Senior-Level Positions: Lead Engineer, Engineering Manager, or Principal Engineer. These roles involve leading teams, strategic planning, and high-level decision-making.

- Specialization Areas: Robotics, Automotive Engineering, Aerospace Engineering, Energy Systems, or HVAC (Heating, Ventilation, and Air Conditioning). Specializing in these areas allows engineers to focus on specific technologies and industries.

- Management Roles: Project Manager, Engineering Manager, or Director of Engineering. These positions require overseeing engineering projects and aligning them with business objectives.

- Continued Education: Pursuing advanced degrees or specialized certifications can lead to more advanced roles and higher salaries.

3.5 Tips for Success

To excel as a mechanical engineer, consider these strategies:

- Hands-On Experience: Gain practical experience through internships, co-op programs, and hands-on projects to enhance your engineering skills.

- Stay Current with Technology: Keep up with the latest advancements in engineering tools, materials, and technologies through continuous education and professional development.

- Networking: Build a professional network by joining engineering societies (e.g., ASME - American Society of Mechanical Engineers), attending industry conferences, and participating in online forums.

- Focus on Sustainability: Develop expertise in sustainable engineering practices to create environmentally friendly and energy-efficient solutions.

- Improve Problem-Solving Skills: Regularly engage in problem-solving exercises and case studies to sharpen your analytical thinking and creativity.

- Effective Communication: Work on improving your communication skills to effectively convey technical information to non-engineering stakeholders and collaborate efficiently with your team.

By following these tips, you can build a successful and impactful career as a mechanical engineer, contributing innovative solutions to various industries and advancing the field of engineering.

4. Civil Engineer

4.1 Overview of the Role

Civil engineers are responsible for designing, constructing, and maintaining infrastructure projects such as roads, bridges, buildings, and water supply systems. They ensure these structures are safe, efficient, and sustainable. Civil engineers work on a variety of projects, from urban development to environmental protection, playing a crucial role in shaping the physical world.

4.2 Required Skills and Education

To excel as a civil engineer, one needs a strong foundation in engineering principles, practical skills, and project management. Key requirements include:

Technical Skills:

- Structural Analysis: Proficiency in analyzing and designing structures to withstand various loads.

- CAD Software: Experience with AutoCAD, Civil 3D, or similar tools for drafting and designing projects.

- Construction Management: Knowledge of construction methods, materials, and project management techniques.

- Surveying: Skills in land surveying and understanding topographical data.

- Geotechnical Engineering: Understanding soil mechanics and foundation design.

Educational Background:

- Degree: A bachelor's degree in civil engineering or a related field is typically required. Advanced degrees (Master's or Ph.D.) can be advantageous for specialized roles.

- Certifications: Professional Engineer (PE) license is essential for career advancement. Additional certifications like Project Management Professional (PMP) can be beneficial.

- Continued Learning: Participation in workshops, online courses, and professional development programs to stay updated with industry standards and practices.

Soft Skills:

- Problem-Solving: Ability to address engineering challenges and develop practical solutions.

- Communication: Effective communication with team members, clients, and stakeholders.

- Attention to Detail: Precision in planning and executing construction projects.

- Leadership: Leading project teams and managing construction activities.

4.3 Typical Work Environment

Civil engineers can work in diverse settings, including office environments, construction sites, and government agencies. They often split their time between office work (planning and designing) and fieldwork (supervising construction and conducting site inspections). Full-time work is typical, with potential for overtime during project deadlines. Safety is a crucial aspect of their work environment, especially on construction sites.

4.4 Career Path and Growth Opportunities

The career path for civil engineers offers various opportunities for specialization and advancement:

- Entry-Level Positions: Civil Engineer, Structural Engineer, or Site Engineer. These roles focus on developing technical skills and gaining hands-on experience.

- Mid-Level Positions: Senior Civil Engineer, Project Engineer, or Construction Manager. Responsibilities expand to managing projects, overseeing construction, and ensuring compliance with regulations.

- Senior-Level Positions: Lead Engineer, Principal Engineer, or Engineering Manager. These roles involve strategic planning, leadership, and high-level decision-making.

- Specialization Areas: Transportation Engineering, Environmental Engineering, Geotechnical Engineering, Water Resources Engineering, or Structural Engineering. Specializing in these areas allows engineers to focus on specific types of projects and technologies.

- Management Roles: Project Manager, Engineering Director, or Chief Engineer. These positions require overseeing large-scale projects and aligning engineering efforts with organizational goals.

- Continued Education: Pursuing advanced degrees or specialized certifications can lead to more advanced roles and higher salaries.

4.5 Tips for Success

To excel as a civil engineer, consider these strategies:

- Gain Practical Experience: Participate in internships, co-op programs, and on-site training to enhance your practical skills and understanding of real-world projects.

- Stay Updated with Regulations: Keep abreast of local, state, and federal regulations and building codes to ensure compliance in your projects.

- Develop Strong Project Management Skills: Learn project management techniques to effectively plan, execute, and oversee construction projects.

- Focus on Sustainability: Embrace sustainable engineering practices to design eco-friendly and energy-efficient infrastructure.

- Enhance Technical Skills: Regularly update your knowledge in the latest engineering software and tools.

- Build Strong Professional Relationships: Network with other professionals through industry associations (e.g., ASCE - American Society of Civil Engineers) and conferences.

By following these tips, you can build a successful and impactful career as a civil engineer, contributing to the development and improvement of essential infrastructure and enhancing the quality of life in communities.

5. Biotechnologist

5.1 Overview of the Role

Biotechnologists apply biological processes to develop technologies and products that help improve the quality of human life. They work in various fields including healthcare, agriculture, and environmental management. Their work involves manipulating organisms at the molecular level to create new medicines, biofuels, genetically modified crops, and more.

5.2 Required Skills and Education

To succeed as a biotechnologist, a combination of scientific knowledge, technical skills, and practical experience is essential. Key requirements include:

Technical Skills:

- Molecular Biology Techniques: Proficiency in techniques such as PCR, gel electrophoresis, and DNA sequencing.

- Laboratory Skills: Experience with cell culture, microbiology, and biochemistry methods.

- Bioinformatics: Knowledge of software and tools for analyzing biological data.

- Genetic Engineering: Understanding of CRISPR and other gene-editing technologies.

- Analytical Skills: Ability to interpret complex biological data and experimental results.

Educational Background:

- Degree: A bachelor's degree in biotechnology, molecular biology, or a related field is typically required. Advanced degrees (Master's or Ph.D.) are highly beneficial for research and specialized roles.

- Certifications: Relevant certifications in biotechnology can enhance career prospects.

- Continued Learning: Participation in professional development courses, workshops, and conferences to stay current with scientific advancements.

Soft Skills:

- Attention to Detail: Precision in conducting experiments and recording results.

- Problem-Solving: Ability to develop innovative solutions to scientific challenges.

- Communication: Effective communication of research findings to colleagues, stakeholders, and the public.

- Collaboration: Working effectively in multidisciplinary teams.

5.3 Typical Work Environment

Biotechnologists typically work in laboratories, research facilities, and manufacturing plants. They may be employed by pharmaceutical companies, agricultural firms, or academic institutions. Work environments are highly controlled and require strict adherence to safety and ethical standards. Full-time work is common, with potential for extended hours during critical phases of research and development projects.

5.4 Career Path and Growth Opportunities

The career path for biotechnologists offers various opportunities for specialization and advancement:

- Entry-Level Positions: Research Assistant, Laboratory Technician, or Quality Control Analyst. These roles focus on developing technical skills and gaining hands-on experience in laboratory settings.

- Mid-Level Positions: Biotechnologist, Research Scientist, or Process Development Scientist. Responsibilities expand to designing experiments, analyzing data, and contributing to scientific discoveries.

- Senior-Level Positions: Senior Scientist, Principal Scientist, or Laboratory Manager. These roles involve leading research projects, managing laboratory operations, and mentoring junior staff.

- Specialization Areas: Medical Biotechnology, Agricultural Biotechnology, Environmental Biotechnology, or Industrial Biotechnology. Specializing in these areas allows professionals to focus on specific applications and technologies.

- Management Roles: Project Manager, R&D Director, or Chief Scientific Officer (CSO). These positions require overseeing research projects and aligning scientific efforts with organizational goals.

- Continued Education: Pursuing advanced degrees or specialized certifications can lead to more advanced roles and higher salaries.

5.5 Tips for Success

To excel as a biotechnologist, consider these strategies:

- Stay Current with Scientific Literature: Regularly read scientific journals and publications to keep up with the latest research and developments in biotechnology.

- Develop Strong Laboratory Skills: Gain proficiency in essential laboratory techniques through hands-on practice and training.

- Network with Professionals: Build relationships with other scientists and industry professionals through conferences, seminars, and professional organizations (e.g., ASBMB - American Society for Biochemistry and Molecular Biology).

- Focus on Ethical Practices: Ensure that your research adheres to ethical guidelines and safety regulations to maintain integrity and public trust.

- Pursue Interdisciplinary Knowledge: Enhance your expertise by learning about related fields such as bioinformatics, chemistry, and environmental science.

- Contribute to Collaborative Projects: Participate in collaborative research projects to gain diverse experience and insights.

By following these tips, you can build a successful and impactful career as a biotechnologist, contributing to groundbreaking discoveries and innovations that improve human health and the environment.

6. Electrical Engineer

6.1 Overview of the Role

Electrical engineers design, develop, test, and oversee the manufacturing of electrical equipment, systems, and components. This includes everything from small-scale electronics to large power generation systems. They work on projects involving wiring, lighting, motors, and communication systems, ensuring that electrical systems function efficiently and safely.

6.2 Required Skills and Education

To excel as an electrical engineer, a strong foundation in electrical theory, technical skills, and problem-solving abilities is essential. Key requirements include:

Technical Skills:

- Circuit Design: Proficiency in designing and analyzing electrical circuits.

- Electronics: Knowledge of electronic components and systems, including semiconductors, transistors, and microcontrollers.

- Software Tools: Experience with CAD software (e.g., AutoCAD Electrical), simulation tools (e.g., SPICE), and programming languages (e.g., MATLAB, C++).

- Power Systems: Understanding of power generation, transmission, and distribution.

- Control Systems: Skills in designing and implementing control systems and automation.

Educational Background:

- Degree: A bachelor's degree in electrical engineering or a related field is typically required. Advanced degrees (Master's or Ph.D.) can be beneficial for specialized roles.

- Certifications: Professional Engineer (PE) license or certifications such as Certified Electrical Engineer (CEE) can enhance career prospects.

- Continued Learning: Participation in professional development courses, workshops, and industry conferences to stay updated with technological advancements.

Soft Skills:

- Problem-Solving: Strong analytical skills to diagnose and solve electrical issues.

- Communication: Ability to clearly convey technical information to team members, stakeholders, and clients.

- Attention to Detail: Precision in designing and testing electrical systems.

- Project Management: Skills in planning, executing, and overseeing electrical projects.

6.3 Typical Work Environment

Electrical engineers can work in a variety of environments, including offices, laboratories, manufacturing plants, and construction sites. They may be employed by engineering firms, utilities, technology companies, or government agencies. Work often involves a mix of office-based design and analysis as well as fieldwork for testing and troubleshooting. Full-time work is common, with potential for extended hours during project deadlines.

6.4 Career Path and Growth Opportunities

The career path for electrical engineers offers numerous opportunities for advancement and specialization:

- Entry-Level Positions: Electrical Engineer, Test Engineer, or Electronics Technician. These roles focus on developing technical skills and gaining practical experience in designing and testing electrical systems.

- Mid-Level Positions: Senior Electrical Engineer, Project Engineer, or Systems Engineer. Responsibilities expand to managing projects, designing complex systems, and overseeing installation and testing.

- Senior-Level Positions: Lead Engineer, Principal Engineer, or Engineering Manager. These roles involve leading engineering teams, strategic planning, and high-level decision-making.

- Specialization Areas: Power Engineering, Telecommunications, Control Systems, Embedded Systems, or Renewable Energy. Specializing in these areas allows engineers to focus on specific technologies and industries.

- Management Roles: Project Manager, Engineering Director, or Chief Engineer. These positions require overseeing large-scale projects and aligning engineering efforts with business goals.

- Continued Education: Pursuing advanced degrees or specialized certifications can lead to more advanced roles and higher salaries.

6.5 Tips for Success

To excel as an electrical engineer, consider these strategies:

- Stay Updated with Technology: Keep abreast of the latest advancements in electrical engineering through continuous education and professional development.

- Develop Strong Analytical Skills: Regularly practice problem-solving and analytical thinking to enhance your ability to diagnose and resolve complex electrical issues.

- Build a Professional Network: Join professional organizations (e.g., IEEE - Institute of Electrical and Electronics Engineers) and attend industry events to connect with other engineers and industry leaders.

- Gain Hands-On Experience: Participate in internships, co-op programs, and hands-on projects to apply theoretical knowledge to real-world scenarios.

- Focus on Safety Standards: Ensure that all designs and installations comply with safety regulations and industry standards to prevent accidents and ensure reliability.

- Pursue Innovation: Stay curious and innovative, seeking out new ways to improve electrical systems and contribute to advancements in the field.

By following these tips, you can build a successful and impactful career as an electrical engineer, contributing to the development of cutting-edge technologies and reliable electrical systems.

7. Web Developer

7.1 Overview of the Role

Web developers are responsible for designing, coding, and maintaining websites and web applications. They ensure that websites are visually appealing, user-friendly, and function smoothly. Web developers work with various programming languages and technologies to build responsive and dynamic websites, contributing significantly to a company's online presence and functionality.

7.2 Required Skills and Education

To excel as a web developer, one needs a mix of technical skills, creativity, and continuous learning. Key requirements include:

Technical Skills:

- Programming Languages: Proficiency in HTML, CSS, JavaScript, and often other languages like PHP, Ruby, or Python.

- Front-End Frameworks: Knowledge of frameworks like React, Angular, or Vue.js.

- Back-End Technologies: Understanding of server-side technologies such as Node.js, Django, or Ruby on Rails.

- Database Management: Familiarity with databases like MySQL, PostgreSQL, or MongoDB.

- Version Control Systems: Experience with Git and platforms like GitHub or Bitbucket.

Educational Background:

- Degree: A bachelor's degree in computer science, web development, or a related field can be beneficial but is not always required. Many web developers are self-taught or have completed coding bootcamps.

- Certifications: Certifications from recognized platforms (e.g., Google, Microsoft, or Codecademy) can enhance credibility.

- Continued Learning: Engaging in online courses, workshops, and staying updated with new web technologies is crucial.

Soft Skills:

- Creativity: Ability to design visually appealing and engaging websites.

- Problem-Solving: Strong analytical skills to troubleshoot and debug code.

- Communication: Effective communication with clients, designers, and team members.

- Attention to Detail: Precision in coding and testing to ensure website functionality.

7.3 Typical Work Environment

Web developers can work in diverse settings, including tech companies, digital agencies, or as freelancers. They often collaborate with designers, content creators, and project managers. The work environment typically involves a mix of office settings and remote work. Web developers usually work full-time, but freelance work offers flexibility in hours and location.

7.4 Career Path and Growth Opportunities

The career path for web developers offers numerous opportunities for specialization and advancement:

- Entry-Level Positions: Junior Web Developer, Front-End Developer, or Web Designer. These roles focus on developing foundational skills in web development and design.

- Mid-Level Positions: Web Developer, Full-Stack Developer, or Back-End Developer. Responsibilities expand to handling more complex projects and managing entire web applications.

- Senior-Level Positions: Senior Web Developer, Lead Developer, or Technical Lead. These roles involve leading development teams, making strategic technical decisions, and overseeing major projects.

- Specialization Areas: E-commerce Development, Mobile Web Development, Web Security, or UX/UI Design. Specializing in these areas allows developers to focus on specific aspects of web development and enhance their expertise.

- Management Roles: Project Manager, Development Manager, or Chief Technology Officer (CTO). These positions require overseeing web development projects, coordinating with various departments, and aligning technical efforts with business goals.

- Continued Education: Pursuing advanced courses, certifications, and staying updated with the latest web development trends and technologies can lead to higher roles and increased earning potential.

7.5 Tips for Success

To excel as a web developer, consider the following strategies:

- Continuous Learning: The web development field evolves rapidly, so staying updated with the latest technologies, frameworks, and best practices is essential. Regularly participate in online courses, webinars, and workshops.

- Build a Portfolio: Develop a strong portfolio showcasing your projects, skills, and versatility. Include a variety of websites and applications you have built or contributed to.

- Practice Coding: Regularly practice coding through challenges on platforms like LeetCode, HackerRank, or CodeWars to improve your problem-solving skills and stay sharp.

- Focus on User Experience: Prioritize creating websites that are user-friendly, responsive, and accessible. Understand the principles of UX/UI design and apply them to your projects.

- Collaborate Effectively: Work well with designers, content creators, and other developers. Good communication and teamwork are crucial for the success of web development projects.

- Stay Security-Conscious: Understand web security principles and practices. Ensure that your websites and applications are secure and protect user data.

- Get Feedback: Seek feedback from users, peers, and clients to improve your work continuously. Use this feedback to refine your skills and deliver better web solutions.

By following these tips, you can build a successful and fulfilling career as a web developer, creating innovative and impactful websites and applications that meet the needs of users and businesses alike.

8. Cybersecurity Specialist

8.1 Overview of the Role

Cybersecurity specialists are responsible for protecting an organization's computer systems and networks from cyber threats. They implement security measures, monitor systems for vulnerabilities, respond to incidents, and ensure compliance with security standards. Their role is crucial in safeguarding sensitive information and maintaining the integrity and confidentiality of data.

8.2 Required Skills and Education

To excel as a cybersecurity specialist, a combination of technical expertise, education, and practical experience is essential. Key requirements include:

Technical Skills:

- Network Security: Proficiency in securing networks, firewalls, and VPNs.

- Threat Analysis: Skills in identifying, analyzing, and mitigating cyber threats.

- Security Tools: Experience with tools like SIEM (Security Information and Event Management), IDS/IPS (Intrusion Detection/Prevention Systems), and antivirus software.

- Cryptography: Understanding of encryption techniques and secure communication protocols.

- Incident Response: Ability to respond to and manage security breaches effectively.

Educational Background:

- Degree: A bachelor's degree in cybersecurity, computer science, or a related field is typically required. Advanced degrees (Master's or Ph.D.) can be beneficial for specialized roles.

- Certifications: Industry certifications such as Certified Information Systems Security Professional (CISSP), Certified Ethical Hacker (CEH), or CompTIA Security+ can enhance career prospects.

- Continued Learning: Participation in professional development courses, workshops, and industry conferences to stay updated with the latest security trends and technologies.

Soft Skills:

- Attention to Detail: Precision in monitoring systems and identifying potential threats.

- Problem-Solving: Strong analytical skills to address and resolve security issues.

- Communication: Ability to communicate security protocols and incidents effectively to non-technical stakeholders.

- Adaptability: Staying updated with the constantly evolving cybersecurity landscape.

8.3 Typical Work Environment

Cybersecurity specialists can work in a variety of environments, including corporate offices, government agencies, and security firms. They may also work remotely, particularly in roles that involve monitoring and analyzing security systems. The work often involves full-time hours with the potential for extended hours during security incidents or breaches. Collaboration with IT departments and other security professionals is common, and maintaining a high level of confidentiality and trust is essential.

8.4 Career Path and Growth Opportunities

The career path for cybersecurity specialists offers numerous opportunities for advancement and specialization:

- Entry-Level Positions: Security Analyst, IT Security Consultant, or Network Administrator. These roles focus on developing foundational skills in cybersecurity and gaining practical experience.

- Mid-Level Positions: Cybersecurity Specialist, Security Engineer, or Incident Responder. Responsibilities expand to designing and implementing security measures, and managing security incidents.

- Senior-Level Positions: Senior Security Analyst, Cybersecurity Manager, or Chief Information Security Officer (CISO). These roles involve leading security teams, strategic planning, and high-level decision-making.

- Specialization Areas: Penetration Testing, Digital Forensics, Cloud Security, or Application Security. Specializing in these areas allows professionals to focus on specific aspects of cybersecurity and enhance their expertise.

- Management Roles: Security Director, Information Security Director, or VP of Information Security. These positions require overseeing comprehensive security programs and aligning them with organizational goals.

- Continued Education: Pursuing advanced degrees or specialized certifications can lead to more advanced roles and higher salaries.

8.5 Tips for Success

To excel as a cybersecurity specialist, consider these strategies:

- Continuous Learning: Stay updated with the latest cybersecurity threats, tools, and best practices through continuous education and professional development.

- Develop a Hacker Mindset: Understand the tactics, techniques, and procedures used by cybercriminals to better anticipate and defend against attacks.

- Build a Strong Professional Network: Join professional organizations (e.g., ISC2, ISACA) and attend industry events to connect with other cybersecurity professionals and stay informed about industry developments.

- Gain Hands-On Experience: Participate in internships, capture-the-flag (CTF) competitions, and hands-on projects to apply theoretical knowledge to real-world scenarios.

- Focus on Certifications: Obtain industry-recognized certifications to validate your skills and enhance your credibility.

- Stay Ethical: Always adhere to ethical guidelines and legal standards in your cybersecurity practices to maintain integrity and trust.

- Develop Incident Response Skills: Practice and refine your skills in responding to security incidents to minimize damage and recover quickly from breaches.

By following these tips, you can build a successful and impactful career as a cybersecurity specialist, protecting organizations from cyber threats and contributing to the overall security of the digital landscape.

9. Environmental Scientist

9.1 Overview of the Role

Environmental scientists study the natural environment and develop solutions to environmental problems. They work to protect human health, preserve natural resources, and improve environmental quality. Their work involves conducting research, collecting and analyzing data, and advising policymakers and the public on environmental issues.

9.2 Required Skills and Education

To excel as an environmental scientist, a blend of scientific knowledge, technical skills, and practical experience is essential. Key requirements include:

Technical Skills:

- Data Analysis: Proficiency in analyzing environmental data using statistical software and GIS (Geographic Information Systems).

- Fieldwork Techniques: Skills in sampling, monitoring, and conducting environmental assessments.

- Laboratory Skills: Experience with laboratory equipment and procedures for analyzing soil, water, and air samples.

- Environmental Regulations: Understanding of environmental laws and regulations at the local, state, and federal levels.

- Research Methods: Ability to design and conduct scientific research projects.

Educational Background:

- Degree: A bachelor's degree in environmental science, biology, chemistry, or a related field is typically required. Advanced degrees (Master's or Ph.D.) can be beneficial for specialized roles and research positions.

- Certifications: Certifications such as Registered Environmental Scientist (RES) or Certified Environmental Professional (CEP) can enhance career prospects.

- Continued Learning: Participation in professional development courses, workshops, and conferences to stay updated with the latest environmental research and technologies.

Soft Skills:

- Problem-Solving: Strong analytical skills to develop effective solutions to environmental problems.

- Communication: Ability to communicate scientific findings to policymakers, stakeholders, and the public.

- Attention to Detail: Precision in data collection and analysis to ensure accurate results.

- Teamwork: Working effectively in multidisciplinary teams on research and conservation projects.

9.3 Typical Work Environment

Environmental scientists can work in a variety of settings, including government agencies, private consulting firms, non-profit organizations, and research institutions. They may divide their time between office work (analyzing data and writing reports) and fieldwork (collecting samples and monitoring environmental conditions). Full-time work is common, with potential for extended hours during field studies or research projects.

9.4 Career Path and Growth Opportunities

The career path for environmental scientists offers various opportunities for specialization and advancement:

- Entry-Level Positions: Environmental Technician, Research Assistant, or Field Analyst. These roles focus on developing foundational skills in environmental science and gaining practical experience.

 Mid Level Positions: Environmental Scientist, Conservation Scientist, or Environmental Consultant. Responsibilities expand to designing and conducting research projects, analyzing data, and advising on environmental policies.

- Senior-Level Positions: Senior Environmental Scientist, Project Manager, or Environmental Program Director. These roles involve leading research teams, managing projects, and making strategic decisions.

- Specialization Areas: Wildlife Biology, Environmental Toxicology, Hydrology, or Climate Science. Specializing in these areas allows scientists to focus on specific aspects of environmental science and enhance their expertise.

- Management Roles: Environmental Director, Chief Environmental Officer, or Research Director. These positions require overseeing large-scale environmental programs and aligning them with organizational goals.

- Continued Education: Pursuing advanced degrees or specialized certifications can lead to more advanced roles and higher salaries.

9.5 Tips for Success

To excel as an environmental scientist, consider these strategies:

- Stay Informed on Environmental Issues: Keep up with current environmental news, research, and policies to understand the latest challenges and developments.

- Develop Strong Analytical Skills: Enhance your ability to analyze and interpret environmental data through continuous practice and training.

- Engage in Fieldwork: Gain hands-on experience through field studies, internships, and volunteer opportunities to understand real-world environmental conditions.

- Build a Professional Network: Join professional organizations (e.g., Ecological Society of America, Society for Conservation Biology) and attend conferences to connect with other environmental scientists and stay informed about industry trends.

- Communicate Effectively: Improve your ability to communicate complex scientific information to non-scientists, including policymakers, stakeholders, and the public.

- Focus on Interdisciplinary Collaboration: Work with professionals from other fields, such as economics, public health, and urban planning, to develop comprehensive solutions to environmental problems.

- Commit to Lifelong Learning: Continuously update your knowledge and skills through professional development courses, certifications, and advanced degrees.

By following these tips, you can build a successful and impactful career as an environmental scientist, contributing to the protection and preservation of the environment for future generations.

Chapter 1 Review

Overview of STEM Careers

In Chapter 1, we explored a variety of careers in the STEM (Science, Technology, Engineering, and Mathematics) fields. These careers are pivotal in driving innovation and technological advancement across multiple industries. Here's a summary of the key points covered for each role:

1. Software Developer

- Overview of the Role: Designing, coding, and testing software applications.

- Required Skills and Education: Proficiency in programming languages (Java, Python, C++), understanding of software development tools, and a degree in computer science or a related field.

- Typical Work Environment: Office or remote settings, team collaboration, and project-based work.

- Career Path and Growth Opportunities: Entry-level to senior roles, specialization in areas like mobile app development, and management positions.

- Tips for Success: Continuous learning, networking, maintaining a portfolio, and seeking mentorship.

2. Data Scientist

- Overview of the Role: Analyzing complex data to aid in decision-making.

- Required Skills and Education: Knowledge of programming languages (Python, R), statistical analysis, data visualization, and a degree in computer science, statistics, or a related field.

- Typical Work Environment: Office settings, often remote, and team-based projects.

- Career Path and Growth Opportunities: Data Analyst to Senior Data Scientist, specialization in machine learning, and management roles.

- Tips for Success: Develop domain knowledge, master data storytelling, stay curious, and focus on ethical data use.

3. Mechanical Engineer

- Overview of the Role: Designing, developing, and testing mechanical systems.

- Required Skills and Education: Proficiency in CAD, understanding of mechanical design, a degree in mechanical engineering, and certifications like PE.

- Typical Work Environment: Office, laboratory, and on-site locations.

- Career Path and Growth Opportunities: Junior Engineer to Senior Mechanical Engineer, specialization areas, and management roles.

- Tips for Success: Gain practical experience, stay current with technology, network, and focus on sustainability.

4. Civil Engineer

- Overview of the Role: Designing and maintaining infrastructure projects.

- Required Skills and Education: Proficiency in CAD, project management, a degree in civil engineering, and certifications like PE.

- Typical Work Environment: Office, laboratory, and field locations.

- Career Path and Growth Opportunities: Entry-level to senior roles, specialization in structural or environmental engineering, and management positions.

- Tips for Success: Gain practical experience, stay updated with regulations, develop strong project management skills, and build strong professional relationships.

5. Biotechnologist

- Overview of the Role: Using biological systems to develop products.

- Required Skills and Education: Laboratory techniques, molecular biology, a degree in biotechnology, and advanced degrees for research roles.

- Typical Work Environment: Laboratories and offices.

- Career Path and Growth Opportunities: Laboratory Technician to Senior Research Scientist, specialization in genetic engineering or pharmaceuticals, and management roles.

- Tips for Success: Stay current with scientific literature, develop strong laboratory skills, focus on ethical practices, and contribute to collaborative projects.

6. Electrical Engineer

- Overview of the Role: Designing and testing electrical systems and equipment.

- Required Skills and Education: Circuit design, digital and analog electronics, a degree in electrical engineering, and certifications like PE.

- Typical Work Environment: Office, laboratory, and on-site locations.

- Career Path and Growth Opportunities: Junior Electrical Engineer to Senior Engineer, specialization areas, and management roles.

- Tips for Success: Stay updated with technology, develop strong analytical skills, focus on safety standards, and pursue innovation.

7. Web Developer

- Overview of the Role: Designing and modifying websites.

- Required Skills and Education: Proficiency in HTML/CSS, JavaScript, server-side languages, and a degree or relevant certification.

- Typical Work Environment: Office or remote settings, team collaboration.

- Career Path and Growth Opportunities: Junior Web Developer to Senior Developer, specialization in front-end or back-end, and management roles.

- Tips for Success: Build a strong portfolio, practice coding, focus on user experience, and stay security-conscious.

8. Cybersecurity Specialist

- Overview of the Role: Protecting computer systems from cyber threats.

- Required Skills and Education: Network security, cryptography, a degree in cybersecurity or related field, and certifications like CISSP.

- Typical Work Environment: Office settings, often remote, team collaboration.

- Career Path and Growth Opportunities: Security Analyst to Senior Cybersecurity Specialist, specialization in incident response or threat intelligence, and management roles.

- Tips for Success: Develop a hacker mindset, build a professional network, focus on ethical practices, and enhance incident response skills.

9. Environmental Scientist

- Overview of the Role: Protecting the environment through research and policy development.

- Required Skills and Education: Data analysis, field sampling, a degree in environmental science or related field, and certifications like CEP.

- Typical Work Environment: Office, laboratory, and field locations.

- Career Path and Growth Opportunities: Environmental Technician to Senior Scientist, specialization in air quality or water resources, and management roles.

- Tips for Success: Stay informed on environmental issues, engage in fieldwork, communicate effectively, and commit to lifelong learning.

Key Takeaways

- Continuous Learning: Staying updated with industry trends and technological advancements is crucial across all STEM careers.

- Networking: Building a professional network through industry events, online forums, and social media can provide valuable opportunities and insights.

- Practical Experience: Gaining hands-on experience through internships, co-op programs, or part-time jobs is essential for skill development and career advancement.

- Certifications and Education: Obtaining relevant certifications and pursuing higher education can enhance career prospects and open up advanced roles.

- Mentorship: Seeking guidance from experienced professionals can provide valuable insights and support throughout your career.

By understanding the roles, required skills, typical work environments, career paths, and tips for success, you can make informed decisions about pursuing a career in the STEM fields covered in this chapter. Whether you are just starting out or looking to advance your career, this guide provides the essential information to help you succeed.

Chapter 2: Medical and Healthcare Careers

10. Registered Nurse

10.1 Overview of the Role

Registered Nurses (RNs) play a crucial role in the healthcare system, providing direct patient care, educating patients and the public about various health conditions, and offering emotional support to patients and their families. They assess patients' conditions, administer medications, assist with diagnostic tests, and collaborate with other healthcare professionals to create and implement patient care plans.

10.2 Required Skills and Education

To become a successful registered nurse, individuals need a mix of technical knowledge, clinical skills, and compassionate care. Key requirements include:

Technical Skills:

- Clinical Knowledge: Understanding of medical terminologies, patient care techniques, and healthcare protocols.

- Medication Administration: Proficiency in safely administering medications and monitoring their effects.

- Patient Assessment: Skills in assessing patient conditions, identifying changes, and responding appropriately.

- Medical Equipment: Familiarity with the use and maintenance of medical equipment (e.g., IV pumps, heart monitors).

- Electronic Health Records (EHR): Knowledge of electronic health record systems for documenting patient care.

Educational Background:

- Degree: An associate's degree in nursing (ADN) or a bachelor's degree in nursing (BSN) from an accredited nursing program is required. A BSN is increasingly preferred by employers.

- Licensure: Passing the National Council Licensure Examination for Registered Nurses (NCLEX-RN) is mandatory to obtain a nursing license.

- Certifications: Specialty certifications (e.g., Certified Emergency Nurse, Certified Pediatric Nurse) can enhance career prospects.

- Continued Learning: Engaging in continuing education courses to keep up with advancements in nursing practices and healthcare technologies.

Soft Skills:

- Communication: Effective verbal and written communication with patients, families, and healthcare teams.

- Compassion: Empathy and compassion in providing patient-centered care.

- Critical Thinking: Strong problem-solving and decision-making abilities.

- Attention to Detail: Precision in administering treatments and recording patient information.

- Physical Stamina: Ability to handle the physical demands of the job, including long hours and potential lifting of patients.

10.3 Typical Work Environment

Registered nurses work in a variety of healthcare settings, including hospitals, clinics, nursing homes, and private practices. They may also work in schools, community health centers, and government agencies. The work environment is often fast-paced and physically demanding, requiring long shifts, including nights, weekends, and holidays. RNs frequently collaborate with physicians, specialists, and other healthcare professionals to provide comprehensive patient care.

10.4 Career Path and Growth Opportunities

The career path for registered nurses offers numerous opportunities for specialization and advancement:

- Entry-Level Positions: Staff Nurse, Charge Nurse, or Clinical Nurse. These roles focus on developing clinical skills and gaining practical experience in patient care.

- Mid-Level Positions: Nurse Supervisor, Nurse Educator, or Case Manager. Responsibilities expand to managing nursing teams, educating patients and staff, and coordinating patient care.

- Senior-Level Positions: Nurse Practitioner, Clinical Nurse Specialist, or Nurse Manager. These roles involve advanced clinical practice, leadership, and strategic planning.

- Specialization Areas: Critical Care Nursing, Pediatric Nursing, Oncology Nursing, or Geriatric Nursing. Specializing in these areas allows nurses to focus on specific patient populations and enhance their expertise.

- Management Roles: Director of Nursing, Chief Nursing Officer (CNO), or Healthcare Administrator. These positions require overseeing nursing departments, managing budgets, and aligning nursing practices with organizational goals.

- Continued Education: Pursuing advanced degrees (e.g., MSN, DNP) or specialized certifications can lead to higher roles and increased salaries.

10.5 Tips for Success

To excel as a registered nurse, consider the following strategies:

- Prioritize Patient Care: Always focus on providing compassionate and patient-centered care. Build strong relationships with patients and their families to enhance their healthcare experience.

- Stay Updated: Continuously update your knowledge and skills through continuing education, workshops, and professional development courses.

- Develop Strong Communication Skills: Effective communication is crucial for collaborating with healthcare teams, educating patients, and ensuring clear documentation.

- Manage Stress Effectively: Nursing can be stressful, so develop healthy coping mechanisms, such as regular exercise, mindfulness, and seeking support from colleagues.

- Embrace Technology: Familiarize yourself with the latest healthcare technologies and electronic health records to improve efficiency and patient care.

- Seek Specialization: Consider pursuing certifications in specialized areas of nursing to advance your career and increase your expertise.

- Network and Mentor: Build a professional network through nursing associations (e.g., American Nurses Association) and seek mentorship from experienced nurses to gain insights and career guidance.

By following these tips, you can build a successful and fulfilling career as a registered nurse, making a significant impact on patient care and the healthcare system.

11. Physician Assistant

11.1 Overview of the Role

Physician Assistants (PAs) are healthcare professionals who practice medicine under the supervision of physicians and surgeons. They perform a variety of tasks, including diagnosing illnesses, developing and managing treatment plans, prescribing medications, and often serving as a patient's principal healthcare provider. PAs work in various medical settings and play a crucial role in enhancing healthcare accessibility and quality.

11.2 Required Skills and Education

To become a successful physician assistant, a combination of medical knowledge, clinical skills, and interpersonal abilities is essential. Key requirements include:

Technical Skills:

- Medical Knowledge: Strong understanding of medical principles, anatomy, physiology, and clinical procedures.

- Diagnostic Skills: Ability to assess patient symptoms and diagnose conditions accurately.

- Treatment Planning: Skills in developing and implementing effective treatment plans.

- Pharmacology: Knowledge of medications, their effects, and appropriate prescribing practices.

- Procedural Skills: Competence in performing clinical procedures such as suturing, casting, and administering injections.

Educational Background:

- Degree: A master's degree from an accredited physician assistant program is required. These programs typically take about two years to complete and include both classroom instruction and clinical rotations.

- Licensure: Passing the Physician Assistant National Certifying Exam (PANCE) is mandatory to obtain licensure. Continuing Medical Education (CME) and recertification exams are required periodically.

- Certifications: Additional certifications in specialty areas (e.g., surgery, emergency medicine) can enhance career prospects.

- Continued Learning: Participation in professional development courses and workshops to keep up with medical advancements.

Soft Skills:

- Communication: Effective communication with patients, families, and healthcare teams.

- Empathy: Providing compassionate care and support to patients.

- Critical Thinking: Strong problem-solving and decision-making abilities.

- Attention to Detail: Precision in patient assessment, diagnosis, and treatment.

- Teamwork: Collaborating effectively with physicians, nurses, and other healthcare professionals.

11.3 Typical Work Environment

Physician assistants work in a variety of healthcare settings, including hospitals, clinics, private practices, and specialty care centers. They may also work in rural or underserved areas to improve access to healthcare. The work environment is often fast-paced and can be physically demanding, with long hours, including nights, weekends, and holidays. PAs frequently collaborate with physicians and other healthcare providers to deliver comprehensive patient care.

11.4 Career Path and Growth Opportunities

The career path for physician assistants offers numerous opportunities for specialization and advancement:

- Entry-Level Positions: PA-C (Physician Assistant-Certified), typically working in general medicine or primary care settings to build foundational skills.

- Mid-Level Positions: Senior PA, specializing in areas such as surgery, emergency medicine, or pediatrics. Responsibilities expand to more complex cases and independent patient management.

- Senior-Level Positions: Lead PA or PA Supervisor, overseeing other physician assistants and managing clinical operations within a department or practice.

- Specialization Areas: Orthopedics, Cardiology, Dermatology, Psychiatry, or Oncology. Specializing in these areas allows PAs to focus on specific patient populations and medical conditions.

- Management Roles: Clinical Director, Healthcare Administrator, or PA Program Director. These positions require overseeing clinical programs, managing healthcare teams, and contributing to policy development.

- Continued Education: Pursuing advanced certifications or doctoral degrees (e.g., Doctor of Medical Science) can lead to higher roles and increased salaries.

11.5 Tips for Success

To excel as a physician assistant, consider the following strategies:

- Prioritize Patient Care: Focus on delivering high-quality, patient-centered care. Build strong relationships with patients and their families to enhance trust and communication.

- Stay Updated: Continuously update your medical knowledge and skills through continuing medical education, professional development courses, and staying current with medical research.

- Develop Strong Interpersonal Skills: Effective communication and empathy are crucial for building rapport with patients and collaborating with healthcare teams.

- Embrace Technology: Familiarize yourself with the latest medical technologies and electronic health records to improve efficiency and patient care.

- Seek Specialization: Consider pursuing additional certifications in specialized areas of interest to advance your career and enhance your expertise.

- Network and Mentor: Build a professional network through medical associations (e.g., American Academy of Physician Assistants) and seek mentorship from experienced healthcare providers to gain insights and career guidance.

- Focus on Work-Life Balance: Manage stress and maintain a healthy work-life balance to ensure long-term productivity and job satisfaction.

By following these tips, you can build a successful and fulfilling career as a physician assistant, making a significant impact on patient care and the healthcare system.

12. Pharmacist

12.1 Overview of the Role

Pharmacists are healthcare professionals responsible for dispensing medications, providing drug information, and advising patients on the safe and effective use of prescriptions. They play a critical role in ensuring that medications are used appropriately and help manage patients' overall health by offering counsel on lifestyle changes, medication management, and potential drug interactions.

12.2 Required Skills and Education

To excel as a pharmacist, a combination of technical knowledge, clinical skills, and interpersonal abilities is essential. Key requirements include:

Technical Skills:

- Pharmacology: Deep understanding of drug mechanisms, therapeutic uses, side effects, and interactions.

- Medication Dispensing: Proficiency in accurately dispensing medications and managing pharmacy operations.

- Patient Counseling: Skills in educating patients about their medications, including proper usage, potential side effects, and storage.

- Compounding: Ability to prepare customized medications when necessary.

- Healthcare Technology: Familiarity with electronic health records (EHRs) and pharmacy management software.

Educational Background:

- Degree: A Doctor of Pharmacy (Pharm.D.) degree from an accredited pharmacy school is required.

- Licensure: Passing the North American Pharmacist Licensure Examination (NAPLEX) and state-specific exams (e.g., Multistate Pharmacy Jurisprudence Examination) is mandatory for licensure.

- Certifications: Additional certifications in specialty areas (e.g., Certified Diabetes Educator, Board Certified Pharmacotherapy Specialist) can enhance career prospects.

- Continued Learning: Participation in continuing education courses to keep up with advancements in pharmacology and pharmacy practice.

Soft Skills:

- Attention to Detail: Precision in dispensing medications and managing patient records.

- Communication: Effective communication with patients, healthcare providers, and pharmacy staff.

- Empathy: Providing compassionate care and support to patients.

- Problem-Solving: Ability to address medication-related issues and patient concerns.

- Management: Skills in managing pharmacy operations and staff.

12.3 Typical Work Environment

Pharmacists work in a variety of settings, including retail pharmacies, hospitals, clinics, and long-term care facilities. They may also work in pharmaceutical companies, government agencies, or academic institutions. The work environment is typically clean and well-lit, with a focus on safety and accuracy. Pharmacists often work full-time, with potential for evening, weekend, and holiday shifts, especially in 24-hour pharmacy locations.

12.4 Career Path and Growth Opportunities

The career path for pharmacists offers numerous opportunities for specialization and advancement:

- Entry-Level Positions: Staff Pharmacist or Clinical Pharmacist, focusing on dispensing medications and providing patient care.

- Mid-Level Positions: Senior Pharmacist, Pharmacy Manager, or Clinical Specialist, taking on more responsibilities in patient care, management, and specialized areas.

- Senior-Level Positions: Pharmacy Director, Chief Pharmacist, or Consultant Pharmacist, leading pharmacy departments, managing complex operations, and providing expert advice.

- Specialization Areas: Oncology Pharmacy, Geriatric Pharmacy, Pediatric Pharmacy, or Infectious Disease Pharmacy. Specializing in these areas allows pharmacists to focus on specific patient populations and therapeutic areas.

- Management Roles: Pharmacy Manager, Director of Pharmacy, or Healthcare Administrator. These positions involve overseeing pharmacy operations, managing budgets, and ensuring compliance with regulations.

- Continued Education: Pursuing advanced certifications or degrees (e.g., MBA in Healthcare Management) can lead to higher roles and increased salaries.

12.5 Tips for Success

To excel as a pharmacist, consider the following strategies:

- Prioritize Patient Safety: Always focus on ensuring the safe and effective use of medications. Double-check prescriptions, educate patients, and stay vigilant for potential drug interactions.

- Stay Updated: Continuously update your knowledge and skills through continuing education, professional development courses, and staying current with medical research and pharmaceutical advancements.

- Develop Strong Interpersonal Skills: Effective communication and empathy are crucial for building rapport with patients and collaborating with healthcare teams.

- Embrace Technology: Familiarize yourself with the latest pharmacy management software and electronic health records to improve efficiency and patient care.

- Seek Specialization: Consider pursuing additional certifications in specialized areas of interest to advance your career and enhance your expertise.

- Network and Mentor: Build a professional network through pharmacy associations (e.g., American Pharmacists Association) and seek mentorship from experienced pharmacists to gain insights and career guidance.

- Focus on Work-Life Balance: Manage stress and maintain a healthy work-life balance to ensure long-term productivity and job satisfaction.

By following these tips, you can build a successful and fulfilling career as a pharmacist, making a significant impact on patient health and the healthcare system.

13. Physical Therapist

13.1 Overview of the Role

Physical therapists (PTs) are healthcare professionals who help patients improve their movement and manage pain. They are involved in the rehabilitation of individuals who have injuries, disabilities, or chronic conditions that affect their physical function. PTs develop personalized treatment plans using exercises, manual therapy, and various modalities to restore mobility, enhance strength, and improve overall quality of life.

13.2 Required Skills and Education

To become a successful physical therapist, a blend of clinical expertise, technical skills, and compassionate care is essential. Key requirements include:

Technical Skills:

- Anatomy and Physiology: Deep understanding of the human body, musculoskeletal system, and physiological processes.

- Therapeutic Exercise: Proficiency in designing and implementing exercise programs tailored to individual patient needs.

- Manual Therapy: Skills in hands-on techniques to manipulate muscles and joints.

- Modalities: Knowledge of using therapeutic equipment such as ultrasound, electrical stimulation, and heat/cold therapy.

- Patient Assessment: Ability to evaluate patient conditions, set goals, and track progress.

Educational Background:

- Degree: A Doctor of Physical Therapy (DPT) degree from an accredited program is required.

- Licensure: Passing the National Physical Therapy Examination (NPTE) is mandatory for licensure. State-specific requirements may also apply.

- Certifications: Additional certifications in specialty areas (e.g., Orthopedic Clinical Specialist, Sports Certified Specialist) can enhance career prospects.

- Continued Learning: Participation in continuing education courses to keep up with advancements in physical therapy practices and technologies.

Soft Skills:

- Communication: Effective communication with patients, families, and healthcare teams.

- Empathy: Providing compassionate care and support to patients.

- Critical Thinking: Strong problem-solving and decision-making abilities.

- Attention to Detail: Precision in developing and adjusting treatment plans.

- Physical Stamina: Ability to handle the physical demands of the job, including lifting and assisting patients.

13.3 Typical Work Environment

Physical therapists work in a variety of settings, including hospitals, outpatient clinics, rehabilitation centers, nursing homes, schools, and private practices. They may also provide home health services. The work environment is typically well-lit and equipped with various therapeutic tools and equipment. PTs often work full-time, with potential for evening and weekend shifts to accommodate patient schedules. The role is physically demanding, requiring the ability to stand for long periods and assist patients with exercises and movements.

13.4 Career Path and Growth Opportunities

The career path for physical therapists offers numerous opportunities for specialization and advancement:

- Entry-Level Positions: Staff Physical Therapist, focusing on developing clinical skills and gaining practical experience in patient care.

- Mid-Level Positions: Senior Physical Therapist, Clinical Specialist, or Rehabilitation Coordinator, taking on more responsibilities in patient management and specialized care.

- Senior-Level Positions: Lead Physical Therapist, Clinic Director, or Rehabilitation Manager, overseeing clinical operations, managing staff, and ensuring quality care.

- Specialization Areas: Orthopedics, Sports Medicine, Neurology, Pediatrics, Geriatrics, or Cardiovascular and Pulmonary Physical Therapy. Specializing in these areas allows PTs to focus on specific patient populations and conditions.

- Management Roles: Clinic Director, Rehabilitation Services Director, or Healthcare Administrator. These positions involve overseeing rehabilitation programs, managing budgets, and aligning therapy services with organizational goals.

- Continued Education: Pursuing advanced certifications or degrees (e.g., PhD in Physical Therapy) can lead to higher roles and increased salaries.

13.5 Tips for Success

To excel as a physical therapist, consider the following strategies:

- Prioritize Patient Care: Focus on providing patient-centered care by building strong relationships with patients and their families, understanding their goals, and tailoring treatment plans accordingly.

- Stay Updated: Continuously update your knowledge and skills through continuing education, professional development courses, and staying current with medical research.

- Develop Strong Interpersonal Skills: Effective communication and empathy are crucial for building rapport with patients and collaborating with healthcare teams.

- Embrace Technology: Familiarize yourself with the latest therapeutic equipment and techniques to improve patient outcomes.

- Seek Specialization: Consider pursuing additional certifications in specialized areas of interest to advance your career and enhance your expertise.

- Network and Mentor: Build a professional network through physical therapy associations (e.g., American Physical Therapy Association) and seek mentorship from experienced therapists to gain insights and career guidance.

  - Focus on Work-Life Balance: Manage stress and maintain a healthy work-life balance to ensure long-term productivity and job satisfaction.

By following these tips, you can build a successful and fulfilling career as a physical therapist, making a significant impact on patient health and mobility.

14. Medical Laboratory Technologist

14.1 Overview of the Role

Medical laboratory technologists, also known as clinical laboratory technologists, play a vital role in the healthcare system by performing complex tests and procedures on blood, tissue, and other body fluids. These tests help diagnose, treat, and prevent diseases. Medical lab technologists operate sophisticated equipment, analyze test results, and ensure the accuracy and reliability of the data.

14.2 Required Skills and Education

To become a successful medical laboratory technologist, a combination of technical proficiency, scientific knowledge, and attention to detail is essential. Key requirements include:

Technical Skills:

- Laboratory Techniques: Proficiency in conducting various tests such as hematology, microbiology, immunology, and clinical chemistry.

- Equipment Operation: Skills in using and maintaining laboratory instruments like microscopes, automated analyzers, and spectrophotometers.

- Quality Control: Ensuring accuracy and precision in test results through rigorous quality control procedures.

- Data Analysis: Ability to interpret and analyze test results accurately.

- Safety Protocols: Knowledge of safety procedures and regulations to handle biological specimens and hazardous materials.

Educational Background:

- Degree: A bachelor's degree in medical laboratory science, clinical laboratory science, or a related field is typically required.

- Licensure: Depending on the state, licensure or certification may be required. Certification options include the American Society for Clinical Pathology (ASCP) certification.

- Certifications: Specialty certifications (e.g., Molecular Biology, Cytotechnology) can enhance career prospects.

- Continued Learning: Participation in continuing education to keep up with advancements in laboratory techniques and technology.

Soft Skills:

- Attention to Detail: Precision in performing tests and recording results.

- Analytical Thinking: Strong problem-solving and analytical skills to interpret data.

- Communication: Effective communication with healthcare providers to convey test results and collaborate on patient care.

- Organization: Excellent organizational skills to manage multiple tests and ensure timely processing.

- Teamwork: Ability to work collaboratively with other laboratory staff and healthcare professionals.

14.3 Typical Work Environment

Medical laboratory technologists work in various healthcare settings, including hospitals, diagnostic laboratories, clinics, and research institutions. The work environment is typically clean, well-lit, and equipped with advanced laboratory instruments. Technologists may work full-time, with potential for evening, weekend, and holiday shifts to accommodate the needs of 24-hour facilities. The role involves standing for long periods, handling biological samples, and adhering to strict safety protocols to prevent contamination and ensure accuracy.

14.4 Career Path and Growth Opportunities

The career path for medical laboratory technologists offers various opportunities for specialization and advancement:

- Entry-Level Positions: Medical Laboratory Technologist, focusing on developing technical skills and gaining practical experience in laboratory settings.

- Mid-Level Positions: Senior Medical Technologist, Lead Technologist, or Laboratory Supervisor, taking on more responsibilities in test interpretation, quality control, and team management.

- Senior-Level Positions: Laboratory Manager, Clinical Laboratory Director, or Research Scientist, overseeing laboratory operations, managing staff, and leading research projects.

- Specialization Areas: Molecular Biology, Microbiology, Hematology, Clinical Chemistry, or Cytotechnology. Specializing in these areas allows technologists to focus on specific types of tests and enhance their expertise.

- Management Roles: Laboratory Director, Pathology Lab Manager, or Healthcare Administrator. These positions involve overseeing laboratory departments, managing budgets, and ensuring compliance with regulations.

- Continued Education: Pursuing advanced degrees (e.g., Master's in Clinical Laboratory Science) or specialized certifications can lead to higher roles and increased salaries.

14.5 Tips for Success

To excel as a medical laboratory technologist, consider the following strategies:

- Prioritize Accuracy and Precision: Ensure the highest level of accuracy and precision in performing tests and recording results. Double-check your work and adhere to quality control procedures.

- Stay Updated: Continuously update your knowledge and skills through continuing education, professional development courses, and staying current with medical research and laboratory advancements.

- Develop Strong Analytical Skills: Enhance your ability to analyze and interpret test results accurately through continuous practice and training.

- Embrace Technology: Familiarize yourself with the latest laboratory instruments and software to improve efficiency and accuracy.

- Seek Specialization: Consider pursuing additional certifications in specialized areas of interest to advance your career and enhance your expertise.

- Network and Mentor: Build a professional network through laboratory associations (e.g., American Society for Clinical Laboratory Science) and seek mentorship from experienced technologists to gain insights and career guidance.

- Focus on Safety: Adhere to safety protocols and regulations to ensure a safe working environment for yourself and others.

By following these tips, you can build a successful and fulfilling career as a medical laboratory technologist, making a significant impact on patient care and the healthcare system.

15. Radiologic Technologist

15.1 Overview of the Role

Radiologic technologists, also known as radiographers, are healthcare professionals who perform diagnostic imaging examinations, such as X-rays, MRI scans, CT scans, and mammograms. They work closely with radiologists and other healthcare providers to diagnose and monitor various medical conditions. Radiologic technologists ensure that high-quality images are produced while prioritizing patient safety and comfort.

15.2 Required Skills and Education

To become a successful radiologic technologist, a combination of technical proficiency, medical knowledge, and interpersonal skills is essential. Key requirements include:

Technical Skills:

- Imaging Techniques: Proficiency in operating imaging equipment, including X-ray, MRI, and CT machines.

- Radiation Safety: Knowledge of radiation protection principles to minimize exposure to patients and staff.

- Patient Positioning: Skills in positioning patients correctly to obtain the best images and ensure their comfort.

- Image Evaluation: Ability to assess the quality of images and determine if additional images are necessary.

- Medical Terminology: Understanding of medical terminology and anatomy to accurately capture images and assist with diagnoses.

Educational Background:

- Degree: An associate's degree in radiologic technology from an accredited program is typically required. Some positions may require a bachelor's degree.

- Licensure: Passing a certification exam, such as the American Registry of Radiologic Technologists (ARRT) certification, is mandatory for licensure.

- Certifications: Specialty certifications (e.g., MRI, CT) can enhance career prospects.

- Continued Learning: Participation in continuing education to keep up with advancements in imaging technology and techniques.

Soft Skills:

- Communication: Effective communication with patients to explain procedures and with healthcare teams to share findings.

- Compassion: Providing empathetic care and support to patients, especially those who may be anxious or in pain.

- Attention to Detail: Precision in capturing high-quality images and following imaging protocols.

- Problem-Solving: Ability to troubleshoot equipment issues and adapt to unexpected situations.

- Physical Stamina: Ability to handle the physical demands of the job, including standing for long periods and assisting patients.

15.3 Typical Work Environment

Radiologic technologists work in various healthcare settings, including hospitals, outpatient clinics, diagnostic imaging centers, and physician offices. The work environment is typically clean, well-lit, and equipped with advanced imaging technology. Radiologic technologists often work full-time, with potential for evening, weekend, and on-call shifts to accommodate patient needs. The role involves standing for long periods, operating imaging equipment, and ensuring patient safety and comfort.

15.4 Career Path and Growth Opportunities

The career path for radiologic technologists offers various opportunities for specialization and advancement:

- Entry-Level Positions: Radiologic Technologist, focusing on developing technical skills and gaining practical experience in imaging procedures.

- Mid-Level Positions: Senior Radiologic Technologist, Lead Technologist, or Imaging Specialist, taking on more responsibilities in advanced imaging techniques, quality control, and training.

- Senior-Level Positions: Imaging Manager, Radiology Department Supervisor, or Clinical Coordinator, overseeing imaging operations, managing staff, and ensuring compliance with regulations.

- Specialization Areas: MRI Technologist, CT Technologist, Mammography Technologist, or Interventional Radiology Technologist. Specializing in these areas allows technologists to focus on specific imaging modalities and enhance their expertise.

- Management Roles: Radiology Manager, Director of Imaging Services, or Healthcare Administrator. These positions involve overseeing imaging departments, managing budgets, and aligning imaging services with organizational goals.

- Continued Education: Pursuing advanced certifications or degrees (e.g., Bachelor's in Radiologic Sciences) can lead to higher roles and increased salaries.

15.5 Tips for Success

To excel as a radiologic technologist, consider the following strategies:

- Prioritize Patient Care: Focus on providing patient-centered care by explaining procedures clearly, ensuring patient comfort, and addressing any concerns they may have.

- Stay Updated: Continuously update your knowledge and skills through continuing education, professional development courses, and staying current with medical research and imaging advancements.

- Develop Strong Technical Skills: Enhance your proficiency in operating imaging equipment and evaluating image quality through continuous practice and training.

- Embrace Technology: Familiarize yourself with the latest imaging technology and software to improve efficiency and accuracy.

- Seek Specialization: Consider pursuing additional certifications in specialized imaging modalities to advance your career and enhance your expertise.

- Network and Mentor: Build a professional network through radiology associations (e.g., American Society of Radiologic Technologists) and seek mentorship from experienced technologists to gain insights and career guidance.

- Focus on Safety: Adhere to radiation safety protocols and regulations to ensure a safe working environment for yourself and patients.

By following these tips, you can build a successful and fulfilling career as a radiologic technologist, making a significant impact on patient care and the healthcare system.

16. Dental Hygienist

16.1 Overview of the Role

Dental hygienists are essential members of the dental care team who focus on preventive oral healthcare. They perform various tasks, including cleaning teeth, examining patients for signs of oral diseases, and providing other preventive dental care. Dental hygienists also educate patients on ways to improve and maintain good oral health.

16.2 Required Skills and Education

To become a successful dental hygienist, a combination of clinical expertise, technical skills, and interpersonal abilities is essential. Key requirements include:

Technical Skills:

- Clinical Procedures: Proficiency in performing dental cleanings, scaling, root planing, and applying sealants and fluoride treatments.

- Radiography: Skills in taking and interpreting dental X-rays.

- Patient Assessment: Ability to assess patients' oral health, identify signs of diseases, and document findings accurately.

- Infection Control: Knowledge of sterilization techniques and infection control procedures to maintain a safe and clean environment.

- Dental Software: Familiarity with dental practice management software for scheduling, record-keeping, and patient communication.

Educational Background:

- Degree: An associate's degree in dental hygiene from an accredited program is typically required. Some positions may prefer a bachelor's degree.

- Licensure: Passing the National Board Dental Hygiene Examination (NBDHE) and a state or regional clinical board examination is mandatory for licensure.

- Certifications: Additional certifications in areas such as local anesthesia, nitrous oxide sedation, or CPR can enhance career prospects.

- Continued Learning: Participation in continuing education to keep up with advancements in dental hygiene practices and technology.

Soft Skills:

- Communication: Effective communication with patients to explain procedures and oral hygiene practices.

- Compassion: Providing empathetic care and support to patients, especially those who may be anxious or have special needs.

- Attention to Detail: Precision in performing clinical procedures and documenting patient information.

- Critical Thinking: Ability to assess patient needs and make appropriate recommendations for treatment.

- Manual Dexterity: Skilled hand-eye coordination to perform precise dental procedures.

16.3 Typical Work Environment

Dental hygienists work in various settings, including private dental practices, clinics, hospitals, and public health facilities. The work environment is typically clean, well-lit, and equipped with advanced dental instruments. Dental hygienists often work part-time or full-time, with schedules that may include evenings and weekends to accommodate patients' needs. The role involves standing or sitting for long periods and working closely with dentists and other dental staff.

16.4 Career Path and Growth Opportunities

The career path for dental hygienists offers various opportunities for specialization and advancement:

- Entry-Level Positions: Dental Hygienist, focusing on developing clinical skills and gaining practical experience in preventive oral care.

- Mid-Level Positions: Senior Dental Hygienist, Lead Hygienist, or Oral Health Educator, taking on more responsibilities in patient care, education, and training.

- Senior-Level Positions: Dental Hygiene Coordinator, Clinical Instructor, or Public Health Dental Hygienist, overseeing dental hygiene programs, managing staff, and providing community-based oral health services.

- Specialization Areas: Pediatric Dental Hygienist, Orthodontic Hygienist, Periodontal Hygienist, or Geriatric Dental Hygienist. Specializing in these areas allows hygienists to focus on specific patient populations and conditions.

- Management Roles: Dental Office Manager, Dental Program Director, or Healthcare Administrator. These positions involve overseeing dental practice operations, managing budgets, and ensuring compliance with regulations.

- Continued Education: Pursuing advanced degrees (e.g., Bachelor's or Master's in Dental Hygiene) or specialized certifications can lead to higher roles and increased salaries.

16.5 Tips for Success

To excel as a dental hygienist, consider the following strategies:

- Prioritize Patient Care: Focus on providing patient-centered care by building strong relationships with patients, understanding their needs, and tailoring treatment plans accordingly.

- Stay Updated: Continuously update your knowledge and skills through continuing education, professional development courses, and staying current with dental research and advancements.

- Develop Strong Interpersonal Skills: Effective communication and empathy are crucial for building rapport with patients and collaborating with dental teams.

- Embrace Technology: Familiarize yourself with the latest dental instruments and software to improve efficiency and patient care.

- Seek Specialization: Consider pursuing additional certifications in specialized areas of interest to advance your career and enhance your expertise.

- Network and Mentor: Build a professional network through dental hygiene associations (e.g., American Dental Hygienists' Association) and seek mentorship from experienced hygienists to gain insights and career guidance.

- Focus on Prevention: Educate patients on preventive oral care practices, such as proper brushing, flossing, and dietary choices, to help them maintain good oral health.

By following these tips, you can build a successful and fulfilling career as a dental hygienist, making a significant impact on patients' oral health and overall well-being.

17. Occupational Therapist

17.1 Overview of the Role

Occupational therapists (OTs) help individuals of all ages develop, recover, and improve the skills needed for daily living and working. They focus on enabling patients to perform tasks independently through therapeutic use of everyday activities (occupations). OTs work with people who have physical, sensory, cognitive, or emotional disabilities, aiming to enhance their quality of life and promote independence.

17.2 Required Skills and Education

To become a successful occupational therapist, a combination of clinical expertise, creativity, and interpersonal skills is essential. Key requirements include:

Technical Skills:

- Therapeutic Techniques: Proficiency in various therapeutic interventions, including motor skills development, cognitive therapy, and sensory integration.

- Patient Assessment: Ability to evaluate patients' conditions, develop treatment plans, and set realistic goals.

- Adaptive Equipment: Knowledge of adaptive devices and technology to assist patients in performing daily activities.

- Anatomy and Physiology: Understanding of the human body and how disabilities impact function.

- Documentation: Skills in maintaining detailed patient records and documenting progress.

Educational Background:

- Degree: A master's degree in occupational therapy from an accredited program is required. Some positions may require a doctoral degree.

- Licensure: Passing the National Board for Certification in Occupational Therapy (NBCOT) exam is mandatory for licensure. State-specific requirements may also apply.

- Certifications: Additional certifications in specialty areas (e.g., Certified Hand Therapist, Certified Autism Specialist) can enhance career prospects.

- Continued Learning: Participation in continuing education to keep up with advancements in occupational therapy practices and techniques.

Soft Skills:

- Communication: Effective communication with patients, families, and healthcare teams.

- Compassion: Providing empathetic care and support to patients.

- Problem-Solving: Strong problem-solving and critical thinking abilities to develop effective treatment plans.

- Creativity: Innovative thinking to create engaging and effective therapeutic activities.

- Patience: Patience and perseverance in working with patients who may have slow progress.

17.3 Typical Work Environment

Occupational therapists work in various settings, including hospitals, rehabilitation centers, schools, nursing homes, and private practices. They may also provide home health services. The work environment is typically well-equipped with adaptive tools and therapeutic materials. OTs often work full-time, with schedules that may include evenings and weekends to accommodate patients' needs. The role involves standing, moving, and assisting patients with exercises and daily tasks.

17.4 Career Path and Growth Opportunities

The career path for occupational therapists offers various opportunities for specialization and advancement:

- Entry-Level Positions: Occupational Therapist, focusing on developing clinical skills and gaining practical experience in patient care.

- Mid-Level Positions: Senior Occupational Therapist, Clinical Specialist, or Rehabilitation Coordinator, taking on more responsibilities in patient management and specialized care.

- Senior-Level Positions: Lead Occupational Therapist, Clinic Director, or Rehabilitation Manager, overseeing clinical operations, managing staff, and ensuring quality care.

- Specialization Areas: Pediatrics, Geriatrics, Hand Therapy, Neurology, Mental Health, or Occupational Therapy for Autism Spectrum Disorders. Specializing in these areas allows OTs to focus on specific patient populations and conditions.

- Management Roles: Clinic Director, Rehabilitation Services Director, or Healthcare Administrator. These positions involve overseeing rehabilitation programs, managing budgets, and aligning therapy services with organizational goals.

- Continued Education: Pursuing advanced certifications or degrees (e.g., PhD in Occupational Therapy) can lead to higher roles and increased salaries.

17.5 Tips for Success

To excel as an occupational therapist, consider the following strategies:

- Prioritize Patient-Centered Care: Focus on understanding patients' unique needs and goals. Develop personalized treatment plans that address their specific challenges and help them achieve independence.

- Stay Updated: Continuously update your knowledge and skills through continuing education, professional development courses, and staying current with medical research.

- Develop Strong Interpersonal Skills: Effective communication and empathy are crucial for building rapport with patients and collaborating with healthcare teams.

- Embrace Creativity: Use innovative and engaging therapeutic activities to keep patients motivated and involved in their treatment plans.

- Seek Specialization: Consider pursuing additional certifications in specialized areas of interest to advance your career and enhance your expertise.

- Network and Mentor: Build a professional network through occupational therapy associations (e.g., American Occupational Therapy Association) and seek mentorship from experienced therapists to gain insights and career guidance.

- Focus on Holistic Care: Address the physical, emotional, and social aspects of patients' lives to provide comprehensive care and support their overall well-being.

By following these tips, you can build a successful and fulfilling career as an occupational therapist, making a significant impact on patients' lives and helping them achieve greater independence and quality of life.

18. Clinical Psychologist

18.1 Overview of the Role

Clinical psychologists are mental health professionals who diagnose and treat emotional, mental, and behavioral disorders. They use a variety of therapeutic techniques to help individuals manage and overcome mental health issues such as depression, anxiety, and schizophrenia. Clinical psychologists work with patients across the lifespan, providing therapy, conducting assessments, and developing treatment plans tailored to individual needs.

18.2 Required Skills and Education

To become a successful clinical psychologist, a combination of extensive education, clinical training, and interpersonal skills is essential. Key requirements include:

Technical Skills:

- Psychological Assessment: Proficiency in conducting psychological tests and assessments to diagnose mental health conditions.

- Therapeutic Techniques: Expertise in various therapeutic modalities, including cognitive-behavioral therapy (CBT), psychodynamic therapy, and humanistic approaches.

- Research Methods: Knowledge of research design, data analysis, and evidence-based practices.

- Ethics: Understanding of ethical principles and guidelines in clinical practice.

- Clinical Documentation: Skills in maintaining accurate and detailed patient records and treatment plans.

Educational Background:

- Degree: A doctoral degree in psychology (Ph.D. or Psy.D.) from an accredited program is required.

- Licensure: Passing the Examination for Professional Practice in Psychology (EPPP) and fulfilling state-specific licensure requirements are mandatory.

- Certifications: Board certification in clinical psychology from organizations such as the American Board of Professional Psychology (ABPP) can enhance career prospects.

- Continued Learning: Participation in continuing education to keep up with advancements in psychological research and therapy techniques.

Soft Skills:

- Communication: Effective communication with patients, families, and healthcare teams.

- Empathy: Providing compassionate care and understanding patients' perspectives.

- Critical Thinking: Strong problem-solving and analytical skills to develop effective treatment plans.

- Patience: Patience and perseverance in working with patients who may have complex and chronic issues.

- Confidentiality: Maintaining patient confidentiality and trust.

18.3 Typical Work Environment

Clinical psychologists work in various settings, including private practices, hospitals, mental health clinics, schools, and research institutions. The work environment is typically quiet and conducive to private, one-on-one sessions with patients. Clinical psychologists may work full-time or part-time, with schedules that include evenings or weekends to accommodate patients' needs. The role involves conducting therapy sessions, performing assessments, and collaborating with other healthcare providers to ensure comprehensive care.

18.4 Career Path and Growth Opportunities

The career path for clinical psychologists offers numerous opportunities for specialization and advancement:

- Entry-Level Positions: Clinical Psychologist or Therapist, focusing on developing clinical skills and gaining practical experience in therapy and assessment.

- Mid-Level Positions: Senior Clinical Psychologist, Clinical Supervisor, or Program Director, taking on more responsibilities in patient care, supervision, and program management.

- Senior-Level Positions: Chief Psychologist, Clinical Director, or Clinical Consultant, overseeing clinical operations, managing staff, and ensuring the quality of mental health services.

- Specialization Areas: Child and Adolescent Psychology, Neuropsychology, Forensic Psychology, Health Psychology, or Geropsychology. Specializing in these areas allows psychologists to focus on specific populations and conditions.

- Management Roles: Director of Mental Health Services, Head of Psychology Department, or Healthcare Administrator. These positions involve overseeing mental health programs, managing budgets, and aligning services with organizational goals.

- Continued Education: Pursuing advanced certifications or additional degrees can lead to higher roles and increased salaries.

18.5 Tips for Success

To excel as a clinical psychologist, consider the following strategies:

- Prioritize Patient-Centered Care: Focus on understanding patients' unique needs and developing personalized treatment plans. Build strong therapeutic relationships to enhance treatment outcomes.

- Stay Updated: Continuously update your knowledge and skills through continuing education, professional development courses, and staying current with psychological research.

- Develop Strong Interpersonal Skills: Effective communication, empathy, and active listening are crucial for building rapport with patients and collaborating with healthcare teams.

- Embrace Evidence-Based Practice: Use evidence-based therapies and interventions to ensure the highest standard of care.

- Seek Specialization: Consider pursuing additional certifications in specialized areas of interest to advance your career and enhance your expertise.

- Network and Mentor: Build a professional network through psychological associations (e.g., American Psychological

Association) and seek mentorship from experienced psychologists to gain insights and career guidance.

- Maintain Self-Care: Practice self-care to manage stress and prevent burnout, ensuring long-term productivity and job satisfaction.

By following these tips, you can build a successful and fulfilling career as a clinical psychologist, making a significant impact on the mental health and well-being of your patients.

19. Veterinarian

19.1 Overview of the Role

Veterinarians are medical professionals who diagnose, treat, and help prevent diseases and injuries in animals. They work with a variety of animals, including pets, livestock, zoo animals, and wildlife. Veterinarians provide medical care, perform surgeries, and offer advice on proper animal care, nutrition, and breeding. Their role is crucial in ensuring the health and well-being of animals and, by extension, public health.

19.2 Required Skills and Education

To become a successful veterinarian, a combination of medical knowledge, clinical skills, and compassion for animals is essential. Key requirements include:

Technical Skills:

- Medical Knowledge: Deep understanding of animal anatomy, physiology, and common diseases.

- Diagnostic Skills: Proficiency in diagnosing illnesses and injuries using various methods, including physical examinations, lab tests, and imaging techniques.

- Surgical Skills: Ability to perform surgeries ranging from routine spaying and neutering to complex operations.

- Pharmacology: Knowledge of medications and their effects on different animal species.

- Emergency Care: Skills in providing emergency medical care and critical care.

Educational Background:

- Degree: A Doctor of Veterinary Medicine (DVM or VMD) degree from an accredited veterinary school is required.

- Licensure: Passing the North American Veterinary Licensing Examination (NAVLE) is mandatory for licensure. State-specific requirements may also apply.

- Certifications: Additional certifications in specialty areas (e.g., Veterinary Surgery, Veterinary Internal Medicine) can enhance career prospects.

- Continued Learning: Participation in continuing education to keep up with advancements in veterinary medicine and techniques.

Soft Skills:

- Communication: Effective communication with pet owners, veterinary staff, and other healthcare professionals.

- Compassion: Providing empathetic care and support to animals and their owners.

- Problem-Solving: Strong problem-solving and critical thinking abilities to diagnose and treat medical conditions.

- Attention to Detail: Precision in performing medical procedures and documenting patient information.

- Physical Stamina: Ability to handle the physical demands of the job, including standing for long periods and handling animals.

19.3 Typical Work Environment

Veterinarians work in various settings, including private veterinary practices, animal hospitals, research laboratories, zoos, and farms. The work environment is typically clean and well-equipped with medical instruments and diagnostic tools. Veterinarians may work full-time or part-time, with schedules that include evenings, weekends, and on-call shifts to accommodate emergencies. The role involves interacting with animals of all sizes and temperaments, which can be physically demanding and sometimes hazardous.

19.4 Career Path and Growth Opportunities

The career path for veterinarians offers numerous opportunities for specialization and advancement:

- Entry-Level Positions: Associate Veterinarian, focusing on developing clinical skills and gaining practical experience in animal care.

- Mid-Level Positions: Senior Veterinarian, Lead Veterinarian, or Veterinary Specialist, taking on more responsibilities in patient care, surgery, and specialty services.

- Senior-Level Positions: Veterinary Hospital Director, Veterinary Practice Owner, or Veterinary Consultant, overseeing clinical operations, managing staff, and ensuring the quality of veterinary services.

- Specialization Areas: Veterinary Surgery, Veterinary Oncology, Veterinary Dermatology, Exotic Animal Medicine, or Wildlife Medicine. Specializing in these areas allows veterinarians to focus on specific species or medical conditions.

- Management Roles: Veterinary Practice Manager, Director of Veterinary Services, or Research Director. These positions involve overseeing veterinary programs, managing budgets, and aligning services with organizational goals.

- Continued Education: Pursuing advanced certifications or degrees (e.g., PhD in Veterinary Science) can lead to higher roles and increased salaries.

19.5 Tips for Success

To excel as a veterinarian, consider the following strategies:

- Prioritize Animal Welfare: Focus on providing compassionate and ethical care to animals. Build strong relationships with pet owners to understand their needs and concerns.

- Stay Updated: Continuously update your knowledge and skills through continuing education, professional development courses, and staying current with veterinary research.

- Develop Strong Interpersonal Skills: Effective communication, empathy, and active listening are crucial for building rapport with pet owners and collaborating with veterinary teams.

- Embrace Technology: Familiarize yourself with the latest veterinary technology and diagnostic tools to improve efficiency and accuracy.

- Seek Specialization: Consider pursuing additional certifications in specialized areas of interest to advance your career and enhance your expertise.

- Network and Mentor: Build a professional network through veterinary associations (e.g., American Veterinary Medical Association) and seek mentorship from experienced veterinarians to gain insights and career guidance.

- Focus on Self-Care: Practice self-care to manage stress and prevent burnout, ensuring long-term productivity and job satisfaction.

By following these tips, you can build a successful and fulfilling career as a veterinarian, making a significant impact on animal health and well-being.

Chapter 2 Review

Overview of Medical and Healthcare Careers

In Chapter 2, we explored various careers within the medical and healthcare fields. These professions are essential for maintaining and improving public health, providing critical services to individuals of all ages and backgrounds. Here's a summary of the key points covered for each role:

10. Registered Nurse

- Overview of the Role: Providing direct patient care, educating patients, and supporting families.

- Required Skills and Education: Clinical knowledge, medication administration, patient assessment, a nursing degree (ADN or BSN), licensure (NCLEX-RN), and ongoing education.

- Typical Work Environment: Hospitals, clinics, nursing homes, and private practices, with shifts that may include nights, weekends, and holidays.

- Career Path and Growth Opportunities: Entry-level to senior roles, specialization areas like critical care or pediatrics, and management positions.

- Tips for Success: Prioritize patient care, stay updated with continuing education, develop strong communication skills, manage stress effectively, and embrace technology.

11. Physician Assistant

- Overview of the Role: Diagnosing illnesses, developing treatment plans, prescribing medications, and serving as a principal healthcare provider.

- Required Skills and Education: Medical knowledge, diagnostic skills, treatment planning, a master's degree from an accredited PA program, licensure (PANCE), and ongoing CME.

- Typical Work Environment: Hospitals, clinics, private practices, and rural or underserved areas.

- Career Path and Growth Opportunities: Entry-level to senior roles, specialization in areas such as surgery or emergency medicine, and management positions.

- Tips for Success: Prioritize patient care, stay updated, develop strong interpersonal skills, embrace technology, seek specialization, and network for mentorship.

12. Pharmacist

- Overview of the Role: Dispensing medications, providing drug information, and advising on safe medication use.

- Required Skills and Education: Pharmacology, medication dispensing, patient counseling, a Pharm.D. degree, licensure (NAPLEX), and ongoing CE.

- Typical Work Environment: Retail pharmacies, hospitals, clinics, and long-term care facilities.

- Career Path and Growth Opportunities: Entry-level to senior roles, specialization areas like oncology or geriatrics, and management positions.

- Tips for Success: Prioritize patient safety, stay updated, develop strong interpersonal skills, embrace technology, seek specialization, and focus on work-life balance.

13. Physical Therapist

- Overview of the Role: Helping patients improve movement and manage pain through therapeutic exercises and manual therapy.

- Required Skills and Education: Therapeutic techniques, patient assessment, a DPT degree, licensure (NPTE), and ongoing CE.

- Typical Work Environment: Hospitals, outpatient clinics, rehabilitation centers, nursing homes, and home health services.

- Career Path and Growth Opportunities: Entry-level to senior roles, specialization areas like orthopedics or sports medicine, and management positions.

- Tips for Success: Prioritize patient-centered care, stay updated, develop strong interpersonal skills, embrace creativity, seek specialization, and focus on work-life balance.

14. Medical Laboratory Technologist

- Overview of the Role: Performing complex tests and procedures on blood, tissue, and other body fluids to diagnose and prevent diseases.

- Required Skills and Education: Laboratory techniques, equipment operation, data analysis, a bachelor's degree in medical laboratory science, licensure or certification, and ongoing CE.

- Typical Work Environment: Hospitals, diagnostic laboratories, clinics, and research institutions.

- Career Path and Growth Opportunities: Entry-level to senior roles, specialization areas like molecular biology or microbiology, and management positions.

- Tips for Success: Prioritize accuracy and precision, stay updated, develop strong analytical skills, embrace technology, seek specialization, and focus on safety.

15. Radiologic Technologist

- Overview of the Role: Performing diagnostic imaging examinations such as X-rays, MRI scans, CT scans, and mammograms.

- Required Skills and Education: Imaging techniques, radiation safety, patient positioning, a degree in radiologic technology, licensure (ARRT), and ongoing CE.

- Typical Work Environment: Hospitals, outpatient clinics, diagnostic imaging centers, and physician offices.

- Career Path and Growth Opportunities: Entry-level to senior roles, specialization areas like MRI or CT, and management positions.

- Tips for Success: Prioritize patient care, stay updated, develop strong technical skills, embrace technology, seek specialization, and focus on safety.

16. Dental Hygienist

- Overview of the Role: Cleaning teeth, examining patients for oral diseases, and providing preventive dental care.

- Required Skills and Education: Clinical procedures, radiography, patient assessment, an associate's or bachelor's degree in dental hygiene, licensure (NBDHE), and ongoing CE.

- Typical Work Environment: Private dental practices, clinics, hospitals, and public health facilities.

- Career Path and Growth Opportunities: Entry-level to senior roles, specialization areas like pediatric or periodontal hygiene, and management positions.

- Tips for Success: Prioritize patient care, stay updated, develop strong interpersonal skills, embrace technology, seek specialization, and focus on prevention.

17. Occupational Therapist

- Overview of the Role: Helping individuals develop, recover, and improve the skills needed for daily living and working.

- Required Skills and Education: Therapeutic techniques, patient assessment, a master's degree in occupational therapy, licensure (NBCOT), and ongoing CE.

- Typical Work Environment: Hospitals, rehabilitation centers, schools, nursing homes, and private practices.

- Career Path and Growth Opportunities: Entry-level to senior roles, specialization areas like pediatrics or neurology, and management positions.

- Tips for Success: Prioritize patient-centered care, stay updated, develop strong interpersonal skills, embrace creativity, seek specialization, and focus on holistic care.

18. Clinical Psychologist

- Overview of the Role: Diagnosing and treating emotional, mental, and behavioral disorders using various therapeutic techniques.

- Required Skills and Education: Psychological assessment, therapeutic techniques, research methods, a doctoral degree in psychology, licensure (EPPP), and ongoing CE.

- Typical Work Environment: Private practices, hospitals, mental health clinics, schools, and research institutions.

- Career Path and Growth Opportunities: Entry-level to senior roles, specialization areas like neuropsychology or forensic psychology, and management positions.

- Tips for Success: Prioritize patient-centered care, stay updated, develop strong interpersonal skills, embrace evidence-based practice, seek specialization, and maintain self-care.

19. Veterinarian

- Overview of the Role: Diagnosing, treating, and preventing diseases and injuries in animals.

- Required Skills and Education: Medical knowledge, diagnostic skills, surgical skills, a DVM or VMD degree, licensure (NAVLE), and ongoing CE.

- Typical Work Environment: Private veterinary practices, animal hospitals, research laboratories, zoos, and farms.

- Career Path and Growth Opportunities: Entry-level to senior roles, specialization areas like veterinary surgery or oncology, and management positions.

- Tips for Success: Prioritize animal welfare, stay updated, develop strong interpersonal skills, embrace technology, seek specialization, and focus on self-care.

Key Takeaways

- Continuous Learning: Staying updated with industry trends and technological advancements is crucial across all medical and healthcare careers.

- Networking: Building a professional network through industry events, online forums, and professional associations can provide valuable opportunities and insights.

- Practical Experience: Gaining hands-on experience through internships, clinical rotations, or part-time jobs is essential for skill development and career advancement.

- Certifications and Education: Obtaining relevant certifications and pursuing higher education can enhance career prospects and open up advanced roles.

- Patient-Centered Care: Prioritizing the well-being and needs of patients is fundamental to success in healthcare careers.

- Work-Life Balance: Maintaining a healthy work-life balance is crucial for long-term productivity and job satisfaction.

By understanding the roles, required skills, typical work environments, career paths, and tips for success, you can make informed decisions about pursuing a career in the medical and healthcare fields covered in this chapter. Whether you are just starting out or looking to advance your career, this guide provides the essential information to help you succeed.

Chapter 3: Business and Finance Careers

20. Financial Analyst

20.1 Overview of the Role

Financial analysts are experts in evaluating financial data to guide investment decisions and business strategies. They assess financial statements, market conditions, and economic trends to provide insights that help companies and individuals make informed financial choices. Financial analysts work in various settings, including investment banks, insurance companies, mutual funds, and corporations.

20.2 Required Skills and Education

To excel as a financial analyst, you need a combination of strong analytical capabilities, relevant education, and interpersonal skills. Here's an outline of the necessary qualifications:

- Technical Skills:

  - Financial Analysis: Ability to dissect financial reports, balance sheets, and income statements.

  - Valuation Methods: Proficiency in techniques like discounted cash flow (DCF), comparative analysis, and precedent transactions.

  - Financial Modeling: Competence in building robust financial models using Excel and other financial software.

  - Investment Strategies: Understanding of various investment vehicles, risk assessment, and portfolio management principles.

- Software Knowledge: Experience with financial databases and tools such as Bloomberg Terminal, Reuters, and advanced Excel functions.

- Educational Background:

- Degree: A bachelor's degree in finance, economics, accounting, or related fields is typically required. Higher education, such as an MBA or a Master's in Finance, can provide an edge.

- Certifications: Earning certifications such as Chartered Financial Analyst (CFA), Certified Financial Planner (CFP), or Financial Risk Manager (FRM) can significantly boost your credentials.

- Ongoing Education: Engaging in continuous learning through workshops, online courses, and seminars to keep up with evolving financial trends and technologies.

- Soft Skills:

- Analytical Acumen: Exceptional ability to interpret complex financial data and derive actionable insights.

- Detail-Oriented: Keen attention to detail in reviewing financial documents and identifying significant trends.

- Effective Communication: Proficiency in explaining financial concepts and recommendations to clients and colleagues.

- Problem-Solving: Aptitude for developing strategic solutions to financial challenges.

- Time Management: Ability to prioritize tasks and manage time efficiently, especially during busy periods like financial reporting.

20.3 Typical Work Environment

Financial analysts work in diverse professional settings, each with its unique environment and expectations:

- Work Hours: Full-time roles often extend beyond standard hours, particularly during critical reporting periods or when market conditions fluctuate.

- Office Setting: Most analysts work in corporate offices, financial institutions, or government agencies.

- Collaboration: Regular interaction with colleagues, including other analysts, portfolio managers, and corporate executives.

- Data-Driven Tasks: Significant time spent analyzing financial data, forecasting market trends, and preparing detailed reports.

20.4 Career Path and Growth Opportunities

Financial analysts have a variety of paths for career advancement and specialization:

- Entry-Level Roles: Starting positions such as Junior Financial Analyst, Research Analyst, or Investment Analyst.

- Mid-Level Positions: Roles like Senior Financial Analyst, Sector Analyst, or Fund Analyst.

- Advanced Roles: Higher positions including Lead Analyst, Portfolio Manager, or Director of Financial Planning and Analysis.

- Specializations: Focusing on areas such as Mergers and Acquisitions (M&A), Corporate Finance, Risk Management, Wealth Management, or Equity Research.

- Further Education: Advanced certifications or specialized training can open doors to senior roles and niche sectors within finance.

20.5 Tips for Success

To thrive as a financial analyst, consider the following strategies:

- Continuous Learning: Stay abreast of the latest financial developments, market trends, and analytical techniques through ongoing education.

- Networking: Cultivate a professional network through industry conferences, finance groups, and online platforms.

- Hands-On Experience: Gain practical experience through internships, entry-level roles, and real-world financial analysis projects.

- Certifications: Pursue and maintain professional certifications to enhance credibility and career prospects.

- Seek Guidance: Engage with mentors and seasoned professionals for career advice and insight.

- Professional Associations: Join organizations like the CFA Institute for access to resources, training, and networking opportunities.

- Balance and Wellbeing: Maintain a balance between professional responsibilities and personal life to sustain long-term career health.

By adhering to these strategies, you can establish a successful career as a financial analyst, playing a pivotal role in guiding investment decisions and shaping financial strategies for businesses and individuals alike.

21. Accountant

21.1 Overview of the Role

Accountants are financial professionals responsible for preparing and examining financial records, ensuring accuracy, and compliance with applicable laws and regulations. They provide insights into financial health, help manage budgets, and advise on financial planning and tax matters. Accountants work in various settings, including public accounting firms, corporations, government agencies, and non-profit organizations.

21.2 Required Skills and Education

To become a successful accountant, a combination of technical skills, formal education, and soft skills are essential. Here's a comprehensive breakdown:

- Technical Skills:

- Accounting Principles: In-depth knowledge of Generally Accepted Accounting Principles (GAAP) and International Financial Reporting Standards (IFRS).

- Financial Reporting: Expertise in preparing financial statements, balance sheets, income statements, and cash flow statements.

- Taxation: Understanding of tax laws, regulations, and filing requirements.

- Auditing: Proficiency in internal and external auditing processes.

- Software Proficiency: Familiarity with accounting software such as QuickBooks, SAP, and Microsoft Excel.

- *Educational Background:*

- Degree: A bachelor's degree in accounting, finance, or a related field is typically required. Advanced degrees (MBA or Master's in Accounting) can enhance career prospects.

- Certifications: Professional certifications such as Certified Public Accountant (CPA), Certified Management Accountant (CMA), or Chartered Accountant (CA) are highly valued.

- Ongoing Education: Participation in continuing professional education (CPE) to stay updated with the latest accounting standards and regulations.

- *Soft Skills:*

- Attention to Detail: Precision in preparing and reviewing financial documents.

- Analytical Thinking: Ability to interpret financial data and identify trends.

- Communication: Clear and effective communication with clients, colleagues, and stakeholders.

- Problem-Solving: Skills to develop solutions for financial discrepancies and challenges.

- Organizational Skills: Efficient management of multiple tasks and deadlines.

21.3 Typical Work Environment

Accountants typically work in diverse professional environments, each with its unique requirements and atmosphere:

- Work Hours: Generally full-time, with potential for overtime during peak periods such as tax season or financial year-end.

- Office Setting: Work in corporate offices, accounting firms, government buildings, or remotely.

- Team Collaboration: Interaction with other accountants, financial analysts, auditors, and management.

- Compliance and Reporting: Ensuring adherence to financial regulations and timely submission of reports.

21.4 Career Path and Growth Opportunities

The career path of an accountant offers numerous avenues for advancement and specialization:

- Entry-Level Positions: Junior Accountant, Staff Accountant, or Accounts Payable/Receivable Clerk.

- Mid-Level Positions: Senior Accountant, Financial Analyst, or Accounting Manager.

- Advanced Roles: Controller, Finance Director, Chief Financial Officer (CFO), or Partner in an accounting firm.

- Specializations: Forensic Accounting, Tax Accounting, Management Accounting, Auditing, and Financial Planning.

- Further Education: Advanced degrees or certifications in specific areas of accounting can lead to higher-level roles and specialized positions.

21.5 Tips for Success

To excel as an accountant, consider the following strategies:

- Continuous Learning: Stay updated with the latest accounting standards, tax laws, and industry trends through ongoing education.

- Networking: Build a professional network through industry associations, conferences, and online platforms.

- Practical Experience: Gain hands-on experience through internships, entry-level positions, and real-world accounting projects.

- Certifications: Pursue and maintain professional certifications to enhance your skills and career prospects.

- Seek Guidance: Engage with mentors and experienced professionals for career advice and insights.

- Professional Associations: Join organizations like the American Institute of Certified Public Accountants (AICPA) for access to resources, training, and networking opportunities.

- Ethical Standards: Adhere to high ethical standards and maintain integrity in all financial dealings.

By implementing these strategies, you can build a successful and rewarding career as an accountant, playing a vital role in financial management and decision-making for businesses and individuals.

22. Marketing Manager

22.1 Overview of the Role

Marketing Managers oversee the marketing strategies and campaigns for businesses to promote their products or services. They analyze market trends, identify target audiences, develop marketing plans, and coordinate efforts across various channels to increase brand awareness and drive sales. Marketing Managers play a crucial role in aligning marketing efforts with business goals, managing budgets, and leading marketing teams.

22.2 Required Skills and Education

To become a successful marketing manager, a combination of technical skills, formal education, and soft skills are essential. Here's a comprehensive breakdown:

- Technical Skills:

  - Market Research: Proficiency in conducting and analyzing market research to understand consumer behavior and market trends.

  - Strategic Planning: Skills in developing and implementing marketing strategies and plans.

  - Digital Marketing: Knowledge of digital marketing channels, including SEO, SEM, social media, email marketing, and content marketing.

  - Data Analysis: Ability to analyze marketing metrics and data to measure campaign effectiveness and ROI.

  - Brand Management: Experience in managing and building brand identity and positioning.

- Educational Background:

  - Degree: A bachelor's degree in marketing, business administration, or a related field is typically required. An advanced degree (MBA or Master's in Marketing) can provide an edge.

  - Certifications: Professional certifications such as Certified Professional Marketer (CPM), Google Analytics, or HubSpot Content Marketing can enhance your credentials.

  - Ongoing Education: Participation in marketing seminars, workshops, and courses to stay updated with the latest marketing trends and techniques.

- *Soft Skills:*

- Creativity: Ability to develop innovative marketing ideas and campaigns.

- Communication: Strong verbal and written communication skills to convey marketing messages effectively.

- Leadership: Skills to lead and motivate marketing teams and manage cross-functional projects.

- Problem-Solving: Ability to address marketing challenges and find effective solutions.

- Project Management: Organizational skills to manage multiple projects and meet deadlines.

22.3 Typical Work Environment

Marketing Managers typically work in diverse professional environments, each with its unique requirements and atmosphere:

- Work Hours: Generally full-time, with potential for overtime during campaign launches or peak marketing periods.

- Office Setting: Work in corporate offices, marketing agencies, or remotely.

- Team Collaboration: Interaction with marketing teams, sales departments, product development teams, and external vendors.

- Client Interaction: Regular communication with clients to understand their needs and ensure satisfaction with marketing efforts.

22.4 Career Path and Growth Opportunities

The career path of a marketing manager offers numerous avenues for advancement and specialization:

- Entry-Level Positions: Marketing Coordinator, Marketing Assistant, or Social Media Specialist.

- Mid-Level Positions: Marketing Manager, Brand Manager, or Digital Marketing Manager.

- Advanced Roles: Senior Marketing Manager, Director of Marketing, Chief Marketing Officer (CMO), or Vice President of Marketing.

- Specializations: Content Marketing, Digital Marketing, Product Marketing, Brand Management, and Market Research.

- Further Education: Advanced degrees or certifications in specific areas of marketing can lead to higher-level roles and specialized positions.

22.5 Tips for Success

To excel as a marketing manager, consider the following strategies:

- Continuous Learning: Stay updated with the latest marketing trends, tools, and techniques through ongoing education and professional development.

- Networking: Build a professional network through industry associations, conferences, and online platforms.

- Practical Experience: Gain hands-on experience through internships, entry-level positions, and real-world marketing projects.

- Certifications: Pursue and maintain professional certifications to enhance your skills and career prospects.

- Seek Guidance: Engage with mentors and experienced professionals for career advice and insights.

- Professional Associations: Join organizations like the American Marketing Association (AMA) for access to resources, training, and networking opportunities.

- Data-Driven Decisions: Utilize data and analytics to guide marketing strategies and measure success.

By implementing these strategies, you can build a successful and rewarding career as a marketing manager, driving impactful marketing campaigns and contributing to the growth and success of businesses.

23. Human Resources Manager

23.1 Overview of the Role

Human Resources (HR) Managers are responsible for overseeing all aspects of human resources practices and processes within an organization. They manage recruitment, employee relations, performance management, training and development, benefits administration, and compliance with labor laws. HR Managers play a critical role in shaping the company culture, ensuring employee satisfaction, and driving organizational success through effective HR strategies.

23.2 Required Skills and Education

To become a successful HR manager, a combination of technical skills, formal education, and soft skills are essential. Here's a comprehensive breakdown:

- *Technical Skills:*

- Recruitment and Selection: Proficiency in talent acquisition, interviewing, and hiring processes.

- Employee Relations: Skills in managing employee relations, conflict resolution, and fostering a positive work environment.

- Performance Management: Knowledge of performance appraisal systems and techniques.

- HR Compliance: Understanding of labor laws, employment regulations, and compliance requirements.

- HR Software: Familiarity with HR Information Systems (HRIS) such as Workday, ADP, or SAP SuccessFactors.

- *Educational Background:*

- Degree: A bachelor's degree in human resources, business administration, or a related field is typically required. An advanced degree (MBA or Master's in HR) can provide an edge.

- Certifications: Professional certifications such as Professional in Human Resources (PHR), Senior Professional in Human Resources (SPHR), or SHRM Certified Professional (SHRM-CP) can enhance your credentials.

- Ongoing Education: Participation in HR seminars, workshops, and courses to stay updated with the latest HR trends and best practices.

- *Soft Skills:*

- Communication: Strong verbal and written communication skills to interact effectively with employees and management.

- Leadership: Ability to lead and motivate HR teams and manage cross-functional projects.

- Problem-Solving: Skills to address HR challenges and develop effective solutions.

- Empathy and Compassion: Providing support and understanding to employees.

- Organizational Skills: Efficient management of HR tasks, documentation, and deadlines.

23.3 Typical Work Environment

HR Managers typically work in diverse professional environments, each with its unique requirements and atmosphere:

- Work Hours: Generally full-time, with potential for overtime during peak periods such as recruitment drives or policy changes.

- Office Setting: Work in corporate offices, government agencies, non-profits, or remotely.

- Team Collaboration: Interaction with HR teams, department managers, and company leadership.

- Employee Interaction: Regular communication with employees to address concerns, provide guidance, and foster a positive work environment.

23.4 Career Path and Growth Opportunities

The career path of an HR manager offers numerous avenues for advancement and specialization:

- Entry-Level Positions: HR Coordinator, HR Assistant, or Recruiter.

- Mid-Level Positions: HR Manager, Talent Acquisition Manager, or Employee Relations Manager.

- Advanced Roles: Senior HR Manager, Director of Human Resources, Chief Human Resources Officer (CHRO), or VP of HR.

- Specializations: Compensation and Benefits, Talent Management, Employee Development, Labor Relations, and HR Compliance.

- Further Education: Advanced degrees or certifications in specific areas of HR can lead to higher-level roles and specialized positions.

23.5 Tips for Success

To excel as an HR manager, consider the following strategies:

- Continuous Learning: Stay updated with the latest HR trends, tools, and techniques through ongoing education and professional development.

- Networking: Build a professional network through HR associations, conferences, and online platforms.

- Practical Experience: Gain hands-on experience through internships, entry-level positions, and real-world HR projects.

- Certifications: Pursue and maintain professional certifications to enhance your skills and career prospects.

- Seek Guidance: Engage with mentors and experienced professionals for career advice and insights.

- Professional Associations: Join organizations like the Society for Human Resource Management (SHRM) for access to resources, training, and networking opportunities.

- Focus on Employee Engagement: Develop strategies to improve employee satisfaction, retention, and engagement.

By implementing these strategies, you can build a successful and rewarding career as an HR manager, driving effective human resources practices and contributing to the overall success of your organization.

24. Project Manager

24.1 Overview of the Role

Project Managers are responsible for planning, executing, and closing projects, ensuring that the project meets its goals within the given constraints of scope, time, and budget. They coordinate teams, manage resources, communicate with stakeholders, and mitigate risks to ensure successful project completion. Project Managers work across various industries, including construction, IT, healthcare, finance, and more.

24.2 Required Skills and Education

To become a successful project manager, a combination of technical skills, formal education, and soft skills are essential. Here's a comprehensive breakdown:

- Technical Skills:

- Project Planning: Expertise in developing detailed project plans, timelines, and schedules.

- Budget Management: Skills in budgeting, cost estimation, and financial tracking.

- Risk Management: Ability to identify potential risks and develop mitigation strategies.

- Project Management Software: Proficiency in tools such as Microsoft Project, Asana, Trello, or Jira.

- Quality Control: Knowledge of quality assurance processes and standards.

- Educational Background:

- Degree: A bachelor's degree in project management, business administration, engineering, or a related field is typically required. Advanced degrees (MBA or Master's in Project Management) can provide an edge.

- Certifications: Professional certifications such as Project Management Professional (PMP), Certified ScrumMaster (CSM), or PRINCE2 Practitioner are highly valued.

- Ongoing Education: Participation in project management seminars, workshops, and courses to stay updated with the latest methodologies and best practices.

- Soft Skills:

- Leadership: Ability to lead and motivate project teams to achieve goals.

- Communication: Strong verbal and written communication skills to interact effectively with stakeholders and team members.

- Problem-Solving: Skills to address project challenges and develop effective solutions.

- Time Management: Efficient management of project timelines and deadlines.

- Organizational Skills: Ability to manage multiple tasks and ensure all aspects of the project are aligned.

24.3 Typical Work Environment

Project Managers typically work in diverse professional environments, each with its unique requirements and atmosphere:

- Work Hours: Generally full-time, with potential for overtime during critical project phases.

- Office Setting: Work in corporate offices, construction sites, or remotely, depending on the industry.

- Team Collaboration: Interaction with project teams, stakeholders, and clients.

- Dynamic Environment: Managing multiple projects simultaneously and adapting to changing project requirements.

24.4 Career Path and Growth Opportunities

The career path of a project manager offers numerous avenues for advancement and specialization:

- Entry-Level Positions: Project Coordinator, Junior Project Manager, or Assistant Project Manager.

- Mid-Level Positions: Project Manager, Senior Project Manager, or Program Manager.

- Advanced Roles: Project Director, Portfolio Manager, Chief Project Officer (CPO), or VP of Project Management.

- Specializations: IT Project Management, Construction Management, Agile Project Management, Healthcare Project Management, and Financial Project Management.

- Further Education: Advanced degrees or certifications in specific areas of project management can lead to higher-level roles and specialized positions.

24.5 Tips for Success

To excel as a project manager, consider the following strategies:

- Continuous Learning: Stay updated with the latest project management trends, tools, and techniques through ongoing education and professional development.

- Networking: Build a professional network through project management associations, conferences, and online platforms.

- Practical Experience: Gain hands-on experience through internships, entry-level positions, and real-world project management projects.

- Certifications: Pursue and maintain professional certifications to enhance your skills and career prospects.

- Seek Guidance: Engage with mentors and experienced professionals for career advice and insights.

- Professional Associations: Join organizations like the Project Management Institute (PMI) for access to resources, training, and networking opportunities.

- Focus on Communication: Develop strong communication skills to ensure clear and effective project updates and stakeholder engagement.

By implementing these strategies, you can build a successful and rewarding career as a project manager, driving successful project outcomes and contributing to the overall success of your organization.

25. Management Consultant

25.1 Overview of the Role

Management consultants help organizations improve their performance by analyzing existing business problems and developing strategies for improvement. They work with senior management to provide expert advice, support organizational change, optimize business processes, and implement strategic initiatives. Consultants can work in a variety of industries, including finance, healthcare, technology, and government.

25.2 Required Skills and Education

To become a successful management consultant, a combination of analytical skills, formal education, and interpersonal skills are essential. Here's a comprehensive breakdown:

- Technical Skills:

  - Business Analysis: Expertise in analyzing business operations, financial statements, and market trends.

  - Strategic Planning: Skills in developing strategic plans and business models.

  - Data Analysis: Proficiency in data collection, statistical analysis, and interpretation.

  - Project Management: Knowledge of project management principles and methodologies.

  - Software Proficiency: Familiarity with business analysis tools such as Excel, Tableau, and project management software.

- *Educational Background:*

- Degree: A bachelor's degree in business administration, management, economics, or a related field is typically required. Advanced degrees (MBA or Master's in Management) can provide an edge.

- Certifications: Professional certifications such as Certified Management Consultant (CMC) or Project Management Professional (PMP) can enhance your credentials.

- Ongoing Education: Participation in management seminars, workshops, and courses to stay updated with the latest business practices and trends.

- *Soft Skills:*

- Analytical Thinking: Strong analytical skills to diagnose problems and develop effective solutions.

- Communication: Excellent verbal and written communication skills to convey recommendations clearly.

- Leadership: Ability to lead teams and drive organizational change.

- Problem-Solving: Skills to address complex business challenges and develop innovative solutions.

- Interpersonal Skills: Ability to build relationships and work collaboratively with clients and stakeholders.

25.3 *Typical Work Environment*

Management consultants typically work in diverse professional environments, each with its unique requirements and atmosphere:

- Work Hours: Generally full-time, with potential for overtime and travel to client sites.

- Office Setting: Work in corporate offices, consulting firms, or remotely.

- Client Interaction: Frequent interaction with clients to understand their needs and provide tailored solutions.

- Dynamic Environment: Managing multiple projects and adapting to different industries and business challenges.

25.4 Career Path and Growth Opportunities

The career path of a management consultant offers numerous avenues for advancement and specialization:

- Entry-Level Positions: Associate Consultant, Business Analyst, or Junior Consultant.

- Mid-Level Positions: Consultant, Senior Consultant, or Engagement Manager.

- Advanced Roles: Principal Consultant, Director of Consulting, Partner, or Managing Director.

- Specializations: Strategy Consulting, Operations Consulting, IT Consulting, Human Resources Consulting, and Financial Advisory.

- Further Education: Advanced degrees or certifications in specific areas of management consulting can lead to higher-level roles and specialized positions.

25.5 Tips for Success

To excel as a management consultant, consider the following strategies:

- Continuous Learning: Stay updated with the latest business trends, tools, and techniques through ongoing education and professional development.

- Networking: Build a professional network through consulting associations, industry conferences, and online platforms.

- Practical Experience: Gain hands-on experience through internships, entry-level positions, and real-world consulting projects.

- Certifications: Pursue and maintain professional certifications to enhance your skills and career prospects.

- Seek Guidance: Engage with mentors and experienced consultants for career advice and insights.

- Professional Associations: Join organizations like the Institute of Management Consultants USA (IMC USA) for access to resources, training, and networking opportunities.

- Client Focus: Develop strong client management skills to ensure satisfaction and foster long-term relationships.

By implementing these strategies, you can build a successful and rewarding career as a management consultant, helping organizations achieve their goals and improve their overall performance.

26. Entrepreneur

26.1 Overview of the Role

Entrepreneurs are individuals who create and manage new business ventures, taking on financial risks in the hopes of profit. They identify market opportunities, develop innovative products or services, and build companies from the ground up. Entrepreneurs are driven by creativity, vision, and the desire to bring new ideas to life. They play a crucial role in driving economic growth, innovation, and job creation.

26.2 Required Skills and Education

To become a successful entrepreneur, a combination of creative thinking, business acumen, and soft skills are essential. Here's a comprehensive breakdown:

- Technical Skills:

  - Business Planning: Ability to develop comprehensive business plans, including market analysis, financial projections, and strategic goals.

  - Financial Management: Skills in budgeting, financial analysis, and funding acquisition.

  - Marketing: Proficiency in developing marketing strategies, branding, and customer outreach.

  - Operations Management: Knowledge of business operations, supply chain management, and productivity optimization.

  - Technology: Familiarity with relevant technology and software tools for business management.

- Educational Background:

  - Degree: While formal education is not always required, a bachelor's degree in business, entrepreneurship, or a related field can provide valuable knowledge and skills. Many successful entrepreneurs also pursue MBAs to enhance their business acumen.

  - Certifications: Certifications in areas such as project management, digital marketing, or financial planning can be beneficial.

- Ongoing Education: Participation in entrepreneurship workshops, seminars, and courses to stay updated with the latest business trends and practices.

- Soft Skills:

- Creativity and Innovation: Ability to think outside the box and develop unique solutions to market needs.

- Leadership: Strong leadership skills to inspire and manage a team.

- Resilience: Ability to handle setbacks and persist through challenges.

- Networking: Skills in building and maintaining professional relationships.

- Problem-Solving: Aptitude for identifying problems and developing effective solutions.

26.3 Typical Work Environment

Entrepreneurs typically work in dynamic and varied environments, each with its unique requirements and atmosphere:

- Work Hours: Often extended and irregular, especially during the startup phase. Entrepreneurs need to be flexible and adaptable.

- Office Setting: Work can take place in home offices, coworking spaces, corporate offices, or on-site at business locations.

- Team Collaboration: Interaction with co-founders, employees, investors, customers, and other stakeholders.

- Dynamic Environment: Managing multiple aspects of the business simultaneously and adapting to changing market conditions.

26.4 Career Path and Growth Opportunities

The career path of an entrepreneur is unique and can vary greatly depending on the individual's goals, industry, and business model:

- Startup Phase: Identifying opportunities, developing business ideas, and launching a startup.

- Growth Phase: Scaling the business, expanding the customer base, and increasing market share.

- Maturity Phase: Managing a stable and profitable business, exploring new opportunities, and diversifying products or services.

- Exit Strategy: Options include selling the business, merging with another company, or transitioning to a leadership role within the company.

- Serial Entrepreneurship: Many entrepreneurs start multiple ventures over their careers, leveraging their experience to launch new businesses.

26.5 Tips for Success

To excel as an entrepreneur, consider the following strategies:

- Continuous Learning: Stay updated with the latest industry trends, technologies, and business practices through ongoing education.

- Networking: Build a strong professional network through industry events, entrepreneurial organizations, and online platforms.

- Practical Experience: Gain hands-on experience by starting small projects, interning with startups, or working in relevant industries.

- Mentorship: Seek guidance from experienced entrepreneurs and business leaders for advice and support.

- Focus on Customer Needs: Develop products or services that address real market needs and provide value to customers.

- Financial Planning: Maintain careful financial management and seek funding sources such as investors, loans, or grants.

- Adaptability: Be prepared to pivot and adapt your business model in response to market feedback and changing conditions.

- Persistence and Resilience: Stay motivated and persistent through challenges and setbacks.

By following these strategies, you can build a successful and fulfilling career as an entrepreneur, driving innovation and contributing to economic growth through the creation of new businesses and opportunities.

27. Supply Chain Manager

27.1 Overview of the Role

Supply Chain Managers oversee and manage the entire supply chain process, from procurement of raw materials to the delivery of finished products to customers. Their role is critical in ensuring that goods move efficiently through the supply chain, minimizing costs while maximizing customer satisfaction. They coordinate with suppliers, manufacturers, logistics providers, and retailers to streamline operations and implement strategies to improve efficiency and effectiveness.

27.2 Required Skills and Education

To become a successful supply chain manager, a blend of technical expertise, formal education, and interpersonal skills are essential. Here's a detailed breakdown:

- Technical Skills:

  - Logistics and Distribution: Proficiency in managing logistics, warehousing, and distribution networks.

  - Inventory Management: Skills in maintaining optimal inventory levels and minimizing stockouts or overstock situations.

  - Procurement: Expertise in sourcing materials, negotiating with suppliers, and managing vendor relationships.

  - Data Analysis: Ability to analyze supply chain data to identify trends, inefficiencies, and opportunities for improvement.

  - Software Proficiency: Familiarity with supply chain management software (e.g., SAP, Oracle SCM, JDA) and inventory management systems.

- Educational Background:

  - Degree: A bachelor's degree in supply chain management, logistics, business administration, or a related field is typically required. Advanced degrees (MBA or Master's in Supply Chain Management) can provide an advantage.

  - Certifications: Professional certifications such as Certified Supply Chain Professional (CSCP), Certified in Production and Inventory Management (CPIM), or Certified Professional in Supply Management (CPSM) are highly valued.

  - Ongoing Education: Participation in supply chain management seminars, workshops, and courses to stay updated with the latest industry trends and best practices.

- *Soft Skills:*

- Problem-Solving: Ability to identify issues in the supply chain and develop effective solutions.

- Communication: Strong verbal and written communication skills to interact with suppliers, stakeholders, and team members.

- Leadership: Skills to lead and motivate supply chain teams.

- Organizational Skills: Efficient management of multiple tasks and ensuring smooth supply chain operations.

- Analytical Thinking: Ability to interpret complex data and make data-driven decisions.

27.3 Typical Work Environment

Supply Chain Managers typically work in diverse professional environments, each with its unique requirements and atmosphere:

- Work Hours: Generally full-time, with potential for overtime during peak periods or critical projects.

- Office Setting: Work in corporate offices, warehouses, or manufacturing facilities.

- Team Collaboration: Interaction with supply chain teams, procurement managers, logistics providers, and other stakeholders.

- Dynamic Environment: Managing multiple aspects of the supply chain simultaneously and adapting to changing market conditions.

27.4 Career Path and Growth Opportunities

The career path of a supply chain manager offers numerous avenues for advancement and specialization:

- Entry-Level Positions: Supply Chain Analyst, Logistics Coordinator, or Procurement Specialist.

- Mid-Level Positions: Supply Chain Manager, Operations Manager, or Logistics Manager.

- Advanced Roles: Senior Supply Chain Manager, Director of Supply Chain, Vice President of Operations, or Chief Supply Chain Officer (CSCO).

- Specializations: Inventory Management, Procurement, Logistics, Demand Planning, and Distribution Management.

- Further Education: Advanced degrees or certifications in specific areas of supply chain management can lead to higher-level roles and specialized positions.

27.5 Tips for Success

To excel as a supply chain manager, consider the following strategies:

- Continuous Learning: Stay updated with the latest supply chain trends, tools, and techniques through ongoing education and professional development.

- Networking: Build a professional network through supply chain associations, industry conferences, and online platforms.

- Practical Experience: Gain hands-on experience through internships, entry-level positions, and real-world supply chain projects.

- Certifications: Pursue and maintain professional certifications to enhance your skills and career prospects.

- Seek Guidance: Engage with mentors and experienced professionals for career advice and insights.

- Professional Associations: Join organizations like the Council of Supply Chain Management Professionals (CSCMP) for access to resources, training, and networking opportunities.

- Focus on Efficiency: Develop strategies to improve supply chain efficiency, reduce costs, and enhance customer satisfaction.

By implementing these strategies, you can build a successful and rewarding career as a supply chain manager, ensuring efficient and effective movement of goods through the supply chain and contributing to the overall success of your organization.

28. Investment Banker

28.1 Overview of the Role

Investment bankers are financial professionals who assist companies, governments, and other entities in raising capital, merging or acquiring businesses, and executing other financial transactions. They play a critical role in facilitating the buying and selling of securities, providing strategic advice, and managing large financial transactions. Investment bankers work in a high-stakes environment, often dealing with complex financial instruments and sophisticated clients.

28.2 Required Skills and Education

To become a successful investment banker, a combination of technical knowledge, formal education, and interpersonal skills are essential. Here's a comprehensive breakdown:

- Technical Skills:

- Financial Analysis: Expertise in analyzing financial statements, market trends, and economic data.

- Valuation Techniques: Proficiency in valuation methods such as discounted cash flow (DCF), comparable company analysis, and precedent transactions.

- Financial Modeling: Skills in building complex financial models using Excel and other financial software.

- Mergers and Acquisitions (M&A): Understanding of the M&A process, including due diligence, negotiation, and deal structuring.

- Capital Markets: Knowledge of equity and debt capital markets, including initial public offerings (IPOs) and bond issuances.

- Educational Background:

- Degree: A bachelor's degree in finance, economics, business administration, or a related field is typically required. Advanced degrees (MBA or Master's in Finance) are highly valued and often necessary for higher-level positions.

- Certifications: Professional certifications such as Chartered Financial Analyst (CFA) can enhance your credentials.

- Ongoing Education: Participation in finance seminars, workshops, and courses to stay updated with the latest financial trends and regulations.

- Soft Skills:

- Analytical Thinking: Ability to interpret complex financial data and make informed recommendations.

- Attention to Detail: Precision in financial modeling and analysis to ensure accuracy.

- Communication: Strong verbal and written communication skills to present findings and recommendations to clients and stakeholders.

- Negotiation Skills: Ability to negotiate terms and conditions effectively during transactions.

- Time Management: Efficient management of time to handle multiple deals and deadlines.

28.3 Typical Work Environment

Investment bankers typically work in fast-paced and high-pressure environments, each with its unique requirements and atmosphere:

- Work Hours: Generally long hours, including evenings and weekends, especially during deal execution.

- Office Setting: Work primarily in corporate offices of investment banks or financial institutions, with potential travel to client sites.

- Team Collaboration: Interaction with analysts, associates, senior bankers, and clients.

- Dynamic Environment: Managing multiple transactions simultaneously and adapting to rapidly changing market conditions.

28.4 Career Path and Growth Opportunities

The career path of an investment banker offers numerous avenues for advancement and specialization:

- Entry-Level Positions: Analyst or Junior Analyst in investment banking.

- Mid-Level Positions: Associate, Vice President (VP), or Senior Associate.

- Advanced Roles: Director, Managing Director (MD), or Partner.

- Specializations: Mergers and Acquisitions (M&A), Equity Capital Markets (ECM), Debt Capital Markets (DCM), Leveraged Finance, and Structured Finance.

- Further Education: Advanced degrees or certifications in specific areas of finance can lead to higher-level roles and specialized positions.

28.5 Tips for Success

To excel as an investment banker, consider the following strategies:

- Continuous Learning: Stay updated with the latest financial trends, market conditions, and regulatory changes through ongoing education and professional development.

- Networking: Build a robust professional network through industry associations, finance conferences, and online platforms.

- Practical Experience: Gain hands-on experience through internships, entry-level positions, and real-world financial projects.

- Certifications: Pursue and maintain professional certifications to enhance your skills and career prospects.

- Seek Mentorship: Engage with mentors and experienced bankers for career advice and insights.

- Professional Associations: Join organizations like the CFA Institute for access to resources, training, and networking opportunities.

- Focus on Client Relationships: Develop strong relationships with clients to understand their needs and provide tailored financial solutions.

By implementing these strategies, you can build a successful and rewarding career as an investment banker, facilitating significant financial transactions and contributing to the growth and success of businesses and markets.

29. Public Relations Specialist

29.1 Overview of the Role

Public Relations (PR) Specialists are responsible for managing the public image and reputation of their clients or organizations. They create and maintain a favorable public image through media coverage, community involvement, and communication strategies. PR specialists craft press releases, organize events, handle media inquiries, and develop public relations campaigns to promote their clients or organizations effectively.

29.2 Required Skills and Education

To become a successful PR specialist, a combination of technical skills, formal education, and soft skills are essential. Here's a comprehensive breakdown:

- Technical Skills:

  - Media Relations: Expertise in building and maintaining relationships with journalists and media outlets.

  - Writing Skills: Ability to craft compelling press releases, speeches, and other communication materials.

  - Crisis Management: Skills in managing and mitigating negative publicity or crises.

- Social Media Proficiency: Understanding of social media platforms and strategies for engaging audiences online.

- Event Planning: Knowledge of organizing and managing events such as press conferences, product launches, and community outreach programs.

- Educational Background:

- Degree: A bachelor's degree in public relations, communications, journalism, or a related field is typically required. Advanced degrees (Master's in Public Relations or Communications) can provide an advantage.

- Certifications: Professional certifications such as the Accredited in Public Relations (APR) credential can enhance your credentials.

- Ongoing Education: Participation in PR seminars, workshops, and courses to stay updated with the latest industry trends and best practices.

- Soft Skills:

- Communication: Excellent verbal and written communication skills to interact effectively with media, clients, and the public.

- Interpersonal Skills: Ability to build and maintain relationships with various stakeholders.

- Creativity: Developing innovative PR strategies and campaigns.

- Problem-Solving: Skills to address public relations challenges and develop effective solutions.

- Attention to Detail: Precision in crafting messages and managing PR activities.

29.3 Typical Work Environment

PR specialists typically work in diverse professional environments, each with its unique requirements and atmosphere:

- Work Hours: Generally full-time, with potential for overtime during major campaigns or crises.

- Office Setting: Work in corporate offices, PR agencies, government agencies, or non-profit organizations.

- Team Collaboration: Interaction with marketing teams, executives, clients, and media professionals.

- Dynamic Environment: Managing multiple PR activities simultaneously and adapting to changing circumstances.

29.4 Career Path and Growth Opportunities

The career path of a PR specialist offers numerous avenues for advancement and specialization:

- Entry-Level Positions: PR Assistant, Junior PR Specialist, or Communications Coordinator.

- Mid-Level Positions: PR Specialist, Media Relations Manager, or Communications Manager.

- Advanced Roles: Senior PR Specialist, Director of Public Relations, Vice President of Communications, or Chief Communications Officer (CCO).

- Specializations: Media Relations, Crisis Communication, Corporate Communications, Social Media Management, and Event Planning.

- Further Education: Advanced degrees or certifications in specific areas of public relations can lead to higher-level roles and specialized positions.

29.5 Tips for Success

To excel as a PR specialist, consider the following strategies:

- Continuous Learning: Stay updated with the latest public relations trends, tools, and techniques through ongoing education and professional development.

- Networking: Build a professional network through PR associations, industry conferences, and online platforms.

- Practical Experience: Gain hands-on experience through internships, entry-level positions, and real-world PR projects.

- Certifications: Pursue and maintain professional certifications to enhance your skills and career prospects.

- Seek Guidance: Engage with mentors and experienced professionals for career advice and insights.

- Professional Associations: Join organizations like the Public Relations Society of America (PRSA) for access to resources, training, and networking opportunities.

- Focus on Storytelling: Develop strong storytelling skills to create compelling narratives that resonate with audiences.

By implementing these strategies, you can build a successful and rewarding career as a PR specialist, effectively managing public perceptions and contributing to the overall success of your clients or organization.

Chapter 3 Review

Overview of Business and Finance Careers

In Chapter 3, we explored a variety of careers in the business and finance sectors. These careers are essential for driving economic growth, managing financial assets, and ensuring the smooth operation of businesses. Here's a summary of the key points covered for each role:

20. Financial Analyst

- Overview of the Role: Evaluating financial data to guide investment decisions and business strategies.

- Required Skills and Education: Financial analysis, valuation methods, financial modeling, a degree in finance or a related field, and certifications such as CFA.

- Typical Work Environment: Corporate offices, financial institutions, dynamic work setting.

- Career Path and Growth Opportunities: From Junior Financial Analyst to Director of Financial Planning and Analysis, with specializations in areas like Mergers and Acquisitions or Equity Research.

- Tips for Success: Continuous learning, networking, gaining practical experience, obtaining certifications, seeking mentorship, and maintaining work-life balance.

21. Accountant

- Overview of the Role: Preparing and examining financial records to ensure accuracy and compliance.

- Required Skills and Education: Knowledge of GAAP, financial reporting, taxation, a degree in accounting, and certifications such as CPA.

- Typical Work Environment: Corporate offices, accounting firms, and government agencies.

- Career Path and Growth Opportunities: From Junior Accountant to Chief Financial Officer (CFO), with specializations in Forensic Accounting or Tax Accounting.

- Tips for Success: Continuous learning, networking, gaining practical experience, obtaining certifications, adhering to ethical standards, and maintaining organization.

22. Marketing Manager

- Overview of the Role: Overseeing marketing strategies and campaigns to promote products or services.

- Required Skills and Education: Market research, strategic planning, digital marketing, a degree in marketing or business administration, and professional certifications.

- Typical Work Environment: Corporate offices, marketing agencies, or remotely.

- Career Path and Growth Opportunities: From Marketing Coordinator to Chief Marketing Officer (CMO), with specializations in Digital Marketing or Brand Management.

- Tips for Success: Continuous learning, networking, gaining practical experience, obtaining certifications, seeking mentorship, and data-driven decision-making.

23. Human Resources Manager

- Overview of the Role: Managing HR practices and processes, including recruitment, employee relations, and compliance.

- Required Skills and Education: Recruitment, employee relations, performance management, a degree in HR or business administration, and certifications such as PHR or SHRM-CP.

- Typical Work Environment: Corporate offices, government agencies, non-profits.

- Career Path and Growth Opportunities: From HR Coordinator to Chief Human Resources Officer (CHRO), with specializations in Talent Management or Labor Relations.

- Tips for Success: Continuous learning, networking, gaining practical experience, obtaining certifications, focusing on employee engagement, and maintaining a positive work environment.

24. Project Manager

- Overview of the Role: Planning, executing, and closing projects to meet goals within scope, time, and budget constraints.

- Required Skills and Education: Project planning, budget management, risk management, a degree in project management or a related field, and certifications such as PMP.

- Typical Work Environment: Corporate offices, construction sites, or remotely.

- Career Path and Growth Opportunities: From Project Coordinator to Chief Project Officer (CPO), with specializations in IT Project Management or Construction Management.

- Tips for Success: Continuous learning, networking, gaining practical experience, obtaining certifications, seeking mentorship, and developing strong communication skills.

25. Management Consultant

- Overview of the Role: Analyzing business problems and developing strategies for improvement.

- Required Skills and Education: Business analysis, strategic planning, data analysis, a degree in business administration or management, and certifications such as CMC.

- Typical Work Environment: Corporate offices, consulting firms, or remotely.

- Career Path and Growth Opportunities: From Junior Consultant to Managing Director, with specializations in Strategy Consulting or Operations Consulting.

- Tips for Success: Continuous learning, networking, gaining practical experience, obtaining certifications, seeking mentorship, and focusing on client relationships.

26. Entrepreneur

- Overview of the Role: Creating and managing new business ventures, taking on financial risks in the hopes of profit.

- Required Skills and Education: Business planning, financial management, marketing, a degree in business or entrepreneurship, and relevant certifications.

- Typical Work Environment: Home offices, coworking spaces, corporate offices.

- Career Path and Growth Opportunities: From startup phase to serial entrepreneurship, with options for selling the business or diversifying products.

- Tips for Success: Continuous learning, networking, gaining practical experience, seeking mentorship, focusing on customer needs, and maintaining resilience.

27. Supply Chain Manager

- Overview of the Role: Managing the supply chain process from procurement to delivery.

- Required Skills and Education: Logistics, inventory management, procurement, a degree in supply chain management, and certifications such as CSCP.

- Typical Work Environment: Corporate offices, warehouses, manufacturing facilities.

- Career Path and Growth Opportunities: From Supply Chain Analyst to Chief Supply Chain Officer (CSCO), with specializations in Inventory Management or Procurement.

- Tips for Success: Continuous learning, networking, gaining practical experience, obtaining certifications, focusing on efficiency, and engaging in professional associations.

28. Investment Banker

- Overview of the Role: Assisting entities in raising capital, merging or acquiring businesses, and executing financial transactions.

- Required Skills and Education: Financial analysis, valuation techniques, financial modeling, a degree in finance or business administration, and certifications such as CFA.

- Typical Work Environment: Corporate offices, financial institutions.

- Career Path and Growth Opportunities: From Analyst to Managing Director, with specializations in M&A or Capital Markets.

- Tips for Success: Continuous learning, networking, gaining practical experience, obtaining certifications, seeking mentorship, and focusing on client relationships.

29. Public Relations Specialist

- Overview of the Role: Managing the public image and reputation of clients or organizations.

- Required Skills and Education: Media relations, writing skills, crisis management, a degree in public relations or communications, and certifications such as APR.

- Typical Work Environment: Corporate offices, PR agencies, government agencies.

- Career Path and Growth Opportunities: From PR Assistant to Chief Communications Officer (CCO), with specializations in Media Relations or Crisis Communication.

- Tips for Success: Continuous learning, networking, gaining practical experience, obtaining certifications, focusing on storytelling, and engaging with professional associations.

Key Takeaways

- Continuous Learning: Staying updated with industry trends and advancements is crucial across all business and finance careers.

- Networking: Building a professional network through industry events, associations, and online platforms can provide valuable opportunities and insights.

- Practical Experience: Gaining hands-on experience through internships, entry-level positions, and real-world projects is essential for skill development and career advancement.

- Certifications and Education: Obtaining relevant certifications and pursuing higher education can enhance career prospects and open up advanced roles.

- Mentorship: Seeking guidance from experienced professionals can provide valuable insights and support throughout your career.

By understanding the roles, required skills, typical work environments, career paths, and tips for success, you can make informed decisions about pursuing a career in the business and finance fields covered in this chapter. Whether you are just starting out or looking to advance your career, this guide provides the essential information to help you succeed.

Would you like me to remember your preference for continuous learning and networking for future chapters?

Chapter 4: Education Careers

30. Elementary School Teacher

30.1 Overview of the Role

Elementary school teachers are responsible for educating young children in the foundational subjects such as reading, writing, mathematics, science, and social studies. They create lesson plans, assess student performance, and foster a positive and inclusive classroom environment. Elementary school teachers play a crucial role in the early development of children's cognitive and social skills, setting the stage for their future academic success.

30.2 Required Skills and Education

To become a successful elementary school teacher, a combination of educational qualifications, technical skills, and soft skills are essential. Here's a comprehensive breakdown:

- Educational Background:

  - Degree: A bachelor's degree in elementary education or a related field is typically required. Some positions may require a master's degree.

  - Certification: State-specific teaching certification or licensure is mandatory. This often involves passing a series of exams and completing a teacher preparation program.

  - Ongoing Education: Participation in continuing education courses, workshops, and seminars to stay updated with the latest teaching methods and educational trends.

- *Technical Skills:*

- Lesson Planning: Ability to develop comprehensive lesson plans that align with curriculum standards.

- Classroom Management: Skills in managing classroom behavior and maintaining a positive learning environment.

- Assessment: Proficiency in designing and administering tests, quizzes, and other assessment tools to measure student progress.

- Instructional Techniques: Knowledge of various teaching strategies to accommodate diverse learning styles.

- *Soft Skills:*

- Communication: Strong verbal and written communication skills to interact effectively with students, parents, and colleagues.

- Patience and Empathy: Ability to understand and address the individual needs of each student.

- Creativity: Developing engaging and interactive lessons to capture students' interest.

- Organization: Efficiently managing classroom activities, paperwork, and student records.

- Adaptability: Flexibility to adjust teaching methods based on student needs and feedback.

30.3 Typical Work Environment

Elementary school teachers typically work in diverse educational settings, each with its unique requirements and atmosphere:

- Work Hours: Generally full-time, with additional hours for lesson planning, grading, and parent-teacher conferences.

- Classroom Setting: Work in public or private elementary schools, often with access to various educational resources and technology.

- Team Collaboration: Interaction with other teachers, school administrators, and support staff.

- Student Interaction: Frequent direct interaction with students, providing instruction and support.

30.4 Career Path and Growth Opportunities

The career path of an elementary school teacher offers numerous avenues for advancement and specialization:

- Entry-Level Positions: Assistant Teacher, Substitute Teacher, or Classroom Teacher.

- Mid-Level Positions: Lead Teacher, Grade-Level Coordinator, or Curriculum Specialist.

- Advanced Roles: Instructional Coach, Assistant Principal, Principal, or Director of Education.

- Specializations: Special Education, Reading Specialist, ESL (English as a Second Language), or Gifted and Talented Education.

- Further Education: Pursuing advanced degrees or certifications in specific areas of education can lead to higher-level roles and specialized positions.

30.5 Tips for Success

To excel as an elementary school teacher, consider the following strategies:

- Continuous Learning: Stay updated with the latest educational practices, tools, and techniques through ongoing education and professional development.

- Networking: Build a professional network through education associations, conferences, and online platforms.

- Practical Experience: Gain hands-on experience through student teaching, internships, and volunteer work in educational settings.

- Certifications: Pursue and maintain professional certifications to enhance your skills and career prospects.

- Seek Guidance: Engage with mentors and experienced educators for career advice and insights.

- Professional Associations: Join organizations like the National Education Association (NEA) for access to resources, training, and networking opportunities.

- Focus on Student Engagement: Develop strategies to create engaging and inclusive lessons that cater to the diverse needs of your students.

- Reflect and Adapt: Regularly reflect on your teaching practices and be willing to adapt based on student feedback and educational trends.

By implementing these strategies, you can build a successful and fulfilling career as an elementary school teacher, making a significant impact on the lives of young students and contributing to their long-term academic and personal success.

31. High School Teacher

31.1 Overview of the Role

High school teachers are responsible for educating students in grades 9 through 12 in specific subject areas such as mathematics, science, English, history, and more. They develop lesson plans, assess student performance, and prepare students for standardized tests and future academic pursuits. High school teachers also play a crucial role in mentoring students and preparing them for college or career paths.

31.2 Required Skills and Education

To become a successful high school teacher, a combination of educational qualifications, technical skills, and soft skills are essential. Here's a comprehensive breakdown:

- Educational Background:

  - Degree: A bachelor's degree in education or a specific subject area is typically required. Many states also require a master's degree for advanced licensure.

  - Certification: State-specific teaching certification or licensure is mandatory, which usually involves passing a series of exams and completing a teacher preparation program.

  - Ongoing Education: Participation in continuing education courses, workshops, and seminars to stay updated with the latest teaching methods and educational trends.

- Technical Skills:

  - Lesson Planning: Ability to develop comprehensive lesson plans that align with curriculum standards and state requirements.

  - Classroom Management: Skills in managing classroom behavior and maintaining a positive learning environment.

  - Assessment: Proficiency in designing and administering tests, quizzes, and other assessment tools to measure student progress.

- Instructional Techniques: Knowledge of various teaching strategies to accommodate diverse learning styles and abilities.

- *Soft Skills:*

  - Communication: Strong verbal and written communication skills to interact effectively with students, parents, and colleagues.

  - Patience and Empathy: Ability to understand and address the individual needs of each student.

  - Creativity: Developing engaging and interactive lessons to capture students' interest.

  - Organization: Efficiently managing classroom activities, paperwork, and student records.

  - Adaptability: Flexibility to adjust teaching methods based on student needs and feedback.

31.3 Typical Work Environment

High school teachers typically work in diverse educational settings, each with its unique requirements and atmosphere:

- Work Hours: Generally full-time, with additional hours for lesson planning, grading, and parent-teacher conferences. Extra-curricular activities and after-school programs may also require additional time.

- Classroom Setting: Work in public or private high schools, often with access to various educational resources and technology.

- Team Collaboration: Interaction with other teachers, school administrators, and support staff.

- Student Interaction: Frequent direct interaction with students, providing instruction, guidance, and support.

31.4 Career Path and Growth Opportunities

The career path of a high school teacher offers numerous avenues for advancement and specialization:

- Entry-Level Positions: Student Teacher, Substitute Teacher, or Classroom Teacher.

- Mid-Level Positions: Lead Teacher, Department Head, or Curriculum Specialist.

- Advanced Roles: Instructional Coach, Assistant Principal, Principal, or Director of Education.

- Specializations: Special Education, Advanced Placement (AP) Courses, ESL (English as a Second Language), or Subject Area Expertise.

- Further Education: Pursuing advanced degrees or certifications in specific areas of education can lead to higher-level roles and specialized positions.

31.5 Tips for Success

To excel as a high school teacher, consider the following strategies:

- Continuous Learning: Stay updated with the latest educational practices, tools, and techniques through ongoing education and professional development.

- Networking: Build a professional network through education associations, conferences, and online platforms.

- Practical Experience: Gain hands-on experience through student teaching, internships, and volunteer work in educational settings.

- Certifications: Pursue and maintain professional certifications to enhance your skills and career prospects.

- Seek Guidance: Engage with mentors and experienced educators for career advice and insights.

- Professional Associations: Join organizations like the National Education Association (NEA) for access to resources, training, and networking opportunities.

- Focus on Student Engagement: Develop strategies to create engaging and inclusive lessons that cater to the diverse needs of your students.

- Reflect and Adapt: Regularly reflect on your teaching practices and be willing to adapt based on student feedback and educational trends.

By implementing these strategies, you can build a successful and fulfilling career as a high school teacher, making a significant impact on the lives of students and contributing to their long-term academic and personal success.

32. College Professor

32.1 Overview of the Role

College professors are academic professionals responsible for teaching courses, conducting research, and contributing to their academic field. They develop curricula, deliver lectures, assess student performance, and often engage in scholarly activities such as publishing research and presenting at conferences. College professors also mentor students, providing guidance on academic and career goals.

32.2 Required Skills and Education

To become a successful college professor, a combination of advanced education, specialized knowledge, and a range of soft skills are essential. Here's a comprehensive breakdown:

- Educational Background:

- Degree: A doctoral degree (Ph.D.) in the relevant field is typically required for full-time, tenure-track positions. Some positions, particularly in community colleges, may accept a master's degree.

- Research Experience: Significant research experience, including publications in academic journals and presentations at conferences.

- Teaching Certification: While not always required, some institutions may value certification in higher education teaching.

- Technical Skills:

- Subject Matter Expertise: In-depth knowledge of the specific academic field and ongoing engagement with the latest research.

- Curriculum Development: Ability to design and update course materials, including syllabi, lectures, and assignments.

- Research Skills: Proficiency in conducting research, analyzing data, and writing scholarly papers.

- Technology Proficiency: Familiarity with educational technologies, such as Learning Management Systems (LMS) like Blackboard or Canvas, and online teaching tools.

- Soft Skills:

- Communication: Strong verbal and written communication skills for effective teaching and academic writing.

- Mentoring: Ability to guide and support students in their academic and professional development.

- Time Management: Efficiently balancing teaching, research, and administrative responsibilities.

- Critical Thinking: Ability to analyze complex issues and encourage critical thinking in students.

- Collaboration: Working effectively with colleagues in academia and contributing to departmental goals.

32.3 Typical Work Environment

College professors typically work in various higher education settings, each with its unique requirements and atmosphere:

- Work Hours: Generally full-time, with additional hours for research, grading, and student mentoring. Flexibility is often required to accommodate office hours, research commitments, and academic conferences.

- Academic Setting: Work in public or private colleges and universities, community colleges, and online institutions.

- Team Collaboration: Interaction with fellow faculty members, academic committees, and administrative staff.

- Student Interaction: Frequent direct interaction with students through lectures, office hours, and academic advising.

32.4 Career Path and Growth Opportunities

The career path of a college professor offers numerous avenues for advancement and specialization:

- Entry-Level Positions: Adjunct Instructor, Lecturer, or Assistant Professor.

- Mid-Level Positions: Associate Professor, Program Coordinator, or Department Chair.

- Advanced Roles: Full Professor, Dean, or Provost.

- Specializations: Research Focus, Teaching Focus, Administrative Roles, or Interdisciplinary Studies.

- Further Education: Continuing professional development through workshops, conferences, and additional certifications can lead to higher-level roles and specialized positions.

32.5 Tips for Success

To excel as a college professor, consider the following strategies:

- Continuous Learning: Stay updated with the latest research and teaching practices through ongoing education and professional development.

- Networking: Build a professional network through academic associations, conferences, and collaborative research projects.

- Practical Experience: Gain teaching experience through adjunct or part-time positions, internships, and teaching assistantships during graduate studies.

- Research and Publication: Maintain an active research agenda and publish regularly in reputable academic journals.

- Seek Mentorship: Engage with experienced academics for career advice and insights.

- Professional Associations: Join organizations such as the American Association of University Professors (AAUP) for access to resources, training, and networking opportunities.

- Student Engagement: Develop strategies to create engaging and inclusive learning environments that cater to the diverse needs of students.

- Work-Life Balance: Strive to maintain a healthy balance between teaching, research, and personal life to avoid burnout.

By implementing these strategies, you can build a successful and fulfilling career as a college professor, making significant contributions to your academic field and positively impacting the lives of your students.

33. Educational Administrator

33.1 Overview of the Role

Educational administrators are responsible for overseeing the operations and management of educational institutions such as schools, colleges, and universities. They ensure that academic policies and procedures are implemented effectively, manage budgets, supervise staff, and work to create a positive learning environment. Educational administrators play a crucial role in shaping educational standards and practices.

33.2 Required Skills and Education

To become a successful educational administrator, a combination of advanced education, management skills, and soft skills are essential. Here's a comprehensive breakdown:

- Educational Background:

- Degree: A master's degree in education administration, leadership, or a related field is typically required. Some positions may require a doctoral degree (Ed.D. or Ph.D.).

- Certifications: State-specific certifications or licensure may be necessary, particularly for public school administrators.

- Ongoing Education: Participation in leadership seminars, workshops, and courses to stay updated with the latest educational practices and policies.

- Technical Skills:

- Leadership: Strong leadership skills to manage staff, guide decision-making, and foster a collaborative environment.

- Budget Management: Ability to develop and manage budgets, allocate resources efficiently, and ensure financial stability.

- Policy Implementation: Knowledge of educational laws, policies, and procedures to ensure compliance and effective implementation.

- Data Analysis: Skills in analyzing educational data to make informed decisions and improve institutional performance.

- Technology Proficiency: Familiarity with educational software and tools for administration and communication.

- Soft Skills:

- Communication: Excellent verbal and written communication skills to interact effectively with staff, students, parents, and the community.

- Problem-Solving: Ability to address and resolve conflicts, challenges, and issues within the institution.

- Interpersonal Skills: Building and maintaining positive relationships with stakeholders.

- Organizational Skills: Efficiently managing multiple tasks and ensuring smooth operation of the institution.

- Vision and Innovation: Ability to develop and implement strategic plans for institutional growth and improvement.

33.3 Typical Work Environment

Educational administrators typically work in diverse educational settings, each with its unique requirements and atmosphere:

- Work Hours: Generally full-time, with additional hours for meetings, events, and administrative duties. Flexibility is often required to address urgent matters.

- Office Setting: Work in offices within schools, colleges, or universities, with frequent interaction with staff, students, and parents.

- Team Collaboration: Interaction with faculty, administrative staff, and other departments.

- Dynamic Environment: Managing various aspects of the institution simultaneously and adapting to changing educational needs.

33.4 Career Path and Growth Opportunities

The career path of an educational administrator offers numerous avenues for advancement and specialization:

- Entry-Level Positions: Assistant Principal, Academic Coordinator, or Program Director.

- Mid-Level Positions: Principal, Dean, or Director of Admissions.

- Advanced Roles: Superintendent, Provost, Vice President of Academic Affairs, or President.

- Specializations: Curriculum Development, Student Affairs, Institutional Research, or Human Resources.

- Further Education: Advanced degrees or certifications in specific areas of educational administration can lead to higher-level roles and specialized positions.

33.5 Tips for Success

To excel as an educational administrator, consider the following strategies:

- Continuous Learning: Stay updated with the latest educational trends, policies, and technologies through ongoing education and professional development.

- Networking: Build a professional network through educational associations, conferences, and online platforms.

- Practical Experience: Gain hands-on experience through internships, entry-level positions, and real-world administrative projects.

- Certifications: Pursue and maintain professional certifications to enhance your skills and career prospects.

- Seek Guidance: Engage with mentors and experienced administrators for career advice and insights.

- Professional Associations: Join organizations such as the National Association of Secondary School Principals (NASSP) or the American Association of School Administrators (AASA) for access to resources, training, and networking opportunities.

- Focus on Vision and Strategy: Develop and implement strategic plans that align with the institution's goals and mission.

- Cultivate a Positive Environment: Foster a positive and inclusive environment that supports staff and student success.

By implementing these strategies, you can build a successful and fulfilling career as an educational administrator, contributing to the improvement and success of educational institutions and positively impacting the lives of students and staff.

34. School Counselor

34.1 Overview of the Role

School counselors play a critical role in the educational system by providing academic, career, and emotional support to students. They help students develop coping skills, make informed decisions, and plan for their future education and careers. School counselors also work closely with teachers, parents, and administrators to create a supportive and nurturing school environment.

34.2 Required Skills and Education

To become a successful school counselor, a combination of advanced education, counseling skills, and interpersonal skills are essential. Here's a comprehensive breakdown:

- Educational Background:

 - Degree: A master's degree in school counseling, psychology, or a related field is typically required.

- Certification/Licensure: State-specific certification or licensure is mandatory, which usually involves passing a comprehensive exam and completing a certain number of supervised counseling hours.

- Ongoing Education: Participation in continuing education courses, workshops, and seminars to stay updated with the latest counseling practices and trends.

- *Technical Skills:*

- Counseling Techniques: Proficiency in individual and group counseling methods.

- Assessment: Skills in administering and interpreting academic, career, and psychological assessments.

- Career Guidance: Knowledge of career development theories and tools to assist students in planning their future education and careers.

- Crisis Intervention: Ability to provide immediate support and intervention during crises or emergencies.

- *Soft Skills:*

- Communication: Excellent verbal and written communication skills to interact effectively with students, parents, and staff.

- Empathy and Compassion: Ability to understand and address the individual needs and concerns of students.

- Problem-Solving: Skills to help students develop strategies to overcome personal and academic challenges.

- Confidentiality: Maintaining confidentiality and building trust with students.

- Organization: Efficiently managing counseling programs, student records, and administrative tasks.

34.3 Typical Work Environment

School counselors typically work in various educational settings, each with its unique requirements and atmosphere:

- Work Hours: Generally full-time, with additional hours for meetings, events, and crisis intervention. Flexibility is often required to address urgent student needs.

- Office Setting: Work in offices within elementary, middle, or high schools, providing a private and safe space for student counseling.

- Team Collaboration: Interaction with teachers, administrators, parents, and external mental health professionals.

- Student Interaction: Frequent direct interaction with students through counseling sessions, group activities, and classroom guidance.

34.4 Career Path and Growth Opportunities

The career path of a school counselor offers numerous avenues for advancement and specialization:

- Entry-Level Positions: School Counselor, Guidance Counselor, or Career Counselor.

- Mid-Level Positions: Lead Counselor, Counseling Program Coordinator, or Counseling Department Chair.

- Advanced Roles: Director of Counseling Services, School Administrator, or Educational Consultant.

- Specializations: College Counseling, Career Development, Mental Health Counseling, or Substance Abuse Counseling.

- Further Education: Advanced degrees or certifications in specific areas of counseling can lead to higher-level roles and specialized positions.

34.5 Tips for Success

To excel as a school counselor, consider the following strategies:

- Continuous Learning: Stay updated with the latest counseling practices, tools, and techniques through ongoing education and professional development.

- Networking: Build a professional network through counseling associations, conferences, and online platforms.

- Practical Experience: Gain hands-on experience through internships, entry-level positions, and real-world counseling projects.

- Certifications: Pursue and maintain professional certifications to enhance your skills and career prospects.

- Seek Guidance: Engage with mentors and experienced counselors for career advice and insights.

- Professional Associations: Join organizations like the American School Counselor Association (ASCA) for access to resources, training, and networking opportunities.

- Focus on Student Well-Being: Develop strategies to support the academic, career, and personal development of students.

- Maintain Confidentiality: Build trust with students by maintaining confidentiality and providing a safe space for open communication.

By implementing these strategies, you can build a successful and fulfilling career as a school counselor, making a significant impact on the lives of students and contributing to their overall well-being and success.

35. Special Education Teacher

35.1 Overview of the Role

Special education teachers are dedicated professionals who work with students who have a wide range of learning, mental, emotional, and physical disabilities. They adapt general education lessons and teach various subjects to students with mild to moderate disabilities. Special education teachers also teach basic skills, such as literacy and communication techniques, to students with severe disabilities. Their goal is to provide individualized instruction and create a supportive environment that fosters learning and development.

35.2 Required Skills and Education

To become a successful special education teacher, a combination of specialized education, technical skills, and soft skills are essential. Here's a comprehensive breakdown:

- Educational Background:

  - Degree: A bachelor's degree in special education or a related field is typically required. Many positions may also require a master's degree.

  - Certification/Licensure: State-specific certification or licensure in special education is mandatory, which usually involves passing a comprehensive exam and completing a certain number of supervised teaching hours.

- Ongoing Education: Participation in continuing education courses, workshops, and seminars to stay updated with the latest teaching methods and special education practices.

- Technical Skills:

- Individualized Education Plans (IEPs): Ability to develop and implement IEPs tailored to each student's needs.

- Adapted Instruction: Skills in modifying teaching methods and materials to accommodate different learning styles and disabilities.

- Assessment: Proficiency in assessing student progress and adjusting instructional strategies accordingly.

- Behavior Management: Techniques for managing classroom behavior and creating a positive learning environment.

- Assistive Technology: Knowledge of assistive technologies that support student learning and communication.

- Soft Skills:

- Patience and Empathy: Understanding and addressing the individual needs and challenges of students with disabilities.

- Communication: Strong verbal and written communication skills to interact effectively with students, parents, and colleagues.

- Creativity: Developing engaging and innovative lessons that cater to diverse learning needs.

- Organization: Efficiently managing classroom activities, paperwork, and student records.

- Collaboration: Working closely with other teachers, support staff, and parents to support student development.

35.3 Typical Work Environment

Special education teachers typically work in various educational settings, each with its unique requirements and atmosphere:

- Work Hours: Generally full-time, with additional hours for lesson planning, IEP meetings, and parent-teacher conferences.

- Classroom Setting: Work in public or private schools, specialized institutions, or inclusive classrooms, providing a supportive environment tailored to students' needs.

- Team Collaboration: Interaction with general education teachers, school administrators, special education coordinators, and support staff.

- Student Interaction: Frequent direct interaction with students, providing individualized instruction and support.

35.4 Career Path and Growth Opportunities

The career path of a special education teacher offers numerous avenues for advancement and specialization:

- Entry-Level Positions: Special Education Teacher, Resource Teacher, or Inclusion Teacher.

- Mid-Level Positions: Lead Special Education Teacher, Special Education Coordinator, or Department Head.

- Advanced Roles: Instructional Coach, Director of Special Education, School Administrator, or Educational Consultant.

- Specializations: Autism Spectrum Disorders (ASD), Learning Disabilities, Emotional and Behavioral Disorders, or Early Childhood Special Education.

- Further Education: Advanced degrees or certifications in specific areas of special education can lead to higher-level roles and specialized positions.

35.5 Tips for Success

To excel as a special education teacher, consider the following strategies:

- Continuous Learning: Stay updated with the latest special education practices, tools, and techniques through ongoing education and professional development.

- Networking: Build a professional network through special education associations, conferences, and online platforms.

- Practical Experience: Gain hands-on experience through internships, entry-level positions, and real-world teaching projects.

- Certifications: Pursue and maintain professional certifications to enhance your skills and career prospects.

- Seek Guidance: Engage with mentors and experienced special education professionals for career advice and insights.

- Professional Associations: Join organizations like the Council for Exceptional Children (CEC) for access to resources, training, and networking opportunities.

- Focus on Individualized Instruction: Develop and implement effective IEPs that address the unique needs of each student.

- Promote Inclusion: Advocate for inclusive practices that allow students with disabilities to participate fully in general education classrooms and activities.

By implementing these strategies, you can build a successful and fulfilling career as a special education teacher, making a significant impact on the lives of students with disabilities and contributing to their overall development and success.

36. ESL Teacher

36.1 Overview of the Role

English as a Second Language (ESL) teachers specialize in teaching English to non-native speakers. Their primary goal is to help students develop proficiency in reading, writing, speaking, and understanding English. ESL teachers work with students of all ages, from young children to adults, and adapt their teaching methods to meet the diverse linguistic and cultural backgrounds of their students. They play a crucial role in helping students integrate into English-speaking environments and achieve academic and professional success.

36.2 Required Skills and Education

To become a successful ESL teacher, a combination of specialized education, linguistic skills, and cultural sensitivity is essential. Here's a comprehensive breakdown:

- Educational Background:

  - Degree: A bachelor's degree in education, English, linguistics, or a related field is typically required. Many positions may also require a master's degree in TESOL (Teaching English to Speakers of Other Languages) or a related field.

  - Certification: ESL teaching certification, such as TESOL, TEFL (Teaching English as a Foreign Language), or CELTA (Certificate in English Language Teaching to Adults), is often required.

  - Ongoing Education: Participation in professional development courses, workshops, and seminars to stay updated with the latest ESL teaching methods and practices.

- *Technical Skills:*

  - Language Instruction: Proficiency in teaching English grammar, vocabulary, pronunciation, and language skills.

  - Curriculum Development: Ability to design and implement lesson plans that align with language learning objectives.

  - Assessment: Skills in assessing student progress and adjusting instructional strategies accordingly.

  - Technology Integration: Knowledge of educational technology and tools that support language learning, such as language learning apps, online platforms, and interactive whiteboards.

- *Soft Skills:*

  - Communication: Strong verbal and written communication skills to interact effectively with students, parents, and colleagues.

  - Cultural Sensitivity: Understanding and respecting the diverse cultural backgrounds of students.

  - Patience and Empathy: Ability to address the individual needs and challenges of students learning a new language.

  - Creativity: Developing engaging and interactive lessons to capture students' interest.

  - Adaptability: Flexibility to adjust teaching methods based on student needs and feedback.

36.3 Typical Work Environment

ESL teachers typically work in various educational settings, each with its unique requirements and atmosphere:

- Work Hours: Generally full-time, with additional hours for lesson planning, grading, and student support. Part-time and evening classes may also be required, especially in adult education settings.

- Classroom Setting: Work in public or private schools, language institutes, community colleges, universities, and online platforms.

- Team Collaboration: Interaction with other teachers, school administrators, and support staff.

- Student Interaction: Frequent direct interaction with students through classroom instruction, tutoring, and language practice activities.

36.4 Career Path and Growth Opportunities

The career path of an ESL teacher offers numerous avenues for advancement and specialization:

- Entry-Level Positions: ESL Teacher, Language Instructor, or Teaching Assistant.

- Mid-Level Positions: Senior ESL Teacher, Curriculum Developer, or Program Coordinator.

- Advanced Roles: Director of ESL Programs, Academic Advisor, or Educational Consultant.

- Specializations: Business English, Academic English, Test Preparation (e.g., TOEFL, IELTS), or Teaching English to Young Learners.

- Further Education: Advanced degrees or certifications in specific areas of ESL teaching can lead to higher-level roles and specialized positions.

36.5 Tips for Success

To excel as an ESL teacher, consider the following strategies:

- Continuous Learning: Stay updated with the latest ESL teaching practices, tools, and techniques through ongoing education and professional development.

- Networking: Build a professional network through ESL associations, conferences, and online platforms.

- Practical Experience: Gain hands-on experience through internships, entry-level positions, and real-world teaching projects.

- Certifications: Pursue and maintain professional certifications to enhance your skills and career prospects.

- Seek Guidance: Engage with mentors and experienced ESL professionals for career advice and insights.

- Professional Associations: Join organizations like TESOL International Association for access to resources, training, and networking opportunities.

- Focus on Student Engagement: Develop strategies to create engaging and inclusive lessons that cater to the diverse needs of your students.

- Cultural Competence: Foster a culturally inclusive environment by learning about and incorporating students' cultural backgrounds into your teaching.

By implementing these strategies, you can build a successful and fulfilling career as an ESL teacher, making a significant impact on the lives of non-native English speakers and helping them achieve their academic and professional goals.

37. Education Consultant

37.1 Overview of the Role

Education consultants provide expert advice and support to educational institutions, educators, students, and parents. They help improve educational outcomes by developing and implementing effective teaching strategies, curriculum plans, and educational policies. Education consultants work on various projects, including school improvement initiatives, teacher training programs, student counseling, and educational research.

37.2 Required Skills and Education

To become a successful education consultant, a combination of advanced education, specialized knowledge, and a range of soft skills are essential. Here's a comprehensive breakdown:

- Educational Background:

- Degree: A bachelor's degree in education, curriculum and instruction, educational leadership, or a related field is typically required. Many positions also require a master's degree or doctoral degree (Ed.D. or Ph.D.).

- Experience: Significant experience in teaching or educational administration is often required.

- Certifications: Certifications in specific areas of education consulting or specialized training programs can be beneficial.

- Ongoing Education: Participation in professional development courses, workshops, and seminars to stay updated with the latest educational practices and trends.

- *Technical Skills:*

- Curriculum Development: Expertise in designing, developing, and evaluating curriculum plans that meet educational standards.

- Educational Assessment: Skills in assessing educational programs, student performance, and instructional effectiveness.

- Data Analysis: Ability to analyze educational data to identify trends, areas for improvement, and to inform decision-making.

- Project Management: Proficiency in managing educational projects, including planning, implementation, and evaluation.

- Policy Development: Knowledge of educational policies and the ability to develop and implement policies that improve educational outcomes.

- *Soft Skills:*

- Communication: Excellent verbal and written communication skills to interact effectively with educators, administrators, parents, and students.

- Problem-Solving: Ability to identify educational challenges and develop effective solutions.

- Leadership: Strong leadership skills to guide and support educational teams and initiatives.

- Interpersonal Skills: Building and maintaining positive relationships with clients and stakeholders.

- Adaptability: Flexibility to adjust consulting strategies based on client needs and feedback.

37.3 Typical Work Environment

Education consultants typically work in various educational settings, each with its unique requirements and atmosphere:

- Work Hours: Generally full-time, with additional hours for meetings, training sessions, and project management.

- Office Setting: Work in offices within educational institutions, consulting firms, or remotely. Travel may be required to client sites, schools, or conferences.

- Team Collaboration: Interaction with teachers, school administrators, policymakers, and other educational professionals.

- Dynamic Environment: Managing multiple projects simultaneously and adapting to changing educational needs.

37.4 Career Path and Growth Opportunities

The career path of an education consultant offers numerous avenues for advancement and specialization:

- Entry-Level Positions: Educational Consultant, Instructional Coordinator, or Curriculum Specialist.

- Mid-Level Positions: Senior Education Consultant, Project Manager, or Education Program Director.

- Advanced Roles: Director of Educational Services, Chief Academic Officer, or Educational Policy Advisor.

- Specializations: Curriculum Development, Teacher Training, Educational Technology, Special Education, or School Improvement.

- Further Education: Advanced degrees or certifications in specific areas of education consulting can lead to higher-level roles and specialized positions.

37.5 Tips for Success

To excel as an education consultant, consider the following strategies:

- Continuous Learning: Stay updated with the latest educational practices, tools, and techniques through ongoing education and professional development.

- Networking: Build a professional network through educational associations, conferences, and online platforms.

- Practical Experience: Gain hands-on experience through internships, entry-level positions, and real-world consulting projects.

- Certifications: Pursue and maintain professional certifications to enhance your skills and career prospects.

- Seek Guidance: Engage with mentors and experienced education professionals for career advice and insights.

- Professional Associations: Join organizations like the American Educational Research Association (AERA) for access to resources, training, and networking opportunities.

- Focus on Client Needs: Develop strategies to address the unique needs and goals of each client, whether it's a school, district, or individual educator.

- Document and Reflect: Keep detailed records of your projects and outcomes, and regularly reflect on your consulting practices to continuously improve.

By implementing these strategies, you can build a successful and fulfilling career as an education consultant, helping to enhance the quality of education and positively impact the lives of students and educators.

38. Librarian

38.1 Overview of the Role

Librarians are information professionals who manage and organize collections of books, journals, electronic resources, and other materials. They assist patrons in finding information, conducting research, and using library resources effectively. Librarians also plan and conduct programs, manage library operations, and contribute to the development and preservation of collections. They play a crucial role in promoting literacy, learning, and access to information.

38.2 Required Skills and Education

To become a successful librarian, a combination of specialized education, technical skills, and interpersonal skills are essential. Here's a comprehensive breakdown:

- Educational Background:

- Degree: A master's degree in library science (MLS) or library and information science (MLIS) from an accredited program is typically required. Some positions, particularly in academic or specialized libraries, may require additional subject-specific degrees.

- Certification: Some states and employers require certification or licensure for librarians.

- Ongoing Education: Participation in professional development courses, workshops, and seminars to stay updated with the latest library practices and technologies.

- *Technical Skills:*

- Information Management: Expertise in cataloging, classification, and organizing library materials.

- Research Skills: Proficiency in conducting research and helping patrons locate and use information.

- Digital Literacy: Knowledge of digital resources, databases, and library management systems (e.g., OPAC, integrated library systems).

- Collection Development: Skills in selecting and acquiring materials that meet the needs of the community.

- Technology Integration: Ability to use and teach various technologies, including e-books, online databases, and digital archiving tools.

- *Soft Skills:*

- Communication: Excellent verbal and written communication skills to interact effectively with patrons, colleagues, and stakeholders.

- Customer Service: Strong commitment to providing high-quality service and support to library users.

- Organization: Efficiently managing library operations, collections, and programs.

- Problem-Solving: Ability to address and resolve issues related to library services and resources.

- Interpersonal Skills: Building and maintaining positive relationships with patrons, staff, and the community.

38.3 Typical Work Environment

Librarians typically work in diverse library settings, each with its unique requirements and atmosphere:

- Work Hours: Generally full-time, with additional hours for events, programs, and community outreach. Some positions may require evening or weekend hours.

- Library Setting: Work in public libraries, academic libraries, school libraries, special libraries (e.g., law, medical), or digital libraries.

- Team Collaboration: Interaction with other librarians, library assistants, volunteers, and administrators.

- Patron Interaction: Frequent direct interaction with patrons, providing assistance, conducting programs, and offering research support.

38.4 Career Path and Growth Opportunities

The career path of a librarian offers numerous avenues for advancement and specialization:

- Entry-Level Positions: Library Assistant, Reference Librarian, or Children's Librarian.

- Mid-Level Positions: Senior Librarian, Branch Manager, or Head of a Specific Department (e.g., Reference, Technical Services).

- Advanced Roles: Library Director, Chief Librarian, or Library System Administrator.

- Specializations: Digital Libraries, Archives and Special Collections, Youth Services, Academic Librarianship, or Information Literacy.

- Further Education: Advanced degrees or certifications in specific areas of librarianship can lead to higher-level roles and specialized positions.

38.5 Tips for Success

To excel as a librarian, consider the following strategies:

- Continuous Learning: Stay updated with the latest library practices, tools, and technologies through ongoing education and professional development.

- Networking: Build a professional network through library associations, conferences, and online platforms.

- Practical Experience: Gain hands-on experience through internships, entry-level positions, and real-world library projects.

- Certifications: Pursue and maintain professional certifications to enhance your skills and career prospects.

- Seek Guidance: Engage with mentors and experienced librarians for career advice and insights.

- Professional Associations: Join organizations like the American Library Association (ALA) for access to resources, training, and networking opportunities.

- Community Engagement: Develop and implement programs and services that meet the needs of your community.

- Advocacy and Outreach: Promote library services and advocate for the value of libraries within your community and beyond.

By implementing these strategies, you can build a successful and fulfilling career as a librarian, making a significant impact on the lives of patrons and contributing to the broader goals of literacy, education, and access to information.

39. Curriculum Developer

39.1 Overview of the Role

Curriculum developers, also known as instructional coordinators or curriculum specialists, design, implement, and evaluate educational programs and instructional materials. They work closely with teachers, administrators, and educational stakeholders to create curricula that meet educational standards and enhance student learning. Curriculum developers also provide training and support to educators on effective teaching strategies and assessment methods.

39.2 Required Skills and Education

To become a successful curriculum developer, a combination of advanced education, specialized knowledge, and various soft skills are essential. Here's a comprehensive breakdown:

- Educational Background:

- Degree: A bachelor's degree in education, curriculum and instruction, or a related field is typically required. Many positions require a master's degree or higher in curriculum development, educational leadership, or a related field.

- Experience: Significant experience in teaching or educational administration is often required.

- Certifications: Certifications in specific areas of curriculum development or instructional design can be beneficial.

- Ongoing Education: Participation in professional development courses, workshops, and seminars to stay updated with the latest educational practices and trends.

- Technical Skills:

  - Curriculum Design: Expertise in developing, organizing, and evaluating curricula that align with educational standards.

  - Educational Assessment: Skills in designing and implementing assessments to measure student learning and curriculum effectiveness.

  - Instructional Strategies: Knowledge of effective teaching methods and strategies to support diverse learning styles.

  - Technology Integration: Proficiency in using educational technology and digital tools to enhance curriculum delivery.

  - Research and Analysis: Ability to conduct educational research and analyze data to inform curriculum decisions.

- Soft Skills:

  - Communication: Excellent verbal and written communication skills to collaborate with educators, administrators, and other stakeholders.

  - Leadership: Strong leadership skills to guide and support educational teams and initiatives.

  - Problem-Solving: Ability to identify educational challenges and develop effective solutions.

  - Creativity: Developing innovative and engaging instructional materials and activities.

  - Collaboration: Building and maintaining positive relationships with educators and stakeholders.

39.3 Typical Work Environment

Curriculum developers typically work in various educational settings, each with its unique requirements and atmosphere:

- Work Hours: Generally full-time, with additional hours for meetings, training sessions, and curriculum evaluation.

- Office Setting: Work in offices within educational institutions, school districts, government agencies, or consulting firms. Some positions may involve travel to different schools or educational facilities.

- Team Collaboration: Interaction with teachers, school administrators, educational consultants, and policymakers.

- Dynamic Environment: Managing multiple projects simultaneously and adapting to changing educational needs and standards.

39.4 Career Path and Growth Opportunities

The career path of a curriculum developer offers numerous avenues for advancement and specialization:

- Entry-Level Positions: Curriculum Developer, Instructional Coordinator, or Education Specialist.

- Mid-Level Positions: Senior Curriculum Developer, Lead Instructional Designer, or Program Manager.

- Advanced Roles: Director of Curriculum and Instruction, Chief Academic Officer, or Educational Consultant.

- Specializations: Subject-Specific Curriculum Development, Digital Learning, Special Education Curriculum, or Adult Education.

- Further Education: Advanced degrees or certifications in specific areas of curriculum development can lead to higher-level roles and specialized positions.

39.5 Tips for Success

To excel as a curriculum developer, consider the following strategies:

- Continuous Learning: Stay updated with the latest educational practices, tools, and techniques through ongoing education and professional development.

- Networking: Build a professional network through educational associations, conferences, and online platforms.

- Practical Experience: Gain hands-on experience through internships, entry-level positions, and real-world curriculum development projects.

- Certifications: Pursue and maintain professional certifications to enhance your skills and career prospects.

- Seek Guidance: Engage with mentors and experienced curriculum developers for career advice and insights.

- Professional Associations: Join organizations like the Association for Supervision and Curriculum Development (ASCD) for access to resources, training, and networking opportunities.

- Focus on Innovation: Develop and implement innovative curriculum solutions that engage students and enhance learning outcomes.

- Evaluate and Reflect: Regularly assess the effectiveness of curricula and make necessary adjustments based on feedback and educational research.

By implementing these strategies, you can build a successful and fulfilling career as a curriculum developer, contributing to the improvement of educational programs and positively impacting student learning and achievement.

Chapter 4 Review

Overview of Education Careers

In Chapter 4, we explored various careers within the education sector, each playing a pivotal role in shaping the future of students and contributing to the overall success of educational institutions. Here's a summary of the key points covered for each role:

30. Elementary School Teacher

- Overview of the Role: Educating young children in foundational subjects and fostering cognitive and social skills.

- Required Skills and Education: Bachelor's degree in elementary education, state certification, lesson planning, classroom management, and adaptability.

- Typical Work Environment: Public or private elementary schools, full-time with additional hours for planning and grading.

- Career Path and Growth Opportunities: From Assistant Teacher to Principal, with specializations in areas like Special Education or Reading Specialist.

- Tips for Success: Continuous learning, networking, practical experience, certifications, seeking guidance, and focusing on student engagement.

31. High School Teacher

- Overview of the Role: Teaching specific subjects to students in grades 9-12, preparing them for standardized tests and future academic pursuits.

- Required Skills and Education: Bachelor's degree in a specific subject, state certification, curriculum development, assessment, and classroom management.

- Typical Work Environment: Public or private high schools, full-time with additional hours for extracurricular activities and student support.

- Career Path and Growth Opportunities: From Classroom Teacher to School Administrator, with specializations in Advanced Placement (AP) courses or Subject Area Expertise.

- Tips for Success: Continuous learning, networking, practical experience, certifications, student engagement, and adaptability.

32. College Professor

- Overview of the Role: Teaching, conducting research, and contributing to academic fields at the collegiate level.

- Required Skills and Education: Doctoral degree, research experience, curriculum development, and teaching certification.

- Typical Work Environment: Colleges and universities, full-time with additional hours for research and mentoring.

- Career Path and Growth Opportunities: From Adjunct Instructor to Dean or Provost, with specializations in Research or Teaching Focus.

- Tips for Success: Continuous learning, networking, practical experience, research and publication, seeking mentorship, and student engagement.

33. Educational Administrator

- Overview of the Role: Overseeing the operations and management of educational institutions, ensuring effective implementation of academic policies.

- Required Skills and Education: Master's degree in educational leadership, leadership skills, budget management, and policy implementation.

- Typical Work Environment: Offices within schools, colleges, or educational agencies, full-time with additional hours for meetings and administrative duties.

- Career Path and Growth Opportunities: From Assistant Principal to Superintendent or Chief Academic Officer, with specializations in Curriculum Development or Student Affairs.

- Tips for Success: Continuous learning, networking, practical experience, certifications, strategic planning, and community engagement.

34. School Counselor

- Overview of the Role: Providing academic, career, and emotional support to students, helping them develop coping skills and make informed decisions.

- Required Skills and Education: Master's degree in school counseling, state certification, counseling techniques, and assessment skills.

- Typical Work Environment: Offices within schools, full-time with additional hours for meetings and crisis intervention.

- Career Path and Growth Opportunities: From School Counselor to Director of Counseling Services, with specializations in College Counseling or Career Development.

- Tips for Success: Continuous learning, networking, practical experience, certifications, student well-being focus, and maintaining confidentiality.

35. Special Education Teacher

- Overview of the Role: Teaching and supporting students with a range of learning, mental, emotional, and physical disabilities.

- Required Skills and Education: Bachelor's degree in special education, state certification, individualized education plans (IEPs), and behavior management.

- Typical Work Environment: Public or private schools, full-time with additional hours for IEP meetings and parent-teacher conferences.

- Career Path and Growth Opportunities: From Special Education Teacher to Director of Special Education, with specializations in Autism Spectrum Disorders or Early Childhood Special Education.

- Tips for Success: Continuous learning, networking, practical experience, certifications, individualized instruction focus, and promoting inclusion.

36. ESL Teacher

- Overview of the Role: Teaching English to non-native speakers, helping them develop proficiency in reading, writing, speaking, and understanding English.

- Required Skills and Education: Bachelor's degree in education or English, ESL teaching certification (TESOL, TEFL, CELTA), and language instruction skills.

- Typical Work Environment: Public or private schools, language institutes, community colleges, and online platforms, full-time with additional hours for lesson planning and student support.

- Career Path and Growth Opportunities: From ESL Teacher to Director of ESL Programs, with specializations in Business English or Test Preparation (TOEFL, IELTS).

- Tips for Success: Continuous learning, networking, practical experience, certifications, cultural competence, and student engagement.

37. Education Consultant

- Overview of the Role: Providing expert advice and support to educational institutions, educators, students, and parents to improve educational outcomes.

- Required Skills and Education: Master's degree in education, significant teaching or administrative experience, curriculum development, and policy development.

- Typical Work Environment: Offices within educational institutions, consulting firms, or remotely, full-time with additional hours for meetings and project management.

- Career Path and Growth Opportunities: From Educational Consultant to Director of Educational Services, with specializations in Teacher Training or Educational Technology.

- Tips for Success: Continuous learning, networking, practical experience, certifications, client needs focus, and documentation and reflection.

38. Librarian

- Overview of the Role: Managing and organizing collections of books, journals, electronic resources, and other materials, assisting patrons with information needs.

- Required Skills and Education: Master's degree in library science (MLS or MLIS), information management, research skills, and digital literacy.

- Typical Work Environment: Public libraries, academic libraries, school libraries, special libraries, and digital libraries, full-time with additional hours for events and programs.

- Career Path and Growth Opportunities: From Library Assistant to Library Director, with specializations in Digital Libraries or Archives and Special Collections.

- Tips for Success: Continuous learning, networking, practical experience, certifications, community engagement, and advocacy and outreach.

39. Curriculum Developer

- Overview of the Role: Designing, implementing, and evaluating educational programs and instructional materials, providing training and support to educators.

- Required Skills and Education: Master's degree in curriculum development, educational assessment, instructional strategies, and technology integration.

- Typical Work Environment: Offices within educational institutions, school districts, government agencies, or consulting firms, full-time with additional hours for curriculum evaluation.

- Career Path and Growth Opportunities: From Curriculum Developer to Director of Curriculum and Instruction, with specializations in Digital Learning or Special Education Curriculum.

- Tips for Success: Continuous learning, networking, practical experience, certifications, innovation focus, and evaluation and reflection.

Key Takeaways

- Continuous Learning: Staying updated with the latest educational trends, tools, and techniques is crucial across all education careers.

- Networking: Building a professional network through educational associations, conferences, and online platforms can provide valuable opportunities and insights.

- Practical Experience: Gaining hands-on experience through internships, entry-level positions, and real-world educational projects is essential for skill development and career advancement.

- Certifications and Education: Obtaining relevant certifications and pursuing higher education can enhance career prospects and open up advanced roles.

- Mentorship: Seeking guidance from experienced professionals can provide valuable insights and support throughout your career.

By understanding the roles, required skills, typical work environments, career paths, and tips for success, you can make informed decisions about pursuing a career in the education fields covered in this chapter. Whether you are just starting out or looking to advance your career, this guide provides the essential information to help you succeed.

Chapter 5: Creative and Media Careers

40. Graphic Designer

40.1 Overview of the Role

Graphic designers create visual content to communicate messages effectively. They design graphics for websites, advertisements, magazines, books, posters, product packaging, logos, and other media. Graphic designers combine art and technology to produce visually appealing and effective designs that meet the needs of their clients or employers. Their work involves selecting colors, images, and typefaces to create cohesive and visually impactful designs.

40.2 Required Skills and Education

To become a successful graphic designer, a combination of technical skills, formal education, and creativity is essential. Here's a comprehensive breakdown:

- Technical Skills:

  - Design Software: Proficiency in design software such as Adobe Creative Suite (Photoshop, Illustrator, InDesign) and other graphic design tools.

  - Typography: Understanding of typography, fonts, and text layout to create visually appealing text elements.

  - Color Theory: Knowledge of color theory and the ability to create harmonious color palettes.

  - Layout and Composition: Skills in arranging visual elements to create balanced and aesthetically pleasing designs.

- Web Design: Familiarity with web design principles and experience with HTML/CSS can be beneficial.

- *Educational Background:*

- Degree: A bachelor's degree in graphic design, visual arts, or a related field is typically required. Some positions may accept an associate degree or certificate with relevant experience.

- Portfolio: A strong portfolio showcasing a variety of design projects is crucial for demonstrating skills and creativity.

- Ongoing Education: Participation in design workshops, online courses, and certification programs to stay updated with the latest design trends and software updates.

- *Soft Skills:*

- Creativity: Ability to develop innovative and visually appealing designs.

- Communication: Strong verbal and written communication skills to understand client needs and present design concepts.

- Attention to Detail: Precision in design work to ensure high-quality and accurate outputs.

- Time Management: Efficiently managing multiple projects and meeting deadlines.

- Problem-Solving: Ability to address design challenges and find effective solutions.

40.3 Typical Work Environment

Graphic designers typically work in diverse settings, each with its unique requirements and atmosphere:

- Work Hours: Generally full-time, with potential for overtime during project deadlines. Freelance graphic designers may have more flexible schedules.

- Office Setting: Work in design studios, advertising agencies, corporate offices, or remotely from home offices.

- Team Collaboration: Interaction with clients, marketing teams, copywriters, and other designers.

- Dynamic Environment: Managing multiple design projects simultaneously and adapting to changing client requirements and feedback.

40.4 Career Path and Growth Opportunities

The career path of a graphic designer offers numerous avenues for advancement and specialization:

- Entry-Level Positions: Junior Graphic Designer, Production Artist, or Graphic Design Intern.

- Mid-Level Positions: Graphic Designer, Senior Graphic Designer, or Art Director.

- Advanced Roles: Creative Director, Design Manager, or Chief Design Officer.

- Specializations: Web Design, UX/UI Design, Motion Graphics, Branding, or Packaging Design.

- Further Education: Advanced degrees or certifications in specific areas of graphic design can lead to higher-level roles and specialized positions.

40.5 Tips for Success

To excel as a graphic designer, consider the following strategies:

- Continuous Learning: Stay updated with the latest design trends, tools, and techniques through ongoing education and professional development.

- Networking: Build a professional network through design associations, industry conferences, and online platforms.

- Practical Experience: Gain hands-on experience through internships, freelance projects, and real-world design challenges.

- Portfolio Development: Continuously update your portfolio with diverse and high-quality design projects to showcase your skills and creativity.

- Seek Feedback: Engage with mentors, peers, and clients to receive constructive feedback and improve your design work.

- Professional Associations: Join organizations like the American Institute of Graphic Arts (AIGA) for access to resources, training, and networking opportunities.

- Focus on Branding: Develop a strong personal brand that reflects your design style and expertise.

- Embrace Technology: Stay proficient with the latest design software and tools to enhance your efficiency and creativity.

By implementing these strategies, you can build a successful and fulfilling career as a graphic designer, creating visually impactful designs that communicate effectively and meet the needs of your clients or employers.

41. Journalist

41.1 Overview of the Role

Journalists play a crucial role in society by gathering, investigating, and reporting news and information to the public. They work across various media platforms, including newspapers, magazines, television, radio, and online news sites. Journalists are responsible for researching stories, conducting interviews, writing articles, and ensuring the accuracy and fairness of their reports. Their work helps inform the public, influence opinions, and contribute to the democratic process.

41.2 Required Skills and Education

To become a successful journalist, a combination of technical skills, formal education, and various soft skills are essential. Here's a comprehensive breakdown:

- Technical Skills:

  - Writing and Reporting: Excellent writing skills to craft clear, engaging, and accurate news stories. Ability to conduct thorough research and verify facts.

  - Interviewing: Proficiency in conducting interviews to gather information from various sources.

  - Editing: Skills in editing and proofreading to ensure clarity, coherence, and error-free content.

  - Multimedia: Knowledge of multimedia tools and platforms, including photography, video production, and social media.

  - Data Journalism: Ability to analyze and interpret data to support investigative journalism and in-depth reporting.

- *Educational Background:*

- Degree: A bachelor's degree in journalism, communications, or a related field is typically required. Some positions may prefer candidates with a master's degree.

- Internships: Gaining practical experience through internships at news organizations is highly beneficial.

- Ongoing Education: Participation in journalism workshops, online courses, and certification programs to stay updated with industry trends and best practices.

- *Soft Skills:*

- Communication: Strong verbal and written communication skills to interact effectively with sources, editors, and audiences.

- Curiosity and Investigative Skills: A natural curiosity and strong investigative skills to uncover and report stories.

- Ethical Judgement: Adherence to journalistic ethics and integrity to ensure fair and unbiased reporting.

- Adaptability: Flexibility to cover breaking news and adjust to the fast-paced nature of the journalism industry.

- Persistence: Determination to pursue leads and overcome obstacles in the reporting process.

41.3 Typical Work Environment

Journalists typically work in diverse environments, each with its unique requirements and atmosphere:

- Work Hours: Often irregular and extended, especially during breaking news or tight deadlines. Journalists may work nights, weekends, and holidays.

- Office Setting: Work in newsrooms, television studios, radio stations, or remotely. Field reporting may require travel to various locations, sometimes under challenging conditions.

- Team Collaboration: Interaction with editors, photographers, videographers, and other journalists.

- Dynamic Environment: Managing multiple stories simultaneously and adapting to rapidly changing news events.

41.4 Career Path and Growth Opportunities

The career path of a journalist offers numerous avenues for advancement and specialization:

- Entry-Level Positions: Reporter, Correspondent, or Junior Journalist.

- Mid-Level Positions: Senior Reporter, News Editor, or Investigative Journalist.

- Advanced Roles: Bureau Chief, Managing Editor, or News Director.

- Specializations: Political Journalism, Sports Journalism, Business Journalism, Investigative Journalism, or Multimedia Journalism.

- Further Education: Advanced degrees or certifications in specific areas of journalism can lead to higher-level roles and specialized positions.

41.5 Tips for Success

To excel as a journalist, consider the following strategies:

- Continuous Learning: Stay updated with the latest journalism practices, tools, and techniques through ongoing education and professional development.

- Networking: Build a professional network through journalism associations, industry conferences, and online platforms.

- Practical Experience: Gain hands-on experience through internships, freelance writing, and real-world reporting projects.

- Certifications: Pursue and maintain professional certifications to enhance your skills and career prospects.

- Seek Mentorship: Engage with experienced journalists for career advice and insights.

- Professional Associations: Join organizations like the Society of Professional Journalists (SPJ) for access to resources, training, and networking opportunities.

- Develop a Beat: Specialize in a particular area of interest (e.g., politics, science, culture) to build expertise and credibility.

- Focus on Accuracy and Fairness: Uphold the highest standards of accuracy, fairness, and integrity in your reporting.

By implementing these strategies, you can build a successful and fulfilling career as a journalist, making a significant impact on society by providing accurate and insightful news coverage.

42. Film Director

42.1 Overview of the Role

Film directors are responsible for the creative and dramatic aspects of a film. They visualize the script while guiding the technical crew and actors to fulfill that vision. A film director makes crucial decisions regarding casting, production design, cinematography, and editing. They oversee the entire filmmaking process, from pre-production through post-production, ensuring that the final product aligns with their artistic vision and the script's intent.

42.2 Required Skills and Education

To become a successful film director, a blend of creative talent, technical knowledge, and leadership skills is essential. Here's a comprehensive breakdown:

- Technical Skills:

- Film Production: Understanding the complete film production process, from pre-production to post-production.

- Cinematography: Knowledge of camera work, lighting, and shot composition to create the desired visual effect.

- Editing: Basic knowledge of film editing techniques and software to understand how scenes fit together.

- Screenwriting: Ability to analyze and interpret scripts to bring the story to life visually.

- Sound Design: Understanding of sound recording, mixing, and editing to enhance the film's audio quality.

- Educational Background:

- Degree: A bachelor's degree in film, media production, or a related field is typically beneficial. Some directors also pursue master's degrees in fine arts (MFA) with a focus on directing.

- Workshops and Courses: Participation in film workshops, directing courses, and film schools to gain hands-on experience and technical skills.

- Internships: Practical experience through internships or assistant roles on film sets to learn the intricacies of filmmaking.

- Soft Skills:

- Creativity: A strong creative vision and the ability to bring stories to life visually.

- Leadership: Strong leadership skills to direct actors and crew effectively.

- Communication: Excellent communication skills to articulate the vision and collaborate with cast and crew.

- Problem-Solving: Ability to make quick decisions and solve problems that arise during production.

- Attention to Detail: Keen eye for detail to ensure every aspect of the film aligns with the vision.

42.3 Typical Work Environment

Film directors typically work in dynamic and diverse environments, each with its unique challenges and atmosphere:

- Work Hours: Often long and irregular, including nights, weekends, and holidays, especially during shooting schedules.

- On-Set: Work on film sets, which can vary from studios to outdoor locations, depending on the script's requirements.

- Office Setting: Pre-production and post-production phases often involve working in offices or editing suites.

- Travel: Travel may be required to various shooting locations, sometimes under challenging conditions.

42.4 Career Path and Growth Opportunities

The career path of a film director offers numerous avenues for advancement and specialization:

- Entry-Level Positions: Assistant Director, Production Assistant, or Script Supervisor.

- Mid-Level Positions: Independent Film Director, Television Director, or Short Film Director.

- Advanced Roles: Feature Film Director, Executive Producer, or Studio Head.

- Specializations: Documentary Filmmaking, Commercial Directing, Music Video Directing, or Animation Directing.

- Further Education: Advanced degrees or continuous professional development through workshops and seminars can lead to higher-level roles and specialized positions.

42.5 Tips for Success

To excel as a film director, consider the following strategies:

- Continuous Learning: Stay updated with the latest film industry trends, techniques, and technologies through ongoing education and professional development.

- Networking: Build a professional network through film festivals, industry events, and online platforms.

- Practical Experience: Gain hands-on experience through internships, assistant roles, and independent film projects.

- Portfolio Development: Create a strong portfolio of short films, commercials, or independent projects to showcase your directing skills.

- Seek Mentorship: Engage with experienced directors and industry professionals for career advice and insights.

- Professional Associations: Join organizations like the Directors Guild of America (DGA) for access to resources, training, and networking opportunities.

- Focus on Storytelling: Develop strong storytelling skills to create compelling and emotionally resonant films.

- Embrace Feedback: Be open to constructive criticism and use it to improve your directing techniques.

By implementing these strategies, you can build a successful and fulfilling career as a film director, bringing your creative visions to life on screen and contributing to the art of filmmaking.

43. Photographer

43.1 Overview of the Role

Photographers capture images that tell a story, convey a message, or preserve memories. They work in various fields, including portrait, commercial, fashion, editorial, event, and nature photography. Photographers use technical expertise, creativity, and composition skills to produce and preserve images that visually record and express events, ideas, and emotions.

43.2 Required Skills and Education

To become a successful photographer, a blend of technical skills, formal education, and artistic talent is essential. Here's a comprehensive breakdown:

- Technical Skills:

  - Camera Operation: Proficiency in using different types of cameras and lenses.

  - Lighting: Knowledge of natural and studio lighting techniques to enhance image quality.

  - Editing Software: Skills in using photo editing software such as Adobe Photoshop, Lightroom, or Capture One.

  - Composition: Understanding of composition techniques to create visually appealing photographs.

  - Post-Processing: Ability to retouch and enhance images to meet clients' needs.

- Educational Background:

  - Degree: While not always required, a degree in photography, fine arts, or a related field can be beneficial.

  - Workshops and Courses: Participation in photography workshops, online courses, and certification programs to gain hands-on experience and technical skills.

  - Internships: Practical experience through internships or assistant roles with professional photographers.

- Soft Skills:

- Creativity: A strong creative vision and the ability to capture unique and compelling images.

- Attention to Detail: Precision in capturing and editing photos to ensure high-quality results.

- Communication: Excellent verbal and written communication skills to understand client needs and present ideas.

- Time Management: Efficiently managing multiple projects and meeting deadlines.

- Customer Service: Building and maintaining positive relationships with clients.

43.3 Typical Work Environment

Photographers typically work in diverse environments, each with its unique challenges and atmosphere:

- Work Hours: Often irregular, including evenings, weekends, and holidays, especially for event photographers.

- On-Location: Work on various locations, including studios, outdoor settings, and client sites.

- Travel: Travel may be required for assignments, especially for nature, travel, and destination event photography.

- Office Setting: Post-processing and client meetings often take place in an office or home office environment.

43.4 Career Path and Growth Opportunities

The career path of a photographer offers numerous avenues for advancement and specialization:

- Entry-Level Positions: Photography Assistant, Junior Photographer, or Studio Assistant.

- Mid-Level Positions: Professional Photographer, Senior Photographer, or Photojournalist.

- Advanced Roles: Studio Owner, Creative Director, or Photography Instructor.

- Specializations: Portrait Photography, Commercial Photography, Fashion Photography, Wedding Photography, or Wildlife Photography.

- Further Education: Advanced degrees or continuous professional development through workshops and seminars can lead to higher-level roles and specialized positions.

43.5 Tips for Success

To excel as a photographer, consider the following strategies:

- Continuous Learning: Stay updated with the latest photography techniques, tools, and trends through ongoing education and professional development.

- Networking: Build a professional network through photography associations, industry events, and online platforms.

- Practical Experience: Gain hands-on experience through internships, assistant roles, and independent photography projects.

- Portfolio Development: Create a strong portfolio showcasing a variety of work to demonstrate your skills and creativity.

- Seek Feedback: Engage with mentors, peers, and clients to receive constructive feedback and improve your photography.

- Professional Associations: Join organizations like the Professional Photographers of America (PPA) for access to resources, training, and networking opportunities.

- Marketing and Branding: Develop a strong personal brand and market your photography services effectively through social media and online portfolios.

- Embrace Technology: Stay proficient with the latest camera equipment, editing software, and digital tools to enhance your efficiency and creativity.

By implementing these strategies, you can build a successful and fulfilling career as a photographer, capturing moments and creating images that inspire, inform, and entertain.

44. Social Media Manager

44.1 Overview of the Role

Social media managers are responsible for planning, implementing, managing, and monitoring a company's social media strategy to increase brand awareness, improve marketing efforts, and drive website traffic. They create and curate content, interact with followers, analyze performance metrics, and stay updated with the latest social media trends. Social media managers play a crucial role in shaping a brand's online presence and engaging with its audience.

44.2 Required Skills and Education

To become a successful social media manager, a combination of technical skills, formal education, and creativity is essential. Here's a comprehensive breakdown:

- *Technical Skills:*

- Content Creation: Ability to create engaging text, image, and video content tailored to different social media platforms.

- Social Media Platforms: Proficiency in using platforms like Facebook, Instagram, Twitter, LinkedIn, Pinterest, TikTok, and YouTube.

- Analytics Tools: Experience with social media analytics tools such as Google Analytics, Hootsuite, Buffer, and social media insights to track and measure performance.

- SEO and SEM: Knowledge of search engine optimization (SEO) and search engine marketing (SEM) to optimize social media content.

- Advertising: Skills in creating and managing social media ad campaigns, including targeting, budgeting, and performance analysis.

- *Educational Background:*

- Degree: A bachelor's degree in marketing, communications, journalism, or a related field is typically required.

- Certifications: Certifications in social media marketing, digital marketing, or related areas can be beneficial.

- Ongoing Education: Participation in workshops, online courses, and industry conferences to stay updated with the latest social media trends and tools.

- Soft Skills:

- Creativity: Ability to develop innovative and engaging content that resonates with the target audience.

- Communication: Strong verbal and written communication skills to interact effectively with followers, clients, and team members.

- Analytical Thinking: Skills to analyze data, derive insights, and make data-driven decisions to improve social media strategies.

- Time Management: Efficiently managing multiple social media accounts and campaigns to meet deadlines.

- Customer Service: Building and maintaining positive relationships with followers and addressing their inquiries or concerns promptly.

44.3 Typical Work Environment

Social media managers typically work in diverse settings, each with its unique requirements and atmosphere:

- Work Hours: Generally full-time, with additional hours for monitoring social media activity, especially during campaigns or major events.

- Office Setting: Work in corporate offices, marketing agencies, or remotely from home offices.

- Team Collaboration: Interaction with marketing teams, content creators, graphic designers, and clients.

- Dynamic Environment: Managing multiple social media accounts and campaigns simultaneously and adapting to changing trends and audience feedback.

44.4 Career Path and Growth Opportunities

The career path of a social media manager offers numerous avenues for advancement and specialization:

- Entry-Level Positions: Social Media Coordinator, Social Media Specialist, or Community Manager.

- Mid-Level Positions: Social Media Manager, Digital Marketing Manager, or Content Manager.

- Advanced Roles: Social Media Director, Head of Social Media, or Chief Marketing Officer (CMO).

- Specializations: Influencer Marketing, Social Media Advertising, Content Strategy, or Brand Management.

- Further Education: Advanced degrees or certifications in specific areas of digital marketing can lead to higher-level roles and specialized positions.

44.5 Tips for Success

To excel as a social media manager, consider the following strategies:

- Continuous Learning: Stay updated with the latest social media trends, tools, and techniques through ongoing education and professional development.

- Networking: Build a professional network through marketing associations, industry conferences, and online platforms.

- Practical Experience: Gain hands-on experience through internships, freelance projects, and real-world social media management.

- Certifications: Pursue and maintain professional certifications to enhance your skills and career prospects.

- Seek Feedback: Engage with mentors, peers, and clients to receive constructive feedback and improve your social media strategies.

- Professional Associations: Join organizations like the Social Media Marketing Society (SMMS) for access to resources, training, and networking opportunities.

- Focus on Analytics: Develop strong analytical skills to track performance, identify trends, and optimize content and strategies.

- Engage Authentically: Foster genuine connections with your audience by being authentic, responsive, and relatable.

By implementing these strategies, you can build a successful and fulfilling career as a social media manager, effectively managing online presence and driving engagement for brands and organizations.

45. Content Writer

45.1 Overview of the Role

Content writers create written material for various platforms, including websites, blogs, social media, marketing materials, and more. Their primary goal is to produce engaging, informative, and persuasive content that aligns with the brand's voice and objectives. Content writers must understand their target audience and craft content that meets their needs while driving traffic and engagement.

45.2 Required Skills and Education

To become a successful content writer, a combination of technical skills, formal education, and creativity is essential. Here's a comprehensive breakdown:

- Technical Skills:

- Writing: Excellent writing skills to create clear, compelling, and grammatically correct content.

- Research: Ability to conduct thorough research to ensure accuracy and depth in content.

- SEO Knowledge: Understanding of search engine optimization (SEO) to improve content visibility and ranking on search engines.

- Editing and Proofreading: Skills to edit and proofread content to ensure it is error-free and polished.

- Content Management Systems (CMS): Familiarity with CMS platforms like WordPress, Drupal, or Joomla for publishing content.

- Educational Background:

- Degree: A bachelor's degree in English, journalism, communications, marketing, or a related field is typically beneficial.

- Certifications: Certifications in content writing, copywriting, or digital marketing can enhance your credentials.

- Ongoing Education: Participation in writing workshops, online courses, and industry conferences to stay updated with the latest trends and best practices.

- Soft Skills:

- Creativity: Ability to generate innovative ideas and create engaging content.

- Attention to Detail: Precision in writing and editing to ensure high-quality content.

- Communication: Strong verbal and written communication skills to understand client needs and present ideas.

- Time Management: Efficiently managing multiple writing projects and meeting deadlines.

- Adaptability: Flexibility to write on a variety of topics and adjust writing style to different audiences and platforms.

45.3 Typical Work Environment

Content writers typically work in diverse settings, each with its unique requirements and atmosphere:

- Work Hours: Generally full-time, with additional hours for meeting deadlines or during peak content production periods. Freelance content writers may have more flexible schedules.

- Office Setting: Work in corporate offices, marketing agencies, media companies, or remotely from home offices.

- Team Collaboration: Interaction with marketing teams, editors, graphic designers, and clients.

- Dynamic Environment: Managing multiple writing projects simultaneously and adapting to changing client requirements and feedback.

45.4 Career Path and Growth Opportunities

The career path of a content writer offers numerous avenues for advancement and specialization:

- Entry-Level Positions: Junior Content Writer, Copywriter, or Blog Writer.

- Mid-Level Positions: Content Writer, Senior Content Writer, or Content Strategist.

- Advanced Roles: Content Manager, Editorial Director, or Chief Content Officer.

- Specializations: Technical Writing, SEO Writing, Copywriting, Blogging, or Scriptwriting.

- Further Education: Advanced degrees or certifications in specific areas of writing can lead to higher-level roles and specialized positions.

45.5 Tips for Success

To excel as a content writer, consider the following strategies:

- Continuous Learning: Stay updated with the latest writing techniques, tools, and trends through ongoing education and professional development.

- Networking: Build a professional network through writing associations, industry conferences, and online platforms.

- Practical Experience: Gain hands-on experience through internships, freelance writing, and real-world writing projects.

- Portfolio Development: Create a strong portfolio showcasing a variety of writing samples to demonstrate your skills and versatility.

- Seek Feedback: Engage with mentors, peers, and clients to receive constructive feedback and improve your writing.

- Professional Associations: Join organizations like the American Writers & Artists Inc. (AWAI) for access to resources, training, and networking opportunities.

- Focus on SEO: Develop strong SEO skills to optimize content for search engines and increase visibility.

- Embrace Technology: Stay proficient with the latest writing and editing software to enhance your efficiency and creativity.

By implementing these strategies, you can build a successful and fulfilling career as a content writer, creating compelling and effective content that engages audiences and meets the needs of your clients or employers.

46. Video Editor

46.1 Overview of the Role

Video editors are responsible for assembling recorded raw material into a finished product suitable for broadcasting. The material may include camera footage, dialogue, sound effects, graphics, and special effects. Video editors work closely with directors, producers, and other creative team members to ensure the final product aligns with the vision and requirements. They play a crucial role in the post-production process, shaping the narrative and enhancing the overall quality of the video.

46.2 Required Skills and Education

To become a successful video editor, a combination of technical skills, formal education, and creative abilities is essential. Here's a comprehensive breakdown:

- Technical Skills:

  - Editing Software: Proficiency in using video editing software such as Adobe Premiere Pro, Final Cut Pro, Avid Media Composer, and DaVinci Resolve.

  - Audio Editing: Skills in editing and synchronizing audio tracks to ensure high-quality sound.

- Color Correction and Grading: Knowledge of color correction and grading to enhance the visual appeal of videos.

- Motion Graphics: Ability to create and incorporate motion graphics and special effects.

- File Management: Efficient management of digital files and media assets.

- *Educational Background:*

- Degree: A bachelor's degree in film production, multimedia, communications, or a related field is typically beneficial.

- Certifications: Certifications in specific editing software or advanced editing techniques can enhance your credentials.

- Ongoing Education: Participation in workshops, online courses, and industry conferences to stay updated with the latest editing trends and tools.

- *Soft Skills:*

- Creativity: A strong creative vision to transform raw footage into compelling stories.

- Attention to Detail: Precision in editing to ensure seamless transitions and high-quality output.

- Communication: Strong verbal and written communication skills to understand project requirements and collaborate with team members.

- Time Management: Efficiently managing multiple projects and meeting tight deadlines.

- Problem-Solving: Ability to address technical issues and find solutions to editing challenges.

46.3 Typical Work Environment

Video editors typically work in diverse settings, each with its unique requirements and atmosphere:

- Work Hours: Generally full-time, with additional hours for meeting deadlines, especially during post-production periods.

- Office Setting: Work in editing studios, production companies, broadcasting companies, or remotely from home offices.

- Team Collaboration: Interaction with directors, producers, cinematographers, and other creative team members.

- Dynamic Environment: Managing multiple projects simultaneously and adapting to feedback and revisions.

46.4 Career Path and Growth Opportunities

The career path of a video editor offers numerous avenues for advancement and specialization:

- Entry-Level Positions: Assistant Editor, Junior Video Editor, or Editorial Intern.

- Mid-Level Positions: Video Editor, Senior Video Editor, or Post-Production Supervisor.

- Advanced Roles: Lead Editor, Editing Director, or Post-Production Manager.

- Specializations: Film Editing, TV Editing, Documentary Editing, Commercial Editing, or Music Video Editing.

- Further Education: Advanced degrees or certifications in specific areas of video editing can lead to higher-level roles and specialized positions.

46.5 Tips for Success

To excel as a video editor, consider the following strategies:

- Continuous Learning: Stay updated with the latest editing techniques, tools, and trends through ongoing education and professional development.

- Networking: Build a professional network through film and media associations, industry events, and online platforms.

- Practical Experience: Gain hands-on experience through internships, freelance projects, and real-world editing assignments.

- Portfolio Development: Create a strong portfolio showcasing a variety of editing projects to demonstrate your skills and versatility.

- Seek Feedback: Engage with mentors, peers, and clients to receive constructive feedback and improve your editing techniques.

- Professional Associations: Join organizations like the Motion Picture Editors Guild (MPEG) for access to resources, training, and networking opportunities.

- Embrace Technology: Stay proficient with the latest editing software and hardware to enhance your efficiency and creativity.

- Storytelling Focus: Develop strong storytelling skills to create engaging and cohesive narratives that resonate with audiences.

By implementing these strategies, you can build a successful and fulfilling career as a video editor, shaping raw footage into compelling visual stories that captivate and engage audiences.

47. Animator

47.1 Overview of the Role

Animators create moving images that tell stories or convey information. They work in various mediums, including 2D, 3D, and stop-motion animation. Animators can be found in multiple industries such as film, television, video games, advertising, and web design. They collaborate with directors, designers, and other artists to bring characters and scenes to life through motion graphics and animation techniques.

47.2 Required Skills and Education

To become a successful animator, a blend of technical skills, formal education, and creativity is essential. Here's a comprehensive breakdown:

- Technical Skills:

  - Animation Software: Proficiency in animation software such as Adobe Animate, Toon Boom Harmony, Maya, Blender, and After Effects.

  - Drawing and Illustration: Strong drawing skills for character design and storyboarding.

  - 3D Modeling and Rigging: Skills in creating and rigging 3D models for animation.

  - Motion Graphics: Ability to create motion graphics and visual effects.

  - Storyboarding: Expertise in creating storyboards to visualize the sequence of events in the animation.

- Educational Background:

- Degree: A bachelor's degree in animation, fine arts, graphic design, or a related field is typically required.

- Certifications: Certifications in specific animation software or advanced animation techniques can enhance your credentials.

- Ongoing Education: Participation in animation workshops, online courses, and industry conferences to stay updated with the latest trends and tools.

- Soft Skills:

- Creativity: A strong creative vision to develop unique and engaging animations.

- Attention to Detail: Precision in animation to ensure smooth and realistic movements.

- Communication: Strong verbal and written communication skills to understand project requirements and collaborate with team members.

- Time Management: Efficiently managing multiple projects and meeting deadlines.

- Problem-Solving: Ability to address technical issues and find solutions to animation challenges.

47.3 Typical Work Environment

Animators typically work in diverse settings, each with its unique requirements and atmosphere:

- Work Hours: Generally full-time, with additional hours for meeting deadlines, especially during the production phase.

- Office Setting: Work in animation studios, film production companies, game development firms, advertising agencies, or remotely from home offices.

- Team Collaboration: Interaction with directors, designers, writers, and other animators.

- Dynamic Environment: Managing multiple animation projects simultaneously and adapting to feedback and revisions.

47.4 Career Path and Growth Opportunities

The career path of an animator offers numerous avenues for advancement and specialization:

- Entry-Level Positions: Junior Animator, Animation Intern, or Character Designer.

- Mid-Level Positions: Animator, Senior Animator, or Animation Supervisor.

- Advanced Roles: Lead Animator, Animation Director, or Creative Director.

- Specializations: 2D Animation, 3D Animation, Visual Effects (VFX), Motion Graphics, or Stop-Motion Animation.

- Further Education: Advanced degrees or certifications in specific areas of animation can lead to higher-level roles and specialized positions.

47.5 Tips for Success

To excel as an animator, consider the following strategies:

- Continuous Learning: Stay updated with the latest animation techniques, tools, and trends through ongoing education and professional development.

- Networking: Build a professional network through animation associations, industry events, and online platforms.

- Practical Experience: Gain hands-on experience through internships, freelance projects, and real-world animation assignments.

- Portfolio Development: Create a strong portfolio showcasing a variety of animation projects to demonstrate your skills and versatility.

- Seek Feedback: Engage with mentors, peers, and clients to receive constructive feedback and improve your animation techniques.

- Professional Associations: Join organizations like the Animation Guild for access to resources, training, and networking opportunities.

- Embrace Technology: Stay proficient with the latest animation software and hardware to enhance your efficiency and creativity.

- Storytelling Focus: Develop strong storytelling skills to create engaging and cohesive narratives that resonate with audiences.

By implementing these strategies, you can build a successful and fulfilling career as an animator, bringing characters and stories to life through captivating and innovative animations.

48. Fashion Designer

48.1 Overview of the Role

Fashion designers create clothing, accessories, and footwear by sketching designs, selecting fabrics, and overseeing the production process. They work to bring their artistic vision to life, blending functionality and aesthetics to create fashion pieces that appeal to consumers. Fashion designers may work in various sectors, including high fashion, ready-to-wear, mass-market clothing, or specialty areas like sportswear or bridal wear.

48.2 Required Skills and Education

To become a successful fashion designer, a combination of creative talent, technical skills, and formal education is essential. Here's a comprehensive breakdown:

- Technical Skills:

- Design Software: Proficiency in using design software such as Adobe Illustrator, Photoshop, and CAD (Computer-Aided Design) programs.

- Sewing and Pattern Making: Skills in sewing and creating patterns to construct garments.

- Fabric and Textile Knowledge: Understanding different fabrics, their properties, and how they behave in different designs.

- Fashion Illustration: Ability to sketch and illustrate design concepts.

- Trend Analysis: Ability to analyze fashion trends and forecast upcoming styles.

- Educational Background:

- Degree: A bachelor's degree in fashion design, fashion merchandising, or a related field is typically required.

- Certifications: Certifications in fashion design, pattern making, or textile design can enhance your credentials.

- Ongoing Education: Participation in fashion workshops, online courses, and industry conferences to stay updated with the latest trends and techniques.

- *Soft Skills:*

- Creativity: A strong creative vision to develop unique and innovative fashion designs.

- Attention to Detail: Precision in design and construction to ensure high-quality garments.

- Communication: Strong verbal and written communication skills to convey design ideas and collaborate with team members.

- Time Management: Efficiently managing multiple design projects and meeting deadlines.

- Business Acumen: Understanding of the fashion industry, market trends, and consumer preferences.

48.3 Typical Work Environment

Fashion designers typically work in diverse settings, each with its unique requirements and atmosphere:

- Work Hours: Generally full-time, with additional hours during fashion shows, product launches, and seasonal deadlines.

- Office Setting: Work in design studios, fashion houses, manufacturing facilities, or remotely from home offices.

- Team Collaboration: Interaction with pattern makers, fabric suppliers, production teams, and marketing departments.

- Dynamic Environment: Managing multiple design projects simultaneously and adapting to feedback and revisions.

48.4 Career Path and Growth Opportunities

The career path of a fashion designer offers numerous avenues for advancement and specialization:

- Entry-Level Positions: Assistant Designer, Fashion Intern, or Pattern Maker.

- Mid-Level Positions: Fashion Designer, Senior Designer, or Design Director.

- Advanced Roles: Creative Director, Head of Design, or Fashion Brand Owner.

- Specializations: Haute Couture, Ready-to-Wear, Sportswear, Bridal Wear, or Accessories Design.

- Further Education: Advanced degrees or certifications in specific areas of fashion design can lead to higher-level roles and specialized positions.

48.5 Tips for Success

To excel as a fashion designer, consider the following strategies:

- Continuous Learning: Stay updated with the latest fashion trends, techniques, and tools through ongoing education and professional development.

- Networking: Build a professional network through fashion associations, industry events, and online platforms.

- Practical Experience: Gain hands-on experience through internships, freelance projects, and real-world design assignments.

- Portfolio Development: Create a strong portfolio showcasing a variety of design projects to demonstrate your skills and versatility.

- Seek Feedback: Engage with mentors, peers, and clients to receive constructive feedback and improve your design techniques.

- Professional Associations: Join organizations like the Council of Fashion Designers of America (CFDA) for access to resources, training, and networking opportunities.

- Embrace Technology: Stay proficient with the latest design software and tools to enhance your efficiency and creativity.

- Market Awareness: Develop an understanding of market trends and consumer preferences to create designs that resonate with your target audience.

By implementing these strategies, you can build a successful and fulfilling career as a fashion designer, creating innovative and stylish clothing and accessories that make a significant impact in the fashion industry.

49. Interior Designer

49.1 Overview of the Role

Interior designers plan, design, and furnish the interiors of residential, commercial, and industrial buildings. They create functional and aesthetically pleasing environments by selecting furniture, lighting, color schemes, and decorative elements. Interior designers work closely with clients to understand their needs and preferences, and then translate those ideas into practical and creative designs. They also coordinate with architects, contractors, and suppliers to ensure the successful implementation of their designs.

49.2 Required Skills and Education

To become a successful interior designer, a combination of creative talent, technical skills, and formal education is essential. Here's a comprehensive breakdown:

- Technical Skills:

- Design Software: Proficiency in using design software such as AutoCAD, SketchUp, Revit, and Adobe Creative Suite.

- Space Planning: Skills in planning and optimizing interior spaces to meet functional and aesthetic requirements.

- Color Theory: Understanding of color theory and the ability to create harmonious color palettes.

- Material Knowledge: Knowledge of different materials, finishes, and textiles used in interior design.

- Building Codes and Regulations: Familiarity with building codes, safety regulations, and accessibility standards.

- Educational Background:

- Degree: A bachelor's degree in interior design, architecture, or a related field is typically required.

- Certifications: Certification from organizations like the National Council for Interior Design Qualification (NCIDQ) can enhance your credentials.

- Ongoing Education: Participation in design workshops, online courses, and industry conferences to stay updated with the latest trends and techniques.

- *Soft Skills:*

- Creativity: A strong creative vision to develop unique and aesthetically pleasing interior designs.

- Attention to Detail: Precision in design and execution to ensure high-quality results.

- Communication: Strong verbal and written communication skills to understand client needs and collaborate with team members.

- Time Management: Efficiently managing multiple design projects and meeting deadlines.

- Problem-Solving: Ability to address design challenges and find practical solutions.

49.3 Typical Work Environment

Interior designers typically work in diverse settings, each with its unique requirements and atmosphere:

- Work Hours: Generally full-time, with additional hours during project deadlines or client meetings.

- Office Setting: Work in design studios, architectural firms, or independently from home offices.

- On-Site: Frequent visits to construction sites, client locations, and supplier showrooms.

- Team Collaboration: Interaction with architects, contractors, suppliers, and clients.

- Dynamic Environment: Managing multiple design projects simultaneously and adapting to feedback and revisions.

49.4 Career Path and Growth Opportunities

The career path of an interior designer offers numerous avenues for advancement and specialization:

- Entry-Level Positions: Interior Design Assistant, Junior Interior Designer, or Design Intern.

- Mid-Level Positions: Interior Designer, Senior Interior Designer, or Project Manager.

- Advanced Roles: Design Director, Principal Designer, or Owner of a Design Firm.

- Specializations: Residential Design, Commercial Design, Hospitality Design, Healthcare Design, or Sustainable Design.

- Further Education: Advanced degrees or certifications in specific areas of interior design can lead to higher-level roles and specialized positions.

49.5 Tips for Success

To excel as an interior designer, consider the following strategies:

- Continuous Learning: Stay updated with the latest design trends, techniques, and tools through ongoing education and professional development.

- Networking: Build a professional network through design associations, industry events, and online platforms.

- Practical Experience: Gain hands-on experience through internships, freelance projects, and real-world design assignments.

- Portfolio Development: Create a strong portfolio showcasing a variety of design projects to demonstrate your skills and versatility.

- Seek Feedback: Engage with mentors, peers, and clients to receive constructive feedback and improve your design techniques.

- Professional Associations: Join organizations like the American Society of Interior Designers (ASID) for access to resources, training, and networking opportunities.

- Embrace Technology: Stay proficient with the latest design software and tools to enhance your efficiency and creativity.

- Client Focus: Develop strong client relationships by understanding their needs, preferences, and budget constraints to deliver customized and satisfactory design solutions.

By implementing these strategies, you can build a successful and fulfilling career as an interior designer, creating functional and beautiful spaces that meet the needs and desires of your clients.

Chapter 5 Review

Overview of Creative and Media Careers

In Chapter 5, we explored various careers within the creative and media sectors, each offering unique opportunities for individuals with artistic talent and a passion for storytelling. Here's a summary of the key points covered for each role:

40. Graphic Designer

- Overview of the Role: Creating visual content for websites, advertisements, magazines, and more.

- Required Skills and Education: Proficiency in design software, typography, color theory, and a strong portfolio. A degree in graphic design or a related field is typically required.

- Typical Work Environment: Full-time in design studios, advertising agencies, or corporate offices; some work remotely.

- Career Path and Growth Opportunities: From Junior Graphic Designer to Creative Director, with specializations in web design, UX/UI design, and branding.

- Tips for Success: Continuous learning, networking, practical experience, portfolio development, and staying updated with design trends.

41. Journalist

- Overview of the Role: Gathering, investigating, and reporting news and information.

- Required Skills and Education: Excellent writing and reporting skills, interviewing, editing, and data journalism. A degree in journalism or communications is typically required.

- Typical Work Environment: Newsrooms, television studios, radio stations, or remotely. Often irregular hours.

- Career Path and Growth Opportunities: From Reporter to Managing Editor, with specializations in political journalism, sports journalism, and investigative journalism.

- Tips for Success: Continuous learning, networking, practical experience, portfolio development, and maintaining journalistic ethics.

42. Film Director

- Overview of the Role: Overseeing the creative and dramatic aspects of film production.

- Required Skills and Education: Knowledge of film production, cinematography, editing, screenwriting, and sound design. A degree in film production or media is beneficial.

- Typical Work Environment: Film sets, studios, and offices; often long and irregular hours.

- Career Path and Growth Opportunities: From Assistant Director to Executive Producer, with specializations in documentary filmmaking, commercial directing, and animation directing.

- Tips for Success: Continuous learning, networking, practical experience, portfolio development, and strong storytelling skills.

43. Photographer

- Overview of the Role: Capturing images for various platforms and purposes.

- Required Skills and Education: Camera operation, lighting, editing software, and composition. A degree in photography or visual arts is beneficial.

- Typical Work Environment: Studios, on-location, or remotely; often irregular hours and travel.

- Career Path and Growth Opportunities: From Photography Assistant to Studio Owner, with specializations in portrait, commercial, fashion, and wildlife photography.

- Tips for Success: Continuous learning, networking, practical experience, portfolio development, and strong marketing skills.

44. Social Media Manager

- Overview of the Role: Managing a company's social media strategy to increase brand awareness and engagement.

- Required Skills and Education: Content creation, social media platforms, analytics tools, and advertising. A degree in marketing or communications is typically required.

- Typical Work Environment: Corporate offices, marketing agencies, or remotely; often full-time with additional hours during campaigns.

- Career Path and Growth Opportunities: From Social Media Coordinator to Social Media Director, with specializations in influencer marketing and social media advertising.

- Tips for Success: Continuous learning, networking, practical experience, certifications, and focus on analytics.

45. Content Writer

- Overview of the Role: Creating written material for various platforms, including websites, blogs, and marketing materials.

- Required Skills and Education: Writing, research, SEO, editing, and content management systems. A degree in English, journalism, or marketing is typically beneficial.

- Typical Work Environment: Corporate offices, marketing agencies, or remotely; often full-time with flexible schedules for freelancers.

- Career Path and Growth Opportunities: From Junior Content Writer to Editorial Director, with specializations in technical writing, copywriting, and blogging.

- Tips for Success: Continuous learning, networking, practical experience, portfolio development, and strong SEO skills.

46. Video Editor

- Overview of the Role: Assembling recorded material into a finished product for broadcasting.

- Required Skills and Education: Editing software, audio editing, color correction, motion graphics, and file management. A degree in film production or multimedia is beneficial.

- Typical Work Environment: Editing studios, production companies, broadcasting companies, or remotely; often full-time with additional hours for deadlines.

- Career Path and Growth Opportunities: From Assistant Editor to Post-Production Manager, with specializations in film, TV, documentary, and commercial editing.

- Tips for Success: Continuous learning, networking, practical experience, portfolio development, and strong storytelling skills.

47. Animator

- Overview of the Role: Creating moving images for films, TV, video games, and other media.

- Required Skills and Education: Animation software, drawing, 3D modeling, motion graphics, and storyboarding. A degree in animation or fine arts is typically required.

- Typical Work Environment: Animation studios, film production companies, game development firms, advertising agencies, or remotely; often full-time with additional hours during production.

- Career Path and Growth Opportunities: From Junior Animator to Creative Director, with specializations in 2D animation, 3D animation, visual effects, and stop-motion animation.

- Tips for Success: Continuous learning, networking, practical experience, portfolio development, and strong storytelling skills.

48. Fashion Designer

- Overview of the Role: Creating clothing, accessories, and footwear.

- Required Skills and Education: Design software, sewing, pattern making, fabric knowledge, and fashion illustration. A degree in fashion design or merchandising is typically required.

- Typical Work Environment: Design studios, fashion houses, manufacturing facilities, or remotely; often full-time with additional hours during fashion shows and product launches.

- Career Path and Growth Opportunities: From Assistant Designer to Creative Director, with specializations in haute couture, ready-to-wear, sportswear, and bridal wear.

- Tips for Success: Continuous learning, networking, practical experience, portfolio development, and market awareness.

49. Interior Designer

- Overview of the Role: Planning, designing, and furnishing interiors of buildings.

- Required Skills and Education: Design software, space planning, color theory, material knowledge, and building codes. A degree in interior design or architecture is typically required.

- Typical Work Environment: Design studios, architectural firms, construction sites, or remotely; often full-time with additional hours for client meetings and project deadlines.

- Career Path and Growth Opportunities: From Interior Design Assistant to Principal Designer, with specializations in residential design, commercial design, hospitality design, and sustainable design.

- Tips for Success: Continuous learning, networking, practical experience, portfolio development, and strong client relationships.

Key Takeaways

- Continuous Learning: Stay updated with the latest trends, techniques, and tools through ongoing education and professional development.

- Networking: Build a professional network through industry associations, conferences, and online platforms.

- Practical Experience: Gain hands-on experience through internships, freelance projects, and real-world assignments.

- Certifications and Education: Obtain relevant certifications and pursue higher education to enhance career prospects and open up advanced roles.

- Mentorship: Seek guidance from experienced professionals for career advice and insights.

- Portfolio Development: Create a strong portfolio showcasing diverse and high-quality work to demonstrate your skills and creativity.

- Market Awareness: Develop an understanding of market trends and consumer preferences to create work that resonates with your target audience.

By understanding the roles, required skills, typical work environments, career paths, and tips for success, you can make informed decisions about pursuing a career in the creative and media fields covered in this chapter. Whether you are just starting out or looking to advance your career, this guide provides the essential information to help you succeed.

Chapter 6: Legal Careers

50. Lawyer

50.1 Overview of the Role

Lawyers, also known as attorneys, are professionals who provide legal advice, represent clients in legal matters, and conduct legal research. They play a crucial role in interpreting laws, advocating for clients, and ensuring justice is served. Lawyers may specialize in various fields such as criminal law, corporate law, family law, intellectual property law, and more. Their duties include drafting legal documents, negotiating settlements, and representing clients in court.

50.2 Required Skills and Education

To become a successful lawyer, a combination of advanced education, technical skills, and various soft skills are essential. Here's a comprehensive breakdown:

- Educational Background:

  - Degree: A bachelor's degree followed by a Juris Doctor (JD) degree from an accredited law school.

  - Bar Examination: Passing the bar examination in the state where you intend to practice.

  - Specializations: Optional further education or certifications in specific areas of law (e.g., tax law, environmental law).

- Technical Skills:

- Legal Research: Proficiency in conducting thorough legal research using online databases and legal libraries.

- Legal Writing: Skills in drafting legal documents such as briefs, contracts, and pleadings.

- Case Management: Ability to manage multiple cases simultaneously, including organizing files, evidence, and schedules.

- Negotiation: Strong negotiation skills to resolve disputes and reach settlements.

- Litigation: Skills in representing clients in court, including presenting evidence, examining witnesses, and making legal arguments.

- Soft Skills:

- Analytical Thinking: Ability to analyze complex legal issues and develop effective strategies.

- Communication: Strong verbal and written communication skills to interact with clients, judges, and other legal professionals.

- Ethics and Integrity: Upholding the highest standards of ethics and confidentiality in legal practice.

- Problem-Solving: Aptitude for solving legal problems and finding effective solutions for clients.

- Interpersonal Skills: Building and maintaining positive relationships with clients, colleagues, and stakeholders.

50.3 Typical Work Environment

Lawyers typically work in diverse settings, each with its unique requirements and atmosphere:

- Work Hours: Generally full-time, with additional hours for research, client meetings, and court appearances. Overtime is common, especially when preparing for trials.

- Office Setting: Work in law firms, corporate legal departments, government agencies, or private practice.

- Courtroom: Frequent appearances in courtrooms for hearings, trials, and other legal proceedings.

- Client Interaction: Regular meetings with clients to provide legal advice, gather information, and discuss case strategies.

- Research and Documentation: Extensive time spent conducting legal research and drafting documents.

50.4 Career Path and Growth Opportunities

The career path of a lawyer offers numerous avenues for advancement and specialization:

- Entry-Level Positions: Associate Attorney, Public Defender, or Law Clerk.

- Mid-Level Positions: Senior Associate, In-House Counsel, or Legal Consultant.

- Advanced Roles: Partner, Chief Legal Officer (CLO), or Judge.

- Specializations: Corporate Law, Criminal Law, Family Law, Intellectual Property Law, Environmental Law, Tax Law, and more.

- Further Education: Advanced degrees (e.g., LL.M.) or certifications in specialized areas of law can lead to higher-level roles and expertise.

50.5 Tips for Success

To excel as a lawyer, consider the following strategies:

- Continuous Learning: Stay updated with the latest legal developments, case laws, and regulations through ongoing education and professional development.

- Networking: Build a professional network through legal associations, industry events, and online platforms.

- Practical Experience: Gain hands-on experience through internships, clerkships, and real-world legal practice.

- Certifications: Pursue and maintain professional certifications to enhance your skills and career prospects.

- Seek Mentorship: Engage with experienced lawyers and mentors for career advice and insights.

- Professional Associations: Join organizations like the American Bar Association (ABA) for access to resources, training, and networking opportunities.

- Client Focus: Develop strong client relationships by understanding their needs, providing clear communication, and delivering effective legal solutions.

- Ethical Practice: Uphold the highest standards of ethics and professionalism in all legal matters.

By implementing these strategies, you can build a successful and fulfilling career as a lawyer, providing valuable legal services and contributing to the justice system.

51. Paralegal

51.1 Overview of the Role

Paralegals, also known as legal assistants, provide essential support to lawyers by conducting legal research, drafting documents, organizing files, and managing cases. They play a crucial role in the legal process by assisting attorneys in preparing for trials, hearings, and other legal proceedings. Paralegals work in various areas of law, including corporate, criminal, family, and real estate law, and must adhere to strict ethical guidelines and confidentiality requirements.

51.2 Required Skills and Education

To become a successful paralegal, a combination of formal education, technical skills, and various soft skills are essential. Here's a comprehensive breakdown:

- Educational Background:

- Degree: An associate's degree in paralegal studies is often required; however, a bachelor's degree in a related field can be beneficial. Some positions may require a paralegal certificate from an ABA-approved program.

- Certifications: Certification from professional organizations such as the National Association of Legal Assistants (NALA) or the National Federation of Paralegal Associations (NFPA) can enhance job prospects.

- Ongoing Education: Participation in continuing education courses to stay updated with the latest legal trends and regulations.

- *Technical Skills:*

- Legal Research: Proficiency in conducting legal research using online databases and legal libraries.

- Document Preparation: Skills in drafting legal documents such as contracts, pleadings, and briefs.

- Case Management: Ability to manage multiple cases, organize files, and maintain accurate records.

- Technology: Familiarity with legal research tools (e.g., LexisNexis, Westlaw), case management software, and office productivity software.

- Knowledge of Legal Procedures: Understanding of court procedures, legal terminology, and case law.

- *Soft Skills:*

- Attention to Detail: Precision in preparing and reviewing legal documents to ensure accuracy.

- Communication: Strong verbal and written communication skills to interact with lawyers, clients, and court personnel.

- Organizational Skills: Efficiently managing files, documents, and schedules.

- Confidentiality: Maintaining strict confidentiality of client information and legal matters.

- Analytical Thinking: Ability to analyze legal issues and provide support in developing case strategies.

51.3 Typical Work Environment

Paralegals typically work in diverse settings, each with its unique requirements and atmosphere:

- Work Hours: Generally full-time, with additional hours required during trial preparation and deadlines.

- Office Setting: Work in law firms, corporate legal departments, government agencies, or non-profit organizations.

- Court Interaction: Some paralegals may need to file documents in court or attend trials and hearings to assist attorneys.

- Client Interaction: Regular interaction with clients to gather information and provide updates on case progress.

- Research and Documentation: Extensive time spent conducting legal research and preparing documents.

51.4 Career Path and Growth Opportunities

The career path of a paralegal offers numerous avenues for advancement and specialization:

- Entry-Level Positions: Paralegal, Legal Assistant, or Legal Secretary.

- Mid-Level Positions: Senior Paralegal, Paralegal Supervisor, or Legal Analyst.

- Advanced Roles: Paralegal Manager, Legal Operations Manager, or Compliance Officer.

- Specializations: Corporate Law, Criminal Law, Family Law, Real Estate Law, Intellectual Property Law, or Immigration Law.

- Further Education: Advanced degrees or certifications in specific areas of law can lead to higher-level roles and specialized positions.

51.5 Tips for Success

To excel as a paralegal, consider the following strategies:

- Continuous Learning: Stay updated with the latest legal trends, tools, and regulations through ongoing education and professional development.

- Networking: Build a professional network through legal associations, industry events, and online platforms.

- Practical Experience: Gain hands-on experience through internships, volunteer work, and real-world legal assignments.

- Certifications: Pursue and maintain professional certifications to enhance your skills and career prospects.

- Seek Mentorship: Engage with experienced paralegals and attorneys for career advice and insights.

- Professional Associations: Join organizations like the National Association of Legal Assistants (NALA) or the National Federation of Paralegal Associations (NFPA) for access to resources, training, and networking opportunities.

- Organizational Skills: Develop strong organizational skills to manage multiple tasks and deadlines efficiently.

- Client Focus: Build strong relationships with clients by understanding their needs and providing clear and timely communication.

By implementing these strategies, you can build a successful and fulfilling career as a paralegal, providing valuable support to attorneys and contributing to the effective operation of the legal system.

52. Judge

52.1 Overview of the Role

Judges are legal professionals who preside over court proceedings, interpret and apply laws, and ensure justice is served. They are responsible for maintaining order in the courtroom, ruling on the admissibility of evidence, guiding the jury, and issuing verdicts and sentences. Judges play a crucial role in the legal system, ensuring that trials are fair and that the rights of all parties are protected. They may specialize in various areas such as criminal, civil, family, or appellate law.

52.2 Required Skills and Education

To become a successful judge, a combination of advanced education, extensive legal experience, and various soft skills are essential. Here's a comprehensive breakdown:

- Educational Background:

  - Degree: A bachelor's degree followed by a Juris Doctor (JD) degree from an accredited law school.

  - Bar Examination: Passing the bar examination in the state where you intend to practice law.

  - Experience: Extensive experience practicing law, typically 5-10 years or more, often as a lawyer, prosecutor, or public defender.

  - Further Education: Some judges pursue a Master of Laws (LL.M.) or other advanced legal degrees.

- Technical Skills:

  - Legal Knowledge: In-depth understanding of legal principles, procedures, and case law.

  - Case Management: Ability to manage court proceedings efficiently, including scheduling and docket control.

  - Decision-Making: Skills in making impartial and well-reasoned decisions based on evidence and legal standards.

  - Writing: Proficiency in writing clear and concise legal opinions, rulings, and instructions.

- Soft Skills:

  - Analytical Thinking: Ability to analyze complex legal issues and interpret laws accurately.

  - Communication: Strong verbal and written communication skills to interact effectively with lawyers, jurors, defendants, and court personnel.

  - Ethics and Integrity: Upholding the highest standards of ethics and impartiality.

  - Leadership: Ability to maintain authority and control in the courtroom.

  - Interpersonal Skills: Building and maintaining respectful relationships with all courtroom participants.

52.3 Typical Work Environment

Judges typically work in diverse settings, each with its unique requirements and atmosphere:

- Work Hours: Generally full-time, with additional hours for reviewing cases, writing opinions, and preparing for court proceedings.

- Courtroom Setting: Work primarily in courtrooms and chambers, overseeing trials, hearings, and other legal proceedings.

- Office Setting: Time spent in offices for research, case review, and administrative duties.

- Interaction: Regular interaction with lawyers, jurors, defendants, court staff, and sometimes the public.

- Stress Level: High-pressure environment due to the importance of decisions and the need for accuracy and fairness.

52.4 Career Path and Growth Opportunities

The career path of a judge offers numerous avenues for advancement and specialization:

- Entry-Level Positions: Magistrate, Administrative Law Judge, or Trial Judge.

- Mid-Level Positions: Circuit Court Judge, District Court Judge, or Family Court Judge.

- Advanced Roles: Appellate Judge, Supreme Court Justice, or Chief Justice.

- Specializations: Criminal Law, Civil Law, Family Law, Juvenile Law, or Administrative Law.

- Further Education: Advanced degrees or specialized training in specific areas of law can lead to higher-level roles and specialized positions.

52.5 Tips for Success

To excel as a judge, consider the following strategies:

- Continuous Learning: Stay updated with the latest legal developments, case laws, and judicial practices through ongoing education and professional development.

- Networking: Build a professional network through legal associations, judicial conferences, and online platforms.

- Practical Experience: Gain extensive experience in the legal field through practicing law, serving as a prosecutor or public defender, and handling a diverse range of cases.

- Certifications: Pursue and maintain professional certifications to enhance your legal and judicial skills.

- Seek Mentorship: Engage with experienced judges and legal professionals for career advice and insights.

- Professional Associations: Join organizations like the American Judges Association (AJA) for access to resources, training, and networking opportunities.

- Ethical Practice: Uphold the highest standards of ethics, impartiality, and fairness in all judicial matters.

- Community Engagement: Build a positive relationship with the community by participating in outreach programs and promoting understanding of the legal system.

By implementing these strategies, you can build a successful and fulfilling career as a judge, ensuring that justice is served fairly and effectively in the legal system.

53. Legal Secretary

53.1 Overview of the Role

Legal secretaries provide administrative support to lawyers and legal teams, ensuring the smooth operation of law offices and legal departments. They perform a variety of tasks, including preparing legal documents, managing correspondence, scheduling appointments, and maintaining records. Legal secretaries play a crucial role in helping lawyers and paralegals stay organized and efficient, allowing them to focus on their legal work.

53.2 Required Skills and Education

To become a successful legal secretary, a combination of technical skills, formal education, and various soft skills are essential. Here's a comprehensive breakdown:

- Educational Background:

  - Degree: A high school diploma is typically required. An associate's degree or a certificate in legal studies or office administration can be beneficial.

  - Certifications: Certification from professional organizations such as the National Association of Legal Secretaries (NALS) can enhance job prospects.

  - Ongoing Education: Participation in continuing education courses to stay updated with the latest legal and administrative practices.

- *Technical Skills:*

- Document Preparation: Proficiency in preparing and formatting legal documents such as briefs, contracts, and pleadings.

- Office Software: Skills in using office software, including Microsoft Office Suite (Word, Excel, Outlook) and legal management software.

- Typing and Dictation: High typing speed and accuracy, along with experience in taking dictation and transcribing legal correspondence.

- Legal Terminology: Understanding of legal terminology and procedures.

- Record Keeping: Ability to maintain and organize legal files and records efficiently.

- *Soft Skills:*

- Attention to Detail: Precision in preparing and reviewing legal documents to ensure accuracy.

- Communication: Strong verbal and written communication skills to interact with lawyers, clients, and court personnel.

- Organizational Skills: Efficiently managing multiple tasks, schedules, and deadlines.

- Confidentiality: Maintaining strict confidentiality of client information and legal matters.

- Interpersonal Skills: Building and maintaining positive relationships with clients, colleagues, and other stakeholders.

53.3 Typical Work Environment

Legal secretaries typically work in diverse settings, each with its unique requirements and atmosphere:

- Work Hours: Generally full-time, with additional hours required during busy periods or trial preparations.

- Office Setting: Work in law firms, corporate legal departments, government agencies, or non-profit organizations.

- Interaction: Regular interaction with lawyers, paralegals, clients, and court personnel.

- Documentation and Filing: Extensive time spent preparing documents, managing correspondence, and maintaining records.

53.4 Career Path and Growth Opportunities

The career path of a legal secretary offers numerous avenues for advancement and specialization:

- Entry-Level Positions: Legal Secretary, Legal Assistant, or Administrative Assistant.

- Mid-Level Positions: Senior Legal Secretary, Executive Legal Assistant, or Office Manager.

- Advanced Roles: Paralegal, Legal Administrator, or Legal Operations Manager.

- Specializations: Corporate Law, Criminal Law, Family Law, Real Estate Law, Intellectual Property Law, or Immigration Law.

- Further Education: Advanced degrees or certifications in specific areas of law or office administration can lead to higher-level roles and specialized positions.

53.5 Tips for Success

To excel as a legal secretary, consider the following strategies:

- Continuous Learning: Stay updated with the latest legal practices, office technologies, and administrative techniques through ongoing education and professional development.

- Networking: Build a professional network through legal associations, industry events, and online platforms.

- Practical Experience: Gain hands-on experience through internships, volunteer work, and real-world administrative assignments.

- Certifications: Pursue and maintain professional certifications to enhance your skills and career prospects.

- Seek Mentorship: Engage with experienced legal secretaries and legal professionals for career advice and insights.

- Professional Associations: Join organizations like the National Association of Legal Secretaries (NALS) for access to resources, training, and networking opportunities.

- Organizational Skills: Develop strong organizational skills to manage multiple tasks, schedules, and deadlines efficiently.

- Client Focus: Build strong relationships with clients by understanding their needs and providing clear and timely communication.

By implementing these strategies, you can build a successful and fulfilling career as a legal secretary, providing valuable administrative support to legal teams and contributing to the effective operation of the legal system.

54. Compliance Officer

54.1 Overview of the Role

Compliance officers ensure that organizations adhere to laws, regulations, and internal policies. They play a critical role in maintaining the integrity and ethical standards of a company by developing, implementing, and managing compliance programs. Compliance officers work across various industries, including finance, healthcare, manufacturing, and government. Their duties include conducting audits, assessing risk, providing training, and addressing compliance issues.

54.2 Required Skills and Education

To become a successful compliance officer, a combination of formal education, technical skills, and various soft skills are essential. Here's a comprehensive breakdown:

- Educational Background:

  - Degree: A bachelor's degree in business, finance, law, or a related field is typically required. Some positions may require a master's degree or a Juris Doctor (JD).

  - Certifications: Professional certifications such as Certified Compliance & Ethics Professional (CCEP), Certified Regulatory Compliance Manager (CRCM), or Certified Internal Auditor (CIA) can enhance job prospects.

  - Ongoing Education: Participation in continuing education courses to stay updated with the latest compliance regulations and practices.

- Technical Skills:

- Regulatory Knowledge: In-depth understanding of relevant laws, regulations, and industry standards.

- Risk Assessment: Ability to identify and assess compliance risks within an organization.

- Auditing: Skills in conducting internal audits to ensure compliance with policies and regulations.

- Policy Development: Expertise in developing and implementing compliance policies and procedures.

- Data Analysis: Proficiency in analyzing data to identify trends and areas of non-compliance.

- Soft Skills:

- Attention to Detail: Precision in reviewing documents and processes to ensure compliance.

- Communication: Strong verbal and written communication skills to convey compliance requirements and provide training.

- Ethics and Integrity: Upholding the highest standards of ethics and confidentiality.

- Problem-Solving: Ability to address compliance issues and find effective solutions.

- Interpersonal Skills: Building and maintaining positive relationships with employees, management, and regulatory bodies.

54.3 Typical Work Environment

Compliance officers typically work in diverse settings, each with its unique requirements and atmosphere:

- Work Hours: Generally full-time, with additional hours required during audits or regulatory inspections.

- Office Setting: Work in corporate offices, financial institutions, healthcare facilities, or government agencies.

- Interaction: Regular interaction with employees, management, external auditors, and regulatory bodies.

- Documentation and Reporting: Extensive time spent preparing reports, conducting audits, and maintaining compliance records.

54.4 Career Path and Growth Opportunities

The career path of a compliance officer offers numerous avenues for advancement and specialization:

- Entry-Level Positions: Compliance Analyst, Compliance Coordinator, or Junior Compliance Officer.

- Mid-Level Positions: Compliance Officer, Senior Compliance Officer, or Compliance Manager.

- Advanced Roles: Chief Compliance Officer (CCO), Director of Compliance, or Regulatory Affairs Manager.

- Specializations: Financial Compliance, Healthcare Compliance, Environmental Compliance, Data Protection Compliance, or Corporate Ethics.

- Further Education: Advanced degrees or certifications in specific areas of compliance can lead to higher-level roles and specialized positions.

54.5 Tips for Success

To excel as a compliance officer, consider the following strategies:

- Continuous Learning: Stay updated with the latest compliance regulations, industry standards, and best practices through ongoing education and professional development.

- Networking: Build a professional network through compliance associations, industry events, and online platforms.

- Practical Experience: Gain hands-on experience through internships, compliance projects, and real-world assignments.

- Certifications: Pursue and maintain professional certifications to enhance your skills and career prospects.

- Seek Mentorship: Engage with experienced compliance professionals for career advice and insights.

- Professional Associations: Join organizations like the Society of Corporate Compliance and Ethics (SCCE) for access to resources, training, and networking opportunities.

- Ethical Practice: Uphold the highest standards of ethics, integrity, and confidentiality in all compliance matters.

- Risk Management: Develop strong risk management skills to identify, assess, and mitigate compliance risks effectively.

By implementing these strategies, you can build a successful and fulfilling career as a compliance officer, ensuring that your organization adheres to legal and ethical standards and operates with integrity.

55. Court Reporter

55.1 Overview of the Role

Court reporters, also known as stenographers, are responsible for creating verbatim transcriptions of legal proceedings, meetings, and other events where accurate records are essential. They capture spoken dialogue using specialized equipment such as stenotype machines, digital recorders, and voice writing equipment. Court reporters play a crucial role in the judicial system by ensuring that accurate and complete records are maintained, which are used for legal references, appeals, and archival purposes.

55.2 Required Skills and Education

To become a successful court reporter, a combination of technical skills, formal education, and various soft skills are essential. Here's a comprehensive breakdown:

- Educational Background:

  - Degree: An associate's degree or a postsecondary certificate in court reporting from an accredited program is typically required.

  - Certifications: Certification from professional organizations such as the National Court Reporters Association (NCRA) or state-level certifications can enhance job prospects.

  - Licensing: Some states require court reporters to be licensed or certified.

- Technical Skills:

- Stenography: Proficiency in using stenotype machines to transcribe spoken words into written text.

- Voice Writing: Skills in using voice writing equipment to repeat spoken dialogue for transcription.

- Typing Speed and Accuracy: High typing speed (typically 225 words per minute) and accuracy are crucial.

- Real-Time Reporting: Ability to provide real-time transcription services for live proceedings.

- Editing and Proofreading: Skills in reviewing and editing transcripts to ensure accuracy and completeness.

- Soft Skills:

- Attention to Detail: Precision in capturing and transcribing spoken words accurately.

- Listening Skills: Excellent listening skills to accurately capture dialogue, even in fast-paced or noisy environments.

- Communication: Strong verbal and written communication skills to interact with legal professionals and clients.

- Confidentiality: Maintaining strict confidentiality of sensitive information and legal proceedings.

- Time Management: Efficiently managing transcription tasks and meeting deadlines.

55.3 Typical Work Environment

Court reporters typically work in diverse settings, each with its unique requirements and atmosphere:

- Work Hours: Generally full-time, with additional hours required during lengthy trials or urgent transcription requests.

- Courtroom Setting: Work primarily in courtrooms, capturing live testimony and proceedings.

- Office Setting: Time spent in offices for reviewing, editing, and finalizing transcripts.

- Remote Work: Some court reporters may work remotely, especially for freelance or real-time captioning services.

- Travel: Occasional travel to different courtrooms or legal venues may be required.

55.4 Career Path and Growth Opportunities

The career path of a court reporter offers numerous avenues for advancement and specialization:

- Entry-Level Positions: Junior Court Reporter, Legal Transcriber, or Court Reporting Intern.

- Mid-Level Positions: Certified Court Reporter, Real-Time Captioner, or Freelance Court Reporter.

- Advanced Roles: Senior Court Reporter, Court Reporting Supervisor, or Court Reporting Instructor.

- Specializations: Real-Time Reporting, Broadcast Captioning, CART (Communication Access Real-Time Translation) Provider, or Medical Transcription.

- Further Education: Advanced certifications and continuing education in specific areas of court reporting can lead to higher-level roles and specialized positions.

55.5 Tips for Success

To excel as a court reporter, consider the following strategies:

- Continuous Learning: Stay updated with the latest court reporting techniques, tools, and best practices through ongoing education and professional development.

- Networking: Build a professional network through court reporting associations, industry events, and online platforms.

- Practical Experience: Gain hands-on experience through internships, freelance work, and real-world transcription assignments.

- Certifications: Pursue and maintain professional certifications to enhance your skills and career prospects.

- Seek Mentorship: Engage with experienced court reporters and legal professionals for career advice and insights.

- Professional Associations: Join organizations like the National Court Reporters Association (NCRA) for access to resources, training, and networking opportunities.

- Technology Proficiency: Stay proficient with the latest stenography and voice writing equipment to enhance your efficiency and accuracy.

- Accuracy Focus: Develop strong accuracy and attention to detail to ensure high-quality transcriptions.

By implementing these strategies, you can build a successful and fulfilling career as a court reporter, providing essential transcription services that contribute to the integrity and functionality of the legal system.

56. Mediator

56.1 Overview of the Role

Mediators are professionals who facilitate negotiations and conflict resolution between disputing parties. They help individuals, groups, or organizations reach mutually acceptable agreements by guiding discussions, identifying underlying issues, and suggesting possible solutions. Mediators play a critical role in resolving disputes without the need for litigation, thus saving time, costs, and preserving relationships.

56.2 Required Skills and Education

To become a successful mediator, a combination of conflict resolution skills, legal knowledge, and interpersonal abilities is essential. Key requirements include:

Technical Skills:

- Conflict Resolution: Proficiency in negotiation, arbitration, and mediation techniques.

- Legal Knowledge: Understanding of relevant laws and regulations, especially if mediating in areas like family law, business, or labor disputes.

- Analytical Skills: Ability to analyze complex situations, identify core issues, and develop effective solutions.

- Documentation: Skills in drafting agreements and documenting the mediation process.

Educational Background:

- Degree: A bachelor's degree in law, psychology, conflict resolution, or a related field is typically required. Advanced degrees (e.g., JD, MA in Dispute Resolution) are beneficial.

- Certifications: Certification from a recognized mediation training program can enhance career prospects.

- Continued Learning: Participation in continuing education courses to stay updated with mediation practices and legal developments.

Soft Skills:

- Communication: Effective communication skills to facilitate discussions and convey ideas clearly.

- Empathy: Providing understanding and sensitivity to the emotions and perspectives of disputing parties.

- Neutrality: Maintaining impartiality and fairness throughout the mediation process.

- Patience: Patience and perseverance in working through conflicts and reaching resolutions.

- Problem-Solving: Strong problem-solving and critical thinking abilities to guide parties toward mutually acceptable solutions.

56.3 Typical Work Environment

Mediators work in a variety of settings, including law firms, private practices, government agencies, community mediation centers, and corporate offices. The work environment is typically an office or conference room where private and confidential discussions can take place. Mediators may work full-time or part-time, with schedules that include evenings or weekends to accommodate the availability of the disputing parties. The role involves facilitating discussions, drafting agreements, and sometimes traveling to different locations for mediation sessions.

56.4 Career Path and Growth Opportunities

The career path for mediators offers various opportunities for specialization and advancement:

- Entry-Level Positions: Assistant Mediator, focusing on developing mediation skills and gaining practical experience under the supervision of experienced mediators.

- Mid-Level Positions: Mediator, Senior Mediator, or Conflict Resolution Specialist, taking on more responsibilities in managing cases and facilitating complex disputes.

- Senior-Level Positions: Lead Mediator, Mediation Program Director, or Mediation Consultant, overseeing mediation programs, managing staff, and ensuring the quality of mediation services.

- Specialization Areas: Family Mediation, Workplace Mediation, Commercial Mediation, or International Mediation. Specializing in these areas allows mediators to focus on specific types of disputes and enhance their expertise.

- Management Roles: Director of Dispute Resolution Services, Head of Mediation Department, or Legal Services Manager. These positions involve overseeing mediation programs, managing budgets, and aligning services with organizational goals.

- Continued Education: Pursuing advanced certifications or degrees (e.g., LLM in Dispute Resolution) can lead to higher roles and increased salaries.

56.5 Tips for Success

To excel as a mediator, consider the following strategies:

- Prioritize Neutrality and Impartiality: Focus on maintaining neutrality and impartiality throughout the mediation process to build trust with the disputing parties.

- Stay Updated: Continuously update your knowledge and skills through continuing education, professional development courses, and staying current with legal and mediation practices.

- Develop Strong Interpersonal Skills: Effective communication, empathy, and active listening are crucial for building rapport with disputing parties and facilitating discussions.

- Embrace Conflict Resolution Techniques: Familiarize yourself with various conflict resolution techniques and adapt them to suit different situations and parties.

- Seek Specialization: Consider pursuing additional certifications in specialized areas of mediation to advance your career and enhance your expertise.

- Network and Mentor: Build a professional network through mediation associations (e.g., Association for Conflict Resolution) and seek mentorship from experienced mediators to gain insights and career guidance.

- Focus on Ethical Practices: Adhere to ethical guidelines and standards in mediation to ensure fairness, confidentiality, and integrity in the process.

By following these tips, you can build a successful and fulfilling career as a mediator, making a significant impact on resolving disputes and fostering positive outcomes for the parties involved.

57. Patent Examiner

57.1 Overview of the Role

Patent examiners are professionals who review patent applications to determine whether they comply with the legal standards and technical requirements for patentability. They analyze the novelty, usefulness, and non-obviousness of inventions, ensuring that patents are granted only for truly innovative and deserving inventions. Patent examiners play a crucial role in protecting intellectual property and fostering innovation.

57.2 Required Skills and Education

To become a successful patent examiner, a combination of technical knowledge, analytical skills, and attention to detail is essential. Key requirements include:

Technical Skills:

- Scientific and Technical Expertise: Proficiency in a specific field of science or engineering relevant to the inventions being reviewed.

- Legal Knowledge: Understanding of patent laws, regulations, and guidelines.

- Research Skills: Ability to conduct thorough searches of existing patents and scientific literature to assess the novelty and non-obviousness of inventions.

- Analytical Skills: Ability to evaluate complex technical information and apply legal standards to determine patentability.

- Documentation: Skills in drafting detailed reports and legal documents.

Educational Background:

- Degree: A bachelor's degree in a relevant scientific or engineering field is typically required. Advanced degrees (e.g., master's or Ph.D.) can be beneficial.

- Certifications: While specific certifications are not typically required, specialized training in intellectual property law or patent examination can enhance career prospects.

- Continued Learning: Participation in continuing education to stay updated with advancements in technology and changes in patent laws.

Soft Skills:

- Attention to Detail: Precision in reviewing patent applications and conducting prior art searches.

- Communication: Effective written and verbal communication skills to interact with patent applicants, attorneys, and colleagues.

- Critical Thinking: Strong problem-solving and analytical skills to assess the patentability of inventions.

- Time Management: Ability to manage a large volume of applications and meet deadlines.

- Independence: Capability to work independently and make informed decisions.

57.3 Typical Work Environment

Patent examiners typically work in office settings, either in government patent offices or private intellectual property firms. The work environment is usually quiet and conducive to detailed analysis and research. Patent examiners may work full-time, with standard office hours, although deadlines and workload may require occasional overtime. Remote work or telecommuting options may be available in some organizations.

57.4 Career Path and Growth Opportunities

The career path for patent examiners offers various opportunities for specialization and advancement:

- Entry-Level Positions: Junior Patent Examiner, focusing on developing expertise in patent examination procedures and gaining practical experience in reviewing applications.

- Mid-Level Positions: Patent Examiner, Senior Patent Examiner, or Supervisory Patent Examiner, taking on more complex cases and mentoring junior examiners.

- Senior-Level Positions: Lead Patent Examiner, Patent Quality Assurance Specialist, or Patent Office Manager, overseeing examination processes, ensuring quality control, and managing staff.

- Specialization Areas: Biotechnology, Software, Mechanical Engineering, Pharmaceuticals, or Electrical Engineering. Specializing in these areas allows examiners to focus on specific types of inventions and enhance their expertise.

- Management Roles: Director of Patent Examination, Chief Patent Examiner, or Intellectual Property Manager. These positions involve overseeing patent examination departments, managing budgets, and aligning services with organizational goals.

- Continued Education: Pursuing advanced degrees or specialized training in intellectual property law can lead to higher roles and increased salaries.

57.5 Tips for Success

To excel as a patent examiner, consider the following strategies:

- Stay Updated: Continuously update your knowledge and skills through continuing education, professional development courses, and staying current with technological advancements and changes in patent laws.

- Develop Strong Research Skills: Enhance your ability to conduct thorough and effective prior art searches to assess the novelty and non-obviousness of inventions.

- Pay Attention to Detail: Maintain a high level of accuracy and precision in reviewing patent applications and drafting reports.

- Improve Communication Skills: Develop effective written and verbal communication skills to interact with applicants, attorneys, and colleagues clearly and professionally.

- Seek Specialization: Consider specializing in a specific technical field to advance your career and enhance your expertise.

- Network and Mentor: Build a professional network through intellectual property associations (e.g., American Intellectual Property Law Association) and seek mentorship from experienced patent examiners to gain insights and career guidance.

- Focus on Time Management: Develop strong time management skills to handle a large volume of applications efficiently and meet deadlines.

By following these tips, you can build a successful and fulfilling career as a patent examiner, making a significant impact on protecting intellectual property and promoting innovation.

58. Law Librarian

58.1 Overview of the Role

Law librarians are specialized librarians who manage legal information resources and provide research support to legal professionals, students, and the public. They play a crucial role in organizing, maintaining, and accessing legal databases, archives, and collections. Law librarians assist with legal research, support teaching and learning in law schools, and help legal practitioners stay informed about new laws and legal precedents.

58.2 Required Skills and Education

To become a successful law librarian, a combination of legal knowledge, library science expertise, and research skills is essential. Key requirements include:

Technical Skills:

- Legal Research: Proficiency in conducting legal research using various databases, such as Westlaw, LexisNexis, and HeinOnline.

- Information Management: Skills in organizing, cataloging, and maintaining legal information resources and databases.

- Library Science: Knowledge of library management principles, including cataloging, classification, and digital library systems.

- Technology Proficiency: Ability to use and manage library software, digital archives, and online research tools.

- Instructional Skills: Capability to teach legal research methods and tools to law students and legal professionals.

Educational Background:

- Degree: A master's degree in library science (MLS or MLIS) from an accredited program is typically required. Some positions may also require a Juris Doctor (JD) degree or equivalent legal education.

- Certifications: Certification from organizations such as the American Association of Law Libraries (AALL) can enhance career prospects.

- Continued Learning: Participation in continuing education to stay updated with advancements in legal research tools and library science practices.

Soft Skills:

- Communication: Effective communication skills to interact with legal professionals, students, and the public.

- Attention to Detail: Precision in managing legal information and conducting research.

- Analytical Thinking: Strong analytical skills to interpret and synthesize legal information.

- Problem-Solving: Ability to assist users with complex legal research questions and find relevant information.

- Customer Service: Providing excellent service and support to library users.

58.3 Typical Work Environment

Law librarians work in various settings, including law schools, law firms, corporate legal departments, government agencies, and public libraries. The work environment is typically quiet and conducive to research and study, equipped with extensive collections of legal texts, journals, and online resources. Law librarians may work full-time or part-time, with standard office hours, although some positions may require evening or weekend shifts to accommodate users' needs.

58.4 Career Path and Growth Opportunities

The career path for law librarians offers various opportunities for specialization and advancement:

- Entry-Level Positions: Reference Librarian or Legal Research Librarian, focusing on developing research skills and gaining practical experience in managing legal information.

- Mid-Level Positions: Senior Law Librarian, Legal Research Coordinator, or Digital Resources Librarian, taking on more responsibilities in managing collections, training users, and overseeing digital resources.

- Senior-Level Positions: Head of Legal Research, Library Director, or Chief Information Officer, overseeing library operations, managing staff, and ensuring the quality of research services.

- Specialization Areas: Academic Law Librarianship, Corporate Law Librarianship, Government Law Librarianship, or Digital Law Librarianship. Specializing in these areas allows librarians to focus on specific types of legal information and user needs.

- Management Roles: Library Director, Director of Information Services, or Knowledge Manager. These positions involve overseeing library departments, managing budgets, and aligning services with organizational goals.

- Continued Education: Pursuing advanced certifications or degrees (e.g., LLM in Legal Information Management) can lead to higher roles and increased salaries.

58.5 Tips for Success

To excel as a law librarian, consider the following strategies:

- Stay Updated: Continuously update your knowledge and skills through continuing education, professional development courses, and staying current with legal research tools and library science advancements.

- Develop Strong Research Skills: Enhance your ability to conduct thorough and effective legal research using various databases and resources.

- Pay Attention to Detail: Maintain a high level of accuracy and precision in managing legal information and conducting research.

- Improve Communication Skills: Develop effective communication skills to interact with users clearly and professionally, providing excellent customer service.

- Seek Specialization: Consider specializing in a specific area of law librarianship to advance your career and enhance your expertise.

- Network and Mentor: Build a professional network through library and legal associations (e.g., American Association of Law Libraries) and seek mentorship from experienced law librarians to gain insights and career guidance.

- Embrace Technology: Familiarize yourself with the latest library software, digital archives, and online research tools to improve efficiency and user support.

By following these tips, you can build a successful and fulfilling career as a law librarian, making a significant impact on legal research and education.

59. Forensic Scientist

59.1 Overview of the Role

Forensic scientists are professionals who apply scientific principles and techniques to analyze physical evidence from crime scenes. They play a critical role in the criminal justice system by helping to solve crimes and support legal investigations. Forensic scientists work in various specialties, including DNA analysis, toxicology, ballistics, and trace evidence, providing crucial information that can link suspects to crimes, determine cause of death, and more.

59.2 Required Skills and Education

To become a successful forensic scientist, a combination of scientific expertise, analytical skills, and attention to detail is essential. Key requirements include:

Technical Skills:

- Laboratory Techniques: Proficiency in laboratory methods and techniques specific to forensic analysis, such as DNA extraction, chromatography, and spectrometry.

- Evidence Handling: Skills in collecting, preserving, and documenting physical evidence from crime scenes.

- Data Analysis: Ability to interpret complex data and draw accurate conclusions from forensic tests.

- Report Writing: Skills in drafting detailed and accurate reports that clearly explain forensic findings.

- Legal Knowledge: Understanding of legal procedures and the rules of evidence to ensure the admissibility of forensic results in court.

Educational Background:

- Degree: A bachelor's degree in forensic science, chemistry, biology, or a related field is typically required. Advanced degrees (e.g., master's or Ph.D.) can be beneficial for career advancement.

- Certifications: Certification from organizations such as the American Board of Criminalistics (ABC) can enhance career prospects.

- Continued Learning: Participation in continuing education to stay updated with advancements in forensic science techniques and technologies.

Soft Skills:

- Attention to Detail: Precision in analyzing evidence and documenting findings to ensure accuracy and reliability.

- Communication: Effective written and verbal communication skills to convey findings clearly to law enforcement, attorneys, and in court.

- Critical Thinking: Strong problem-solving and analytical skills to interpret forensic evidence.

- Ethics: High ethical standards to ensure integrity and impartiality in forensic investigations.

- Teamwork: Ability to collaborate with other forensic scientists, law enforcement, and legal professionals.

59.3 Typical Work Environment

Forensic scientists work in various settings, including crime laboratories, medical examiner offices, police departments, and government agencies. The work environment is typically a laboratory equipped with advanced scientific instruments and tools. Forensic scientists may also visit crime scenes to collect evidence. The role often involves handling potentially hazardous materials, requiring strict adherence to safety protocols. Forensic scientists usually work full-time, with standard office hours, although they may need to be available for on-call work or to testify in court.

59.4 Career Path and Growth Opportunities

The career path for forensic scientists offers various opportunities for specialization and advancement:

- Entry-Level Positions: Forensic Technician or Junior Forensic Scientist, focusing on developing laboratory skills and gaining practical experience in forensic analysis.

- Mid-Level Positions: Forensic Scientist, Senior Forensic Scientist, or Crime Scene Investigator, taking on more complex cases and specialized forensic analyses.

- Senior-Level Positions: Lead Forensic Scientist, Forensic Laboratory Manager, or Chief Forensic Scientist, overseeing forensic operations, managing staff, and ensuring the quality of forensic analyses.

- Specialization Areas: DNA Analysis, Toxicology, Ballistics, Trace Evidence, or Digital Forensics. Specializing in these areas allows forensic scientists to focus on specific types of evidence and enhance their expertise.

- Management Roles: Laboratory Director, Director of Forensic Services, or Crime Lab Supervisor. These positions involve overseeing forensic laboratories, managing budgets, and ensuring compliance with regulations.

- Continued Education: Pursuing advanced certifications or degrees (e.g., Master's in Forensic Science) can lead to higher roles and increased salaries.

59.5 Tips for Success

To excel as a forensic scientist, consider the following strategies:

- Prioritize Accuracy and Precision: Ensure the highest level of accuracy and precision in conducting forensic analyses and documenting findings.

- Stay Updated: Continuously update your knowledge and skills through continuing education, professional development courses, and staying current with advancements in forensic science.

- Develop Strong Analytical Skills: Enhance your ability to analyze and interpret forensic evidence accurately through continuous practice and training.

- Embrace Technology: Familiarize yourself with the latest forensic technologies and laboratory instruments to improve efficiency and accuracy.

- Seek Specialization: Consider pursuing additional certifications in specialized areas of forensic science to advance your career and enhance your expertise.

- Network and Mentor: Build a professional network through forensic science associations (e.g., American Academy of Forensic Sciences) and seek mentorship from experienced forensic scientists to gain insights and career guidance.

- Maintain Ethical Standards: Adhere to high ethical standards and integrity in your forensic work to ensure credibility and reliability in legal proceedings.

By following these tips, you can build a successful and fulfilling career as a forensic scientist, making a significant impact on the criminal justice system and contributing to the resolution of criminal cases.

Chapter 6 Review

Overview of Legal Careers

In Chapter 6, we explored various careers within the legal field. These professions are critical to the functioning of the judicial system and offer numerous opportunities for individuals interested in law and justice. Here's a summary of the key points covered for each role:

50. Lawyer

- Overview of the Role: Lawyers provide legal advice, represent clients in court, draft legal documents, and negotiate settlements.

- Required Skills and Education: Strong analytical and research skills, excellent communication, a Juris Doctor (JD) degree, and passing the bar exam.

- Typical Work Environment: Law firms, corporate legal departments, government agencies, or private practice, often involving long hours and high-stress situations.

- Career Path and Growth Opportunities: Associate to Partner in law firms, specialization in areas like corporate law or criminal defense, and potential for judicial appointments or senior legal roles in corporations.

- Tips for Success: Continuously update legal knowledge, develop strong networking skills, seek mentorship, and maintain a high level of ethical standards.

51. Paralegal

- Overview of the Role: Paralegals assist lawyers by conducting legal research, drafting documents, and organizing case files.

- Required Skills and Education: Strong organizational and research skills, excellent writing ability, an associate's degree or certificate in paralegal studies.

- Typical Work Environment: Law firms, corporate legal departments, government agencies, often working regular office hours with some overtime.

- Career Path and Growth Opportunities: Entry-level paralegal to senior paralegal or paralegal manager, specialization in areas like litigation or real estate, and potential to transition to a legal consultant or law school.

- Tips for Success: Develop strong attention to detail, continuously update legal knowledge, build strong relationships with lawyers, and seek certification from recognized paralegal organizations.

52. Judge

- Overview of the Role: Judges preside over court proceedings, interpret laws, and make rulings.

- Required Skills and Education: Extensive legal experience, strong decision-making and leadership skills, a Juris Doctor (JD) degree, and significant experience as a practicing lawyer.

- Typical Work Environment: Courtrooms, chambers, and offices, often with a high level of responsibility and pressure.

- Career Path and Growth Opportunities: Lawyer to Judge, with opportunities for advancement to higher courts such as appellate or supreme courts, and potential for administrative roles within the judiciary.

- Tips for Success: Maintain high ethical standards, develop strong legal acumen, seek mentorship from experienced judges, and engage in continuous legal education.

53. Legal Secretary

- Overview of the Role: Legal secretaries perform administrative duties such as managing schedules, preparing legal documents, and communicating with clients.

- Required Skills and Education: Strong organizational and communication skills, proficiency in legal terminology and office software, typically a high school diploma with specialized training.

- Typical Work Environment: Law firms, corporate legal departments, government agencies, often with regular office hours.

- Career Path and Growth Opportunities: Entry-level legal secretary to senior legal secretary or office manager, potential for specialization in areas like litigation or corporate law.

- Tips for Success: Develop strong attention to detail, enhance computer and software skills, build strong working relationships with legal professionals, and continuously update knowledge of legal procedures.

54. Compliance Officer

- Overview of the Role: Compliance officers ensure that organizations adhere to legal standards and internal policies.

- Required Skills and Education: Strong analytical skills, understanding of regulatory requirements, a bachelor's degree in law, business, or related field, and certification in compliance.

- Typical Work Environment: Corporate settings, financial institutions, healthcare organizations, often involving regular office hours and occasional travel.

- Career Path and Growth Opportunities: Entry-level compliance analyst to senior compliance officer or compliance manager, with opportunities for specialization in areas like financial compliance or healthcare compliance.

- Tips for Success: Stay updated with regulatory changes, develop strong attention to detail, build strong ethical standards, and seek certification from recognized compliance organizations.

55. Court Reporter

- Overview of the Role: Court reporters create verbatim transcripts of legal proceedings, meetings, and other events.

- Required Skills and Education: Proficiency in stenography or voice writing, excellent listening and typing skills, typically a postsecondary certificate or associate's degree.

- Typical Work Environment: Courtrooms, legal offices, and freelance environments, often requiring sitting for long periods.

- Career Path and Growth Opportunities: Entry-level court reporter to senior court reporter or court reporting manager, with opportunities to specialize in areas like CART (Communication Access Real-time Translation) or broadcast captioning.

- Tips for Success: Develop strong attention to detail, enhance typing speed and accuracy, stay updated with technological advancements, and seek certification from recognized court reporting organizations.

56. Mediator

- Overview of the Role: Mediators facilitate negotiations and conflict resolution between disputing parties.

- Required Skills and Education: Conflict resolution skills, legal knowledge, strong communication skills, typically a bachelor's degree in law, psychology, or related field, and certification in mediation.

- Typical Work Environment: Offices, legal settings, and freelance environments, often involving flexible hours to accommodate parties' schedules.

- Career Path and Growth Opportunities: Entry-level mediator to senior mediator or mediation program director, with opportunities for specialization in areas like family mediation or commercial mediation.

- Tips for Success: Prioritize neutrality and impartiality, stay updated with conflict resolution techniques, develop strong interpersonal skills, seek specialization, and build a professional network.

57. Patent Examiner

- Overview of the Role: Patent examiners review patent applications to determine their compliance with legal standards and technical requirements.

- Required Skills and Education: Scientific and technical expertise, legal knowledge, strong research skills, a bachelor's degree in a relevant field, and specialized training in intellectual property law.

- Typical Work Environment: Government patent offices, intellectual property firms, often involving detailed analysis and research.

- Career Path and Growth Opportunities: Entry-level patent examiner to senior patent examiner or supervisory patent examiner, with opportunities for specialization in areas like biotechnology or software patents.

- Tips for Success: Stay updated with technological advancements, develop strong research skills, maintain high attention to detail, improve communication skills, and seek specialization.

58. Law Librarian

- Overview of the Role: Law librarians manage legal information resources and provide research support to legal professionals, students, and the public.

- Required Skills and Education: Legal research skills, information management expertise, a master's degree in library science, and knowledge of legal databases.

- Typical Work Environment: Law schools, law firms, corporate legal departments, and government agencies, often involving a quiet and research-focused environment.

- Career Path and Growth Opportunities: Entry-level reference librarian to senior law librarian or library director, with opportunities for specialization in digital resources or academic law librarianship.

- Tips for Success: Stay updated with legal research tools, develop strong research skills, improve communication skills, seek specialization, and embrace technology.

59. Forensic Scientist

- Overview of the Role: Forensic scientists analyze physical evidence from crime scenes to support legal investigations.

- Required Skills and Education: Laboratory techniques, evidence handling, data analysis, a bachelor's degree in forensic science or related field, and certification in forensic specialties.

- Typical Work Environment: Crime laboratories, medical examiner offices, police departments, often involving detailed and potentially hazardous work.

- Career Path and Growth Opportunities: Entry-level forensic technician to senior forensic scientist or laboratory manager, with opportunities for specialization in areas like DNA analysis or toxicology.

- Tips for Success: Prioritize accuracy and precision, stay updated with advancements in forensic science, develop strong analytical skills, embrace technology, and maintain ethical standards.

Key Takeaways

- Continuous Learning: Staying updated with industry trends, legal developments, and technological advancements is crucial across all legal careers.

- Networking: Building a professional network through industry events, online forums, and professional associations can provide valuable opportunities and insights.

- Practical Experience: Gaining hands-on experience through internships, clerkships, or part-time jobs is essential for skill development and career advancement.

- Certifications and Education: Obtaining relevant certifications and pursuing higher education can enhance career prospects and open up advanced roles.

- Ethical Standards: Maintaining high ethical standards and integrity is fundamental to success in legal careers.

- Work-Life Balance: Managing stress and maintaining a healthy work-life balance is crucial for long-term productivity and job satisfaction.

By understanding the roles, required skills, typical work environments, career paths, and tips for success, you can make informed decisions about pursuing a career in the legal fields covered in this chapter. Whether you are just starting out or looking to advance your career, this guide provides the essential information to help you succeed.

Chapter 7: Trades and Technical Careers

60. Electrician

60.1 Overview of the Role

Electricians are skilled tradespeople who specialize in installing, maintaining, and repairing electrical systems in residential, commercial, and industrial settings. They ensure that electrical systems operate safely and efficiently, meeting all relevant codes and regulations. Electricians work with a variety of electrical components, including wiring, circuit breakers, transformers, and lighting fixtures.

60.2 Required Skills and Education

To become a successful electrician, a combination of technical skills, education, and hands-on experience is essential. Key requirements include:

Technical Skills:

- Electrical Knowledge: Understanding of electrical theory, circuits, and wiring practices.

- Technical Aptitude: Proficiency in using tools and equipment such as multimeters, conduit benders, and oscilloscopes.

- Blueprint Reading: Ability to read and interpret blueprints, technical diagrams, and electrical codes.

- Troubleshooting: Skills in diagnosing and solving electrical problems.

- Safety Practices: Knowledge of safety procedures and regulations to prevent accidents and ensure compliance with codes.

Educational Background:

- Education: A high school diploma or equivalent is typically required. Courses in math, physics, and shop are beneficial.

- Apprenticeship: Completion of a formal apprenticeship program, which combines classroom instruction with on-the-job training, is necessary. These programs usually last 4-5 years.

- Licensure: Obtaining a license is required in most states. This typically involves passing a comprehensive exam that tests knowledge of electrical theory, local codes, and safety practices.

- Certifications: Additional certifications (e.g., Master Electrician) can enhance career prospects and demonstrate advanced expertise.

Soft Skills:

- Attention to Detail: Precision in performing installations and repairs to avoid mistakes and ensure safety.

- Communication: Effective communication with clients, contractors, and team members.

- Problem-Solving: Strong problem-solving skills to address electrical issues efficiently.

- Physical Stamina: Ability to perform physically demanding tasks, such as lifting heavy equipment and working in confined spaces.

- Time Management: Efficiently managing time to complete projects on schedule.

60.3 Typical Work Environment

Electricians work in various environments, including construction sites, residential homes, commercial buildings, and industrial facilities. The work can be physically demanding and may involve standing for long periods, climbing ladders, and working in cramped or high spaces. Electricians may work indoors or outdoors, and the job can expose them to potential hazards such as electrical shocks, falls, and burns. Safety protocols and protective gear are essential to minimize risks. Electricians often work full-time, with the potential for overtime and emergency call-outs.

60.4 Career Path and Growth Opportunities

The career path for electricians offers numerous opportunities for specialization and advancement:

- Entry-Level Positions: Apprentice Electrician, focusing on gaining hands-on experience and learning from experienced professionals.

- Mid-Level Positions: Journeyman Electrician, taking on more complex tasks and working independently on projects.

- Senior-Level Positions: Master Electrician or Electrical Contractor, overseeing projects, managing teams, and ensuring compliance with codes and regulations.

- Specialization Areas: Industrial Electrician, Residential Electrician, Commercial Electrician, or Maintenance Electrician. Specializing in these areas allows electricians to focus on specific types of work and enhance their expertise.

- Management Roles: Project Manager, Electrical Inspector, or Construction Manager. These positions involve overseeing larger projects, ensuring quality and safety, and managing budgets.

- Continued Education: Pursuing advanced certifications or degrees (e.g., Bachelor's in Electrical Engineering) can lead to higher roles and increased salaries.

60.5 Tips for Success

To excel as an electrician, consider the following strategies:

- Stay Updated: Continuously update your knowledge and skills through continuing education, professional development courses, and staying current with changes in electrical codes and technology.

- Develop Strong Technical Skills: Enhance your proficiency with electrical systems and tools through continuous practice and training.

- Embrace Safety: Always prioritize safety by following established protocols, using protective gear, and staying informed about potential hazards.

- Build a Professional Network: Establish connections with other electricians, contractors, and industry professionals to gain insights and opportunities.

- Seek Specialization: Consider pursuing additional certifications in specialized areas to advance your career and enhance your expertise.

- Provide Excellent Customer Service: Develop strong communication and interpersonal skills to build positive relationships with clients and ensure customer satisfaction.

- Focus on Quality: Strive for high-quality workmanship in all projects to build a strong reputation and ensure long-term success.

By following these tips, you can build a successful and fulfilling career as an electrician, making a significant impact on various construction and maintenance projects and contributing to the safety and functionality of electrical systems.

61. Plumber

61.1 Overview of the Role

Plumbers are skilled tradespeople who install, repair, and maintain plumbing systems in residential, commercial, and industrial buildings. Their work includes installing pipes, fixtures, and appliances, diagnosing plumbing issues, and ensuring that plumbing systems operate efficiently and safely. Plumbers play a crucial role in maintaining the infrastructure of water supply, drainage, and heating systems.

61.2 Required Skills and Education

To become a successful plumber, a combination of technical skills, education, and hands-on experience is essential. Key requirements include:

Technical Skills:

- Plumbing Knowledge: Understanding of plumbing systems, water supply networks, and drainage systems.

- Technical Aptitude: Proficiency in using plumbing tools and equipment, such as pipe cutters, wrenches, and soldering equipment.

- Blueprint Reading: Ability to read and interpret blueprints, technical diagrams, and plumbing codes.

- Troubleshooting: Skills in diagnosing and solving plumbing issues efficiently.

- Safety Practices: Knowledge of safety procedures and regulations to prevent accidents and ensure compliance with codes.

Educational Background:

- Education: A high school diploma or equivalent is typically required. Courses in math, science, and shop are beneficial.

- Apprenticeship: Completion of a formal apprenticeship program, which combines classroom instruction with on-the-job training, is necessary. These programs usually last 4-5 years.

- Licensure: Obtaining a license is required in most states. This typically involves passing a comprehensive exam that tests knowledge of plumbing theory, local codes, and safety practices.

- Certifications: Additional certifications (e.g., Backflow Prevention, Green Plumbing) can enhance career prospects and demonstrate advanced expertise.

Soft Skills:

- Attention to Detail: Precision in performing installations and repairs to avoid mistakes and ensure safety.

- Communication: Effective communication with clients, contractors, and team members.

- Problem-Solving: Strong problem-solving skills to address plumbing issues efficiently.

- Physical Stamina: Ability to perform physically demanding tasks, such as lifting heavy equipment and working in confined spaces.

- Time Management: Efficiently managing time to complete projects on schedule.

61.3 Typical Work Environment

Plumbers work in various environments, including construction sites, residential homes, commercial buildings, and industrial facilities. The work can be physically demanding and may involve standing for long periods, crawling in confined spaces, and working in various weather conditions. Plumbers may work indoors or outdoors, and the job can expose them to potential hazards such as chemicals, hot water, and heavy equipment. Safety protocols and protective gear are essential to minimize risks. Plumbers often work full-time, with the potential for overtime and emergency call-outs.

61.4 Career Path and Growth Opportunities

The career path for plumbers offers numerous opportunities for specialization and advancement:

- Entry-Level Positions: Apprentice Plumber, focusing on gaining hands-on experience and learning from experienced professionals.

- Mid-Level Positions: Journeyman Plumber, taking on more complex tasks and working independently on projects.

- Senior-Level Positions: Master Plumber or Plumbing Contractor, overseeing projects, managing teams, and ensuring compliance with codes and regulations.

- Specialization Areas: Residential Plumber, Commercial Plumber, Industrial Plumber, or Service and Repair Plumber. Specializing in these areas allows plumbers to focus on specific types of work and enhance their expertise.

- Management Roles: Project Manager, Plumbing Inspector, or Construction Manager. These positions involve overseeing larger projects, ensuring quality and safety, and managing budgets.

- Continued Education: Pursuing advanced certifications or degrees (e.g., Associate's in Construction Management) can lead to higher roles and increased salaries.

61.5 Tips for Success

To excel as a plumber, consider the following strategies:

- Stay Updated: Continuously update your knowledge and skills through continuing education, professional development courses, and staying current with changes in plumbing codes and technology.

- Develop Strong Technical Skills: Enhance your proficiency with plumbing systems and tools through continuous practice and training.

- Embrace Safety: Always prioritize safety by following established protocols, using protective gear, and staying informed about potential hazards.

- Build a Professional Network: Establish connections with other plumbers, contractors, and industry professionals to gain insights and opportunities.

- Seek Specialization: Consider pursuing additional certifications in specialized areas to advance your career and enhance your expertise.

- Provide Excellent Customer Service: Develop strong communication and interpersonal skills to build positive relationships with clients and ensure customer satisfaction.

- Focus on Quality: Strive for high-quality workmanship in all projects to build a strong reputation and ensure long-term success.

By following these tips, you can build a successful and fulfilling career as a plumber, making a significant impact on various construction and maintenance projects and contributing to the safety and functionality of plumbing systems.

62. Carpenter

62.1 Overview of the Role

Carpenters are skilled tradespeople who construct, install, and repair structures and fixtures made from wood and other materials. They work on a variety of projects, including building frameworks for houses, installing cabinetry, constructing staircases, and creating furniture. Carpenters play a critical role in the construction and renovation of buildings, ensuring that structures are safe, functional, and aesthetically pleasing.

62.2 Required Skills and Education

To become a successful carpenter, a combination of technical skills, education, and hands-on experience is essential. Key requirements include:

Technical Skills:

- Carpentry Knowledge: Understanding of construction methods, materials, and building codes.

- Technical Aptitude: Proficiency in using carpentry tools and equipment, such as saws, hammers, drills, and levels.

- Blueprint Reading: Ability to read and interpret blueprints, technical diagrams, and construction plans.

- Measurement and Math Skills: Precision in measuring materials and calculating dimensions to ensure accuracy in construction.

- Problem-Solving: Skills in diagnosing and solving construction-related issues efficiently.

Educational Background:

- Education: A high school diploma or equivalent is typically required. Courses in math, mechanical drawing, and shop are beneficial.

- Apprenticeship: Completion of a formal apprenticeship program, which combines classroom instruction with on-the-job training, is necessary. These programs usually last 3-4 years.

- Certifications: Additional certifications (e.g., OSHA safety certification, carpentry certifications) can enhance career prospects and demonstrate advanced expertise.

Soft Skills:

- Attention to Detail: Precision in measuring, cutting, and assembling materials to avoid mistakes and ensure quality.

- Communication: Effective communication with clients, contractors, and team members.

- Physical Stamina: Ability to perform physically demanding tasks, such as lifting heavy materials and working in various positions.

- Time Management: Efficiently managing time to complete projects on schedule.

- Creativity: Innovative thinking to design and build custom structures and fixtures.

62.3 Typical Work Environment

Carpenters work in various environments, including construction sites, residential homes, commercial buildings, and woodworking shops. The work can be physically demanding and may involve standing for long periods, climbing ladders, and working in confined spaces or at heights. Carpenters may work indoors or outdoors, and the job can expose them to potential hazards such as heavy machinery, sharp tools, and falling objects. Safety protocols and protective gear are essential to minimize risks. Carpenters often work full-time, with the potential for overtime and weekend work to meet project deadlines.

62.4 Career Path and Growth Opportunities

The career path for carpenters offers numerous opportunities for specialization and advancement:

- Entry-Level Positions: Apprentice Carpenter, focusing on gaining hands-on experience and learning from experienced professionals.

- Mid-Level Positions: Journeyman Carpenter, taking on more complex tasks and working independently on projects.

- Senior-Level Positions: Master Carpenter or Carpenter Foreman, overseeing projects, managing teams, and ensuring compliance with codes and regulations.

- Specialization Areas: Finish Carpenter, Rough Carpenter, Cabinetmaker, or Furniture Maker. Specializing in these areas allows carpenters to focus on specific types of work and enhance their expertise.

- Management Roles: Project Manager, Construction Supervisor, or General Contractor. These positions involve overseeing larger projects, ensuring quality and safety, and managing budgets.

- Continued Education: Pursuing advanced certifications or degrees (e.g., Associate's in Construction Management) can lead to higher roles and increased salaries.

62.5 Tips for Success

To excel as a carpenter, consider the following strategies:

- Stay Updated: Continuously update your knowledge and skills through continuing education, professional development courses, and staying current with changes in building codes and technology.

- Develop Strong Technical Skills: Enhance your proficiency with carpentry tools and techniques through continuous practice and training.

- Embrace Safety: Always prioritize safety by following established protocols, using protective gear, and staying informed about potential hazards.

- Build a Professional Network: Establish connections with other carpenters, contractors, and industry professionals to gain insights and opportunities.

- Seek Specialization: Consider pursuing additional certifications in specialized areas to advance your career and enhance your expertise.

- Provide Excellent Customer Service: Develop strong communication and interpersonal skills to build positive relationships with clients and ensure customer satisfaction.

- Focus on Quality: Strive for high-quality workmanship in all projects to build a strong reputation and ensure long-term success.

By following these tips, you can build a successful and fulfilling career as a carpenter, making a significant impact on various construction and renovation projects and contributing to the safety and functionality of built environments.

63. HVAC Technician

63.1 Overview of the Role

HVAC (Heating, Ventilation, and Air Conditioning) technicians are skilled tradespeople who install, maintain, and repair heating, cooling, and ventilation systems in residential, commercial, and industrial buildings. They ensure that HVAC systems operate efficiently and safely, providing comfortable indoor environments and maintaining air quality.

63.2 Required Skills and Education

To become a successful HVAC technician, a combination of technical skills, education, and hands-on experience is essential. Key requirements include:

Technical Skills:

- HVAC System Knowledge: Understanding of heating, cooling, and ventilation systems, including boilers, furnaces, heat pumps, air conditioners, and ductwork.

- Technical Aptitude: Proficiency in using tools and equipment such as manifold gauges, voltmeters, and pipe cutters.

- Troubleshooting: Skills in diagnosing and solving HVAC system issues efficiently.

- Blueprint Reading: Ability to read and interpret blueprints, technical diagrams, and HVAC codes.

- Safety Practices: Knowledge of safety procedures and regulations to prevent accidents and ensure compliance with codes.

Educational Background:

- Education: A high school diploma or equivalent is typically required. Courses in math, physics, and shop are beneficial.

- Technical School: Completion of a technical training program or an associate's degree in HVAC technology is often required.

- Apprenticeship: Gaining hands-on experience through an apprenticeship program, which combines classroom instruction with on-the-job training, is highly beneficial.

- Certifications: Obtaining certifications such as EPA Section 608 Certification, NATE (North American Technician Excellence) certification, and state-specific licenses can enhance career prospects and demonstrate advanced expertise.

Soft Skills:

- Attention to Detail: Precision in installing, maintaining, and repairing HVAC systems to ensure efficiency and safety.

- Communication: Effective communication with clients, contractors, and team members.

- Problem-Solving: Strong problem-solving skills to address HVAC issues efficiently.

- Physical Stamina: Ability to perform physically demanding tasks, such as lifting heavy equipment and working in confined spaces.

- Time Management: Efficiently managing time to complete projects on schedule.

63.3 Typical Work Environment

HVAC technicians work in various environments, including residential homes, commercial buildings, and industrial facilities. The work can be physically demanding and may involve standing for long periods, climbing ladders, working in confined spaces, and handling heavy equipment. HVAC technicians may work indoors or outdoors, and the job can expose them to potential hazards such as electrical shocks, refrigerant leaks, and extreme temperatures. Safety protocols and protective gear are essential to minimize risks. HVAC technicians often work full-time, with the potential for overtime and emergency call-outs.

63.4 Career Path and Growth Opportunities

The career path for HVAC technicians offers numerous opportunities for specialization and advancement:

- Entry-Level Positions: HVAC Technician Apprentice, focusing on gaining hands-on experience and learning from experienced professionals.

- Mid-Level Positions: Journeyman HVAC Technician, taking on more complex tasks and working independently on projects.

- Senior-Level Positions: Master HVAC Technician or HVAC Contractor, overseeing projects, managing teams, and ensuring compliance with codes and regulations.

- Specialization Areas: Residential HVAC Technician, Commercial HVAC Technician, Industrial HVAC Technician, or HVAC Service Technician. Specializing in these areas allows technicians to focus on specific types of work and enhance their expertise.

- Management Roles: HVAC Project Manager, HVAC Supervisor, or Construction Manager. These positions involve overseeing larger projects, ensuring quality and safety, and managing budgets.

- Continued Education: Pursuing advanced certifications or degrees (e.g., Associate's in HVAC Technology or Construction Management) can lead to higher roles and increased salaries.

63.5 Tips for Success

To excel as an HVAC technician, consider the following strategies:

- Stay Updated: Continuously update your knowledge and skills through continuing education, professional development courses, and staying current with changes in HVAC technology and codes.

- Develop Strong Technical Skills: Enhance your proficiency with HVAC systems and tools through continuous practice and training.

- Embrace Safety: Always prioritize safety by following established protocols, using protective gear, and staying informed about potential hazards.

- Build a Professional Network: Establish connections with other HVAC technicians, contractors, and industry professionals to gain insights and opportunities.

- Seek Specialization: Consider pursuing additional certifications in specialized areas to advance your career and enhance your expertise.

- Provide Excellent Customer Service: Develop strong communication and interpersonal skills to build positive relationships with clients and ensure customer satisfaction.

- Focus on Quality: Strive for high-quality workmanship in all projects to build a strong reputation and ensure long-term success.

By following these tips, you can build a successful and fulfilling career as an HVAC technician, making a significant impact on various construction and maintenance projects and contributing to the safety and functionality of HVAC systems.

64. Automotive Technician

64.1 Overview of the Role

Automotive technicians are skilled professionals who inspect, maintain, and repair vehicles. They work on various types of vehicles, including cars, trucks, and SUVs, ensuring that they operate safely and efficiently. Automotive technicians diagnose mechanical and electrical problems, perform routine maintenance, and carry out repairs on engines, transmissions, brakes, and other critical vehicle systems.

64.2 Required Skills and Education

To become a successful automotive technician, a combination of technical skills, education, and hands-on experience is essential. Key requirements include:

Technical Skills:

- Mechanical Knowledge: Understanding of vehicle systems, including engines, transmissions, brakes, and electrical systems.

- Diagnostic Skills: Proficiency in using diagnostic tools and equipment to identify vehicle issues.

- Technical Aptitude: Ability to use a variety of tools and equipment, such as wrenches, diagnostic scanners, and hydraulic lifts.

- Problem-Solving: Skills in diagnosing and resolving mechanical and electrical issues efficiently.

- Safety Practices: Knowledge of safety procedures and regulations to prevent accidents and ensure compliance with standards.

Educational Background:

- Education: A high school diploma or equivalent is typically required. Courses in automotive repair, electronics, and mechanical drawing are beneficial.

- Technical School: Completion of a technical training program or an associate's degree in automotive technology is often required.

- Certifications: Obtaining certifications such as ASE (Automotive Service Excellence) certification can enhance career prospects and demonstrate advanced expertise.

- Apprenticeship: Gaining hands-on experience through an apprenticeship program, which combines classroom instruction with on-the-job training, is highly beneficial.

Soft Skills:

- Attention to Detail: Precision in diagnosing problems and performing repairs to ensure vehicle safety and performance.

- Communication: Effective communication with customers, service managers, and team members.

- Time Management: Efficiently managing time to complete repairs and maintenance tasks on schedule.

- Customer Service: Providing excellent customer service to build positive relationships with clients.

- Physical Stamina: Ability to perform physically demanding tasks, such as lifting heavy parts and working in various positions.

64.3 Typical Work Environment

Automotive technicians work in various environments, including repair shops, dealerships, service centers, and garages. The work can be physically demanding and may involve standing for long periods, working in awkward positions, and handling heavy parts. Automotive technicians may work indoors or outdoors, depending on the facility, and the job can expose them to potential hazards such as chemicals, moving parts, and heavy machinery. Safety protocols and protective gear are essential to minimize risks. Automotive technicians often work full-time, with the potential for overtime and weekend work to meet customer demand.

64.4 Career Path and Growth Opportunities

The career path for automotive technicians offers numerous opportunities for specialization and advancement:

- Entry-Level Positions: Automotive Technician Apprentice, focusing on gaining hands-on experience and learning from experienced professionals.

- Mid-Level Positions: Journeyman Automotive Technician, taking on more complex tasks and working independently on repairs and maintenance.

- Senior-Level Positions: Master Automotive Technician or Shop Foreman, overseeing projects, managing teams, and ensuring compliance with standards and regulations.

- Specialization Areas: Engine Specialist, Transmission Specialist, Brake Specialist, or Diagnostic Technician. Specializing in these areas allows technicians to focus on specific types of work and enhance their expertise.

- Management Roles: Service Manager, Shop Manager, or Automotive Service Director. These positions involve overseeing service operations, ensuring quality and safety, and managing budgets.

- Continued Education: Pursuing advanced certifications or degrees (e.g., Bachelor's in Automotive Technology or Business Management) can lead to higher roles and increased salaries.

64.5 Tips for Success

To excel as an automotive technician, consider the following strategies:

- Stay Updated: Continuously update your knowledge and skills through continuing education, professional development courses, and staying current with changes in automotive technology and standards.

- Develop Strong Technical Skills: Enhance your proficiency with vehicle systems and diagnostic tools through continuous practice and training.

- Embrace Safety: Always prioritize safety by following established protocols, using protective gear, and staying informed about potential hazards.

- Build a Professional Network: Establish connections with other automotive technicians, service managers, and industry professionals to gain insights and opportunities.

- Seek Specialization: Consider pursuing additional certifications in specialized areas to advance your career and enhance your expertise.

- Provide Excellent Customer Service: Develop strong communication and interpersonal skills to build positive relationships with customers and ensure customer satisfaction.

- Focus on Quality: Strive for high-quality workmanship in all repairs and maintenance tasks to build a strong reputation and ensure long-term success.

By following these tips, you can build a successful and fulfilling career as an automotive technician, making a significant impact on vehicle safety and performance and contributing to the satisfaction of your customers.

65. Welder

65.1 Overview of the Role

Welders are skilled tradespeople who use high heat to fuse metals together in various construction, manufacturing, and repair projects. They work with different welding techniques, such as MIG, TIG, stick, and arc welding, to join metal parts. Welders play a crucial role in creating and maintaining structures, machinery, and equipment across multiple industries.

65.2 Required Skills and Education

To become a successful welder, a combination of technical skills, education, and hands-on experience is essential. Key requirements include:

Technical Skills:

- Welding Techniques: Proficiency in various welding methods, including MIG, TIG, stick, and arc welding.

- Technical Aptitude: Ability to operate welding equipment and tools, such as torches, grinders, and clamps.

- Blueprint Reading: Ability to read and interpret blueprints, technical diagrams, and welding symbols.

- Metallurgy Knowledge: Understanding of different metals and their properties to ensure proper welding techniques are applied.

- Safety Practices: Knowledge of safety procedures and regulations to prevent accidents and ensure compliance with codes.

Educational Background:

- Education: A high school diploma or equivalent is typically required. Courses in math, science, and shop are beneficial.

- Technical School: Completion of a welding training program or an associate's degree in welding technology is often required.

- Certifications: Obtaining certifications such as AWS (American Welding Society) certification can enhance career prospects and demonstrate advanced expertise.

- Apprenticeship: Gaining hands-on experience through an apprenticeship program, which combines classroom instruction with on-the-job training, is highly beneficial.

Soft Skills:

- Attention to Detail: Precision in performing welds to ensure structural integrity and quality.

- Communication: Effective communication with clients, contractors, and team members.

- Problem-Solving: Strong problem-solving skills to address welding challenges efficiently.

- Physical Stamina: Ability to perform physically demanding tasks, such as lifting heavy materials and working in various positions.

- Time Management: Efficiently managing time to complete welding projects on schedule.

65.3 Typical Work Environment

Welders work in various environments, including construction sites, manufacturing plants, shipyards, and repair shops. The work can be physically demanding and may involve standing for long periods, working in confined spaces, and handling heavy materials. Welders may work indoors or outdoors, and the job can expose them to potential hazards such as intense heat, fumes, and sparks. Safety protocols and protective gear, such as welding helmets, gloves, and aprons, are essential to minimize risks. Welders often work full-time, with the potential for overtime and weekend work to meet project deadlines.

65.4 Career Path and Growth Opportunities

The career path for welders offers numerous opportunities for specialization and advancement:

- Entry-Level Positions: Welder Apprentice, focusing on gaining hands-on experience and learning from experienced professionals.

- Mid-Level Positions: Journeyman Welder, taking on more complex tasks and working independently on welding projects.

- Senior-Level Positions: Master Welder or Welding Foreman, overseeing projects, managing teams, and ensuring compliance with codes and regulations.

- Specialization Areas: Pipe Welder, Structural Welder, Underwater Welder, or Aerospace Welder. Specializing in these areas allows welders to focus on specific types of work and enhance their expertise.

- Management Roles: Welding Inspector, Welding Supervisor, or Welding Engineer. These positions involve overseeing welding operations, ensuring quality and safety, and managing budgets.

- Continued Education: Pursuing advanced certifications or degrees (e.g., Bachelor's in Welding Engineering or Technology) can lead to higher roles and increased salaries.

65.5 Tips for Success

To excel as a welder, consider the following strategies:

- Stay Updated: Continuously update your knowledge and skills through continuing education, professional development courses, and staying current with changes in welding technology and standards.

- Develop Strong Technical Skills: Enhance your proficiency with welding techniques and tools through continuous practice and training.

- Embrace Safety: Always prioritize safety by following established protocols, using protective gear, and staying informed about potential hazards.

- Build a Professional Network: Establish connections with other welders, contractors, and industry professionals to gain insights and opportunities.

- Seek Specialization: Consider pursuing additional certifications in specialized areas to advance your career and enhance your expertise.

- Provide Excellent Workmanship: Strive for high-quality welds in all projects to build a strong reputation and ensure long-term success.

- Maintain Physical Fitness: Stay in good physical condition to handle the demands of the job and work efficiently.

By following these tips, you can build a successful and fulfilling career as a welder, making a significant impact on various construction, manufacturing, and repair projects and contributing to the safety and integrity of metal structures and equipment.

66. Machinist

66.1 Overview of the Role

Machinists are skilled tradespeople who operate and maintain machine tools to produce precision metal parts, instruments, and tools. They work with various materials, including metals, plastics, and composites, and use a variety of machines such as lathes, milling machines, grinders, and CNC (Computer Numerical Control) machines. Machinists play a critical role in manufacturing, ensuring that parts meet exact specifications and quality standards.

66.2 Required Skills and Education

To become a successful machinist, a combination of technical skills, education, and hands-on experience is essential. Key requirements include:

Technical Skills:

- Machining Knowledge: Understanding of machining processes, materials, and tools.

- Technical Aptitude: Proficiency in operating machine tools such as lathes, milling machines, and grinders.

- Blueprint Reading: Ability to read and interpret blueprints, technical diagrams, and engineering drawings.

- Precision Measurement: Skills in using precision measurement tools such as calipers, micrometers, and gauges.

- CNC Programming: Knowledge of CNC programming and operation for automated machining processes.

Educational Background:

- Education: A high school diploma or equivalent is typically required. Courses in math, physics, and shop are beneficial.

- Technical School: Completion of a machining training program or an associate's degree in machining technology is often required.

- Apprenticeship: Gaining hands-on experience through an apprenticeship program, which combines classroom instruction with on-the-job training, is highly beneficial.

- Certifications: Obtaining certifications such as NIMS (National Institute for Metalworking Skills) can enhance career prospects and demonstrate advanced expertise.

Soft Skills:

- Attention to Detail: Precision in machining parts to exact specifications and quality standards.

- Communication: Effective communication with engineers, supervisors, and team members.

- Problem-Solving: Strong problem-solving skills to address machining challenges efficiently.

- Physical Stamina: Ability to perform physically demanding tasks, such as standing for long periods and handling heavy materials.

- Time Management: Efficiently managing time to complete machining tasks on schedule.

66.3 Typical Work Environment

Machinists work in various environments, including manufacturing plants, machine shops, and tool and die facilities.

The work can be physically demanding and may involve standing for long periods, operating heavy machinery, and handling materials. Machinists may work indoors in well-ventilated and well-lit areas, and the job can expose them to potential hazards such as moving parts, sharp tools, and loud noises. Safety protocols and protective gear, such as safety glasses, ear protection, and gloves, are essential to minimize risks. Machinists often work full-time, with the potential for overtime and shift work to meet production demands.

66.4 Career Path and Growth Opportunities

The career path for machinists offers numerous opportunities for specialization and advancement:

- Entry-Level Positions: Machinist Apprentice, focusing on gaining hands-on experience and learning from experienced professionals.

- Mid-Level Positions: Journeyman Machinist, taking on more complex tasks and working independently on machining projects.

- Senior-Level Positions: Master Machinist or Machining Foreman, overseeing projects, managing teams, and ensuring compliance with quality standards and regulations.

- Specialization Areas: CNC Machinist, Tool and Die Maker, Precision Machinist, or Maintenance Machinist. Specializing in these areas allows machinists to focus on specific types of work and enhance their expertise.

- Management Roles: Production Supervisor, Machining Supervisor, or Manufacturing Engineer. These positions involve overseeing machining operations, ensuring quality and safety, and managing budgets.

- Continued Education: Pursuing advanced certifications or degrees (e.g., Bachelor's in Manufacturing Engineering or Industrial Technology) can lead to higher roles and increased salaries.

66.5 Tips for Success

To excel as a machinist, consider the following strategies:

- Stay Updated: Continuously update your knowledge and skills through continuing education, professional development courses, and staying current with advancements in machining technology and techniques.

- Develop Strong Technical Skills: Enhance your proficiency with machining tools and techniques through continuous practice and training.

- Embrace Safety: Always prioritize safety by following established protocols, using protective gear, and staying informed about potential hazards.

- Build a Professional Network: Establish connections with other machinists, engineers, and industry professionals to gain insights and opportunities.

- Seek Specialization: Consider pursuing additional certifications in specialized areas to advance your career and enhance your expertise.

- Provide Excellent Workmanship: Strive for high-quality machining in all projects to build a strong reputation and ensure long-term success.

- Maintain Physical Fitness: Stay in good physical condition to handle the demands of the job and work efficiently.

By following these tips, you can build a successful and fulfilling career as a machinist, making a significant impact on various manufacturing projects and contributing to the production of precision parts and tools that meet high standards of quality and performance.

67. Elevator Installer and Repairer

67.1 Overview of the Role

Elevator installers and repairers are skilled tradespeople responsible for assembling, installing, maintaining, and fixing elevators, escalators, moving walkways, and other types of lifts. They ensure that these systems operate safely and efficiently, meeting all relevant codes and regulations. Their work involves reading blueprints, testing equipment, troubleshooting issues, and performing routine maintenance to prevent breakdowns.

67.2 Required Skills and Education

To become a successful elevator installer and repairer, a combination of technical skills, education, and hands-on experience is essential. Key requirements include:

Technical Skills:

- Mechanical Knowledge: Understanding of mechanical systems, hydraulics, and pneumatics.

- Technical Aptitude: Proficiency in using tools and equipment such as wrenches, multimeters, and hoists.

- Blueprint Reading: Ability to read and interpret blueprints, technical diagrams, and electrical schematics.

- Troubleshooting: Skills in diagnosing and solving mechanical and electrical problems.

- Safety Practices: Knowledge of safety procedures and regulations to prevent accidents and ensure compliance with codes.

Educational Background:

- Education: A high school diploma or equivalent is typically required. Courses in math, physics, and shop are beneficial.

- Apprenticeship: Completion of a formal apprenticeship program, which combines classroom instruction with on-the-job training, is necessary. These programs usually last 4-5 years.

- Licensure: Obtaining a license is required in most states. This typically involves passing a comprehensive exam that tests knowledge of elevator systems, local codes, and safety practices.

- Certifications: Additional certifications (e.g., Qualified Elevator Inspector) can enhance career prospects and demonstrate advanced expertise.

Soft Skills:

- Attention to Detail: Precision in installing and repairing elevators to ensure safety and reliability.

- Communication: Effective communication with clients, contractors, and team members.

- Problem-Solving: Strong problem-solving skills to address technical issues efficiently.

- Physical Stamina: Ability to perform physically demanding tasks, such as lifting heavy equipment and working in confined spaces.

- Time Management: Efficiently managing time to complete projects on schedule.

67.3 Typical Work Environment

Elevator installers and repairers work in various environments, including construction sites, residential buildings, commercial buildings, and industrial facilities. The work can be physically demanding and may involve standing for long periods, working in cramped or high spaces, and handling heavy equipment. They may work indoors or outdoors, and the job can expose them to potential hazards such as electrical shocks, falls, and heavy machinery. Safety protocols and protective gear, such as harnesses, helmets, and gloves, are essential to minimize risks. Elevator installers and repairers often work full-time, with the potential for overtime and emergency call-outs.

67.4 Career Path and Growth Opportunities

The career path for elevator installers and repairers offers numerous opportunities for specialization and advancement:

- Entry-Level Positions: Apprentice Elevator Installer/Repairer, focusing on gaining hands-on experience and learning from experienced professionals.

- Mid-Level Positions: Journeyman Elevator Installer/Repairer, taking on more complex tasks and working independently on installation and repair projects.

- Senior-Level Positions: Master Elevator Installer/Repairer or Elevator Foreman, overseeing projects, managing teams, and ensuring compliance with codes and regulations.

- Specialization Areas: Escalator Technician, Moving Walkway Technician, or Elevator Inspector. Specializing in these areas allows technicians to focus on specific types of lift systems and enhance their expertise.

- Management Roles: Project Manager, Maintenance Supervisor, or Operations Manager. These positions involve overseeing elevator installation and maintenance operations, ensuring quality and safety, and managing budgets.

- Continued Education: Pursuing advanced certifications or degrees (e.g., Bachelor's in Mechanical Engineering or Construction Management) can lead to higher roles and increased salaries.

67.5 Tips for Success

To excel as an elevator installer and repairer, consider the following strategies:

- Stay Updated: Continuously update your knowledge and skills through continuing education, professional development courses, and staying current with changes in elevator technology and codes.

- Develop Strong Technical Skills: Enhance your proficiency with elevator systems and tools through continuous practice and training.

- Embrace Safety: Always prioritize safety by following established protocols, using protective gear, and staying informed about potential hazards.

- Build a Professional Network: Establish connections with other elevator technicians, contractors, and industry professionals to gain insights and opportunities.

- Seek Specialization: Consider pursuing additional certifications in specialized areas to advance your career and enhance your expertise.

- Provide Excellent Customer Service: Develop strong communication and interpersonal skills to build positive relationships with clients and ensure customer satisfaction.

- Focus on Quality: Strive for high-quality workmanship in all projects to build a strong reputation and ensure long-term success.

By following these tips, you can build a successful and fulfilling career as an elevator installer and repairer, making a significant impact on various construction and maintenance projects and contributing to the safety and functionality of lift systems.

68. Wind Turbine Technician

68.1 Overview of the Role

Wind turbine technicians, also known as wind techs, are specialized technicians who install, maintain, and repair wind turbines. Their work is crucial in ensuring the efficient operation of wind farms, which are a key component of renewable energy infrastructure. Wind techs climb to significant heights to inspect, troubleshoot, and fix mechanical, electrical, and hydraulic components of wind turbines.

68.2 Required Skills and Education

To become a successful wind turbine technician, a combination of technical skills, education, and hands-on experience is essential. Key requirements include:

Technical Skills:

- Mechanical Knowledge: Understanding of mechanical systems, including gears, bearings, and hydraulics.

- Electrical Expertise: Proficiency in electrical systems and troubleshooting electrical issues.

- Technical Aptitude: Ability to use various tools and equipment, such as multimeters, torque wrenches, and hydraulic pumps.

- Climbing Skills: Physical ability and comfort with climbing and working at great heights.

- Safety Practices: Knowledge of safety procedures and regulations to prevent accidents and ensure compliance with industry standards.

Educational Background:

- Education: A high school diploma or equivalent is typically required. Courses in math, physics, and shop are beneficial.

- Technical School: Completion of a wind energy technology program or an associate's degree in wind turbine technology is often required.

- Certifications: Obtaining certifications such as OSHA safety certification and specific wind turbine technician certifications can enhance career prospects and demonstrate advanced expertise.

- Training: Hands-on training, often through an apprenticeship or internship, is crucial for gaining practical experience.

Soft Skills:

- Attention to Detail: Precision in inspecting and repairing turbine components to ensure safety and efficiency.

- Communication: Effective communication with team members, engineers, and site managers.

- Problem-Solving: Strong problem-solving skills to address mechanical and electrical issues efficiently.

- Physical Stamina: Ability to perform physically demanding tasks, such as climbing tall structures and working in various weather conditions.

- Time Management: Efficiently managing time to complete maintenance and repair tasks on schedule.

68.3 Typical Work Environment

Wind turbine technicians work in various environments, primarily at wind farms, which may be located in remote or rural areas. The work is physically demanding and involves climbing wind turbine towers, often exceeding 200 feet in height, to perform maintenance and repairs. Technicians work both indoors (in control rooms or maintenance facilities) and outdoors, exposed to all weather conditions. The job can expose them to potential hazards such as falls, electrical shocks, and heavy machinery. Safety protocols and protective gear, such as harnesses, helmets, and gloves, are essential to minimize risks. Wind turbine technicians often work full-time, with the potential for overtime and emergency call-outs.

68.4 Career Path and Growth Opportunities

The career path for wind turbine technicians offers numerous opportunities for specialization and advancement:

- Entry-Level Positions: Wind Turbine Technician Apprentice, focusing on gaining hands-on experience and learning from experienced professionals.

- Mid-Level Positions: Journeyman Wind Turbine Technician, taking on more complex tasks and working independently on maintenance and repair projects.

- Senior-Level Positions: Lead Wind Turbine Technician or Site Supervisor, overseeing projects, managing teams, and ensuring compliance with safety and performance standards.

- Specialization Areas: Blade Repair Technician, Electrical Technician, or Control Systems Technician. Specializing in these areas allows technicians to focus on specific components and enhance their expertise.

- Management Roles: Operations Manager, Wind Farm Manager, or Maintenance Supervisor. These positions involve overseeing wind farm operations, ensuring quality and safety, and managing budgets.

- Continued Education: Pursuing advanced certifications or degrees (e.g., Bachelor's in Renewable Energy Technology or Electrical Engineering) can lead to higher roles and increased salaries.

68.5 Tips for Success

To excel as a wind turbine technician, consider the following strategies:

- Stay Updated: Continuously update your knowledge and skills through continuing education, professional development courses, and staying current with advancements in wind turbine technology and industry standards.

- Develop Strong Technical Skills: Enhance your proficiency with mechanical, electrical, and hydraulic systems through continuous practice and training.

- Embrace Safety: Always prioritize safety by following established protocols, using protective gear, and staying informed about potential hazards.

- Build a Professional Network: Establish connections with other wind turbine technicians, engineers, and industry professionals to gain insights and opportunities.

- Seek Specialization: Consider pursuing additional certifications in specialized areas to advance your career and enhance your expertise.

- Provide Excellent Workmanship: Strive for high-quality maintenance and repair work to build a strong reputation and ensure long-term success.

- Maintain Physical Fitness: Stay in good physical condition to handle the demands of the job and work efficiently.

By following these tips, you can build a successful and fulfilling career as a wind turbine technician, making a significant impact on renewable energy projects and contributing to the sustainability and efficiency of wind energy systems.

69. Solar Photovoltaic Installer

69.1 Overview of the Role

Solar photovoltaic (PV) installers, also known as solar installers, are professionals who assemble, install, and maintain solar panel systems on rooftops or other structures. They ensure that solar panels are positioned correctly to optimize sunlight exposure and electrical output. Solar installers play a vital role in the renewable energy industry by helping to reduce reliance on fossil fuels and promote sustainable energy solutions.

69.2 Required Skills and Education

To become a successful solar PV installer, a combination of technical skills, education, and hands-on experience is essential. Key requirements include:

Technical Skills:

- Electrical Knowledge: Understanding of electrical systems, wiring, and circuits.

- Technical Aptitude: Proficiency in using tools and equipment such as drills, wrenches, and voltage meters.

- Blueprint Reading: Ability to read and interpret blueprints, technical diagrams, and electrical schematics.

- Installation Skills: Skills in assembling and installing solar panels, inverters, and mounting systems.

- Safety Practices: Knowledge of safety procedures and regulations to prevent accidents and ensure compliance with codes.

Educational Background:

- Education: A high school diploma or equivalent is typically required. Courses in math, physics, and shop are beneficial.

- Technical School: Completion of a solar energy technology program or an associate's degree in renewable energy technology is often required.

- Certifications: Obtaining certifications such as NABCEP (North American Board of Certified Energy Practitioners) certification can enhance career prospects and demonstrate advanced expertise.

- Training: Hands-on training, often through an apprenticeship or internship, is crucial for gaining practical experience.

Soft Skills:

- Attention to Detail: Precision in installing and maintaining solar panels to ensure safety and efficiency.

- Communication: Effective communication with clients, contractors, and team members.

- Problem-Solving: Strong problem-solving skills to address installation and maintenance issues efficiently.

- Physical Stamina: Ability to perform physically demanding tasks, such as lifting heavy panels and working on rooftops.

- Time Management: Efficiently managing time to complete installation and maintenance tasks on schedule.

69.3 Typical Work Environment

Solar PV installers work in various environments, primarily on rooftops of residential, commercial, and industrial buildings. The work is physically demanding and involves climbing ladders, working at heights, and handling heavy materials. Solar installers may work indoors during the planning and preparation stages but primarily work outdoors during installations. The job can expose them to potential hazards such as electrical shocks, falls, and extreme weather conditions. Safety protocols and protective gear, such as harnesses, helmets, and gloves, are essential to minimize risks. Solar PV installers often work full-time, with the potential for overtime and weekend work to meet project deadlines.

69.4 Career Path and Growth Opportunities

The career path for solar PV installers offers numerous opportunities for specialization and advancement:

- Entry-Level Positions: Solar PV Installer Apprentice, focusing on gaining hands-on experience and learning from experienced professionals.

- Mid-Level Positions: Journeyman Solar PV Installer, taking on more complex tasks and working independently on installation and maintenance projects.

- Senior-Level Positions: Lead Solar PV Installer or Site Supervisor, overseeing projects, managing teams, and ensuring compliance with safety and performance standards.

- Specialization Areas: Solar Electrician, Solar Project Manager, or Solar Energy Consultant. Specializing in these areas allows installers to focus on specific aspects of solar energy systems and enhance their expertise.

- Management Roles: Operations Manager, Solar Installation Manager, or Maintenance Supervisor. These positions involve overseeing solar installation operations, ensuring quality and safety, and managing budgets.

- Continued Education: Pursuing advanced certifications or degrees (e.g., Bachelor's in Renewable Energy Technology or Electrical Engineering) can lead to higher roles and increased salaries.

69.5 Tips for Success

To excel as a solar PV installer, consider the following strategies:

- Stay Updated: Continuously update your knowledge and skills through continuing education, professional development courses, and staying current with advancements in solar technology and industry standards.

- Develop Strong Technical Skills: Enhance your proficiency with solar energy systems and installation tools through continuous practice and training.

- Embrace Safety: Always prioritize safety by following established protocols, using protective gear, and staying informed about potential hazards.

- Build a Professional Network: Establish connections with other solar PV installers, electricians, and industry professionals to gain insights and opportunities.

- Seek Specialization: Consider pursuing additional certifications in specialized areas to advance your career and enhance your expertise.

- Provide Excellent Customer Service: Develop strong communication and interpersonal skills to build positive relationships with clients and ensure customer satisfaction.

- Focus on Quality: Strive for high-quality installation and maintenance work to build a strong reputation and ensure long-term success.

- Maintain Physical Fitness: Stay in good physical condition to handle the demands of the job and work efficiently.

By following these tips, you can build a successful and fulfilling career as a solar PV installer, making a significant impact on renewable energy projects and contributing to the sustainability and efficiency of solar energy systems.

Chapter 7 Review

Overview of Trades and Technical Careers

In Chapter 7, we explored various trades and technical careers. These professions are essential for building and maintaining the infrastructure and services that support daily life. Trades and technical careers offer hands-on work, opportunities for specialization, and the potential for steady employment and advancement. Here's a summary of the key points covered for each role:

60. Electrician

- Overview of the Role: Installing, maintaining, and repairing electrical systems in various settings.

- Required Skills and Education: Knowledge of electrical systems, proficiency with tools, a high school diploma, completion of an apprenticeship, and licensure.

- Typical Work Environment: Residential, commercial, and industrial sites; often physically demanding and involving safety risks.

- Career Path and Growth Opportunities: Entry-level apprentice to journeyman and master electrician, with specialization areas like industrial or commercial electrical work, and roles in management or project oversight.

- Tips for Success: Stay updated with codes, develop strong technical skills, prioritize safety, build a professional network, and provide excellent customer service.

61. Plumber

- Overview of the Role: Installing, repairing, and maintaining plumbing systems in residential, commercial, and industrial buildings.

- Required Skills and Education: Knowledge of plumbing systems, proficiency with tools, a high school diploma, completion of an apprenticeship, and licensure.

- Typical Work Environment: Construction sites, homes, and businesses; physically demanding and involving potential hazards.

- Career Path and Growth Opportunities: Entry-level apprentice to journeyman and master plumber, with specialization areas like residential or commercial plumbing, and roles in management or inspection.

- Tips for Success: Continuously update skills, embrace safety protocols, build a network, and focus on quality workmanship.

62. Carpenter

- Overview of the Role: Constructing, installing, and repairing structures and fixtures made from wood and other materials.

- Required Skills and Education: Knowledge of construction methods, proficiency with tools, a high school diploma, completion of an apprenticeship, and additional certifications.

- Typical Work Environment: Construction sites, homes, and commercial buildings; physically demanding with exposure to various hazards.

- Career Path and Growth Opportunities: Entry-level apprentice to journeyman and master carpenter, with specialization areas like cabinetry or framing, and roles in project management or construction supervision.

- Tips for Success: Stay updated with building codes, develop technical skills, prioritize safety, network, and provide excellent customer service.

63. HVAC Technician

- Overview of the Role: Installing, maintaining, and repairing heating, ventilation, and air conditioning systems.

- Required Skills and Education: Knowledge of HVAC systems, proficiency with tools, a high school diploma, completion of a technical program, and licensure.

- Typical Work Environment: Residential, commercial, and industrial settings; physically demanding and involving safety risks.

- Career Path and Growth Opportunities: Entry-level apprentice to journeyman and master technician, with specialization areas like residential or commercial HVAC, and roles in management or project oversight.

- Tips for Success: Stay updated with industry advancements, develop technical skills, prioritize safety, network, and provide excellent customer service.

64. Automotive Technician

- Overview of the Role: Inspecting, maintaining, and repairing vehicles.

- Required Skills and Education: Knowledge of vehicle systems, proficiency with tools, a high school diploma, completion of a technical program, and certifications such as ASE.

- Typical Work Environment: Repair shops, dealerships, and service centers; physically demanding and involving potential hazards.

- Career Path and Growth Opportunities: Entry-level apprentice to journeyman and master technician, with specialization areas like engine or transmission repair, and roles in management or service direction.

- Tips for Success: Stay updated with automotive technology, develop technical skills, prioritize safety, network, and provide excellent customer service.

65. Welder

- Overview of the Role: Using high heat to fuse metals together in various construction, manufacturing, and repair projects.

- Required Skills and Education: Knowledge of welding techniques, proficiency with tools, a high school diploma, completion of a technical program, and certifications such as AWS.

- Typical Work Environment: Construction sites, manufacturing plants, and repair shops; physically demanding with exposure to hazards.

- Career Path and Growth Opportunities: Entry-level apprentice to journeyman and master welder, with specialization areas like pipe or structural welding, and roles in management or inspection.

- Tips for Success: Stay updated with welding technology, develop technical skills, prioritize safety, network, and provide excellent workmanship.

66. Machinist

- Overview of the Role: Operating and maintaining machine tools to produce precision metal parts, instruments, and tools.

- Required Skills and Education: Knowledge of machining processes, proficiency with tools, a high school diploma, completion of a technical program, and certifications.

- Typical Work Environment: Manufacturing plants, machine shops, and tool and die facilities; physically demanding with exposure to hazards.

- Career Path and Growth Opportunities: Entry-level apprentice to journeyman and master machinist, with specialization areas like CNC machining or tool making, and roles in management or engineering.

- Tips for Success: Stay updated with machining technology, develop technical skills, prioritize safety, network, and provide excellent workmanship.

67. Elevator Installer and Repairer

- Overview of the Role: Assembling, installing, maintaining, and repairing elevators, escalators, and other types of lifts.

- Required Skills and Education: Knowledge of mechanical and electrical systems, proficiency with tools, a high school diploma, completion of an apprenticeship, and licensure.

- Typical Work Environment: Construction sites, residential and commercial buildings; physically demanding with exposure to hazards.

- Career Path and Growth Opportunities: Entry-level apprentice to journeyman and master installer/repairer, with specialization areas like escalators or moving walkways, and roles in management or inspection.

- Tips for Success: Stay updated with industry advancements, develop technical skills, prioritize safety, network, and provide excellent customer service.

68. Wind Turbine Technician

- Overview of the Role: Installing, maintaining, and repairing wind turbines to ensure efficient operation.

- Required Skills and Education: Knowledge of mechanical and electrical systems, proficiency with tools, a high school diploma, completion of a wind energy program, and certifications.

- Typical Work Environment: Wind farms, often in remote or rural areas; physically demanding with exposure to heights and weather conditions.

- Career Path and Growth Opportunities: Entry-level apprentice to journeyman and lead technician, with specialization areas like blade repair or control systems, and roles in management or operations.

- Tips for Success: Stay updated with wind energy technology, develop technical skills, prioritize safety, network, and provide excellent workmanship.

69. Solar Photovoltaic Installer

- Overview of the Role: Assembling, installing, and maintaining solar panel systems on rooftops or other structures.

- Required Skills and Education: Knowledge of electrical systems, proficiency with tools, a high school diploma, completion of a solar energy program, and certifications.

- Typical Work Environment: Residential, commercial, and industrial rooftops; physically demanding with exposure to heights and weather conditions.

- Career Path and Growth Opportunities: Entry-level apprentice to journeyman and lead installer, with specialization areas like solar energy consulting or project management, and roles in operations or maintenance management.

- Tips for Success: Stay updated with solar technology, develop technical skills, prioritize safety, network, and provide excellent customer service.

Key Takeaways

- Continuous Learning: Staying updated with industry trends, technological advancements, and safety standards is crucial across all trades and technical careers.

- Networking: Building a professional network through industry events, online forums, and professional associations can provide valuable opportunities and insights.

- Practical Experience: Gaining hands-on experience through apprenticeships, internships, or part-time jobs is essential for skill development and career advancement.

- Certifications and Education: Obtaining relevant certifications and pursuing higher education can enhance career prospects and open up advanced roles.

- Safety: Prioritizing safety and adhering to safety protocols is fundamental to success in trades and technical careers.

- Workmanship: Striving for high-quality workmanship in all projects helps build a strong reputation and ensures long-term success.

By understanding the roles, required skills, typical work environments, career paths, and tips for success, you can make informed decisions about pursuing a career in the trades and technical fields covered in this chapter. Whether you are just starting out or looking to advance your career, this guide provides the essential information to help you succeed.

Chapter 8: Hospitality and Service Careers

70. Chef

70.1 Overview of the Role

Chefs are culinary professionals who oversee the preparation, cooking, and presentation of food in restaurants, hotels, and other food service establishments. They create menus, develop recipes, manage kitchen staff, and ensure that meals are prepared to the highest standards. Chefs play a crucial role in providing exceptional dining experiences and maintaining the reputation of their establishments.

70.2 Required Skills and Education

To become a successful chef, a combination of culinary skills, education, and hands-on experience is essential. Key requirements include:

Technical Skills:

- Culinary Knowledge: Proficiency in cooking techniques, food preparation, and presentation.

- Recipe Development: Ability to create and adapt recipes to fit various menus and dietary needs.

- Food Safety: Knowledge of food safety and sanitation regulations to ensure compliance and prevent foodborne illnesses.

- Knife Skills: Expertise in using knives and other kitchen tools efficiently and safely.

- Menu Planning: Skills in designing menus that balance flavor, cost, and nutritional value.

Educational Background:

- Education: A high school diploma or equivalent is typically required. Courses in home economics and food science are beneficial.

- Culinary School: Completion of a culinary arts program or an associate's degree in culinary arts is often required.

- Apprenticeship: Gaining hands-on experience through apprenticeships or internships in professional kitchens is highly beneficial.

- Certifications: Obtaining certifications such as ServSafe or Certified Executive Chef (CEC) can enhance career prospects and demonstrate advanced expertise.

Soft Skills:

- Attention to Detail: Precision in preparing and presenting dishes to ensure consistency and quality.

- Communication: Effective communication with kitchen staff, front-of-house staff, and suppliers.

- Creativity: Innovative thinking to develop new recipes and improve existing ones.

- Leadership: Strong leadership skills to manage and motivate kitchen staff.

- Time Management: Efficiently managing time to prepare and serve meals promptly.

70.3 Typical Work Environment

Chefs work in various environments, including restaurants, hotels, catering companies, and institutional kitchens. The work can be physically demanding and may involve standing for long periods, working in hot and fast-paced conditions, and handling sharp tools. Chefs may work indoors in well-equipped kitchens, and the job can expose them to potential hazards such as burns, cuts, and slips. Safety protocols and protective gear, such as aprons and gloves, are essential to minimize risks. Chefs often work full-time, with the potential for long hours, evenings, weekends, and holidays, especially during peak dining times.

70.4 Career Path and Growth Opportunities

The career path for chefs offers numerous opportunities for specialization and advancement:

- Entry-Level Positions: Line Cook, Prep Cook, or Commis Chef, focusing on developing basic culinary skills and gaining practical experience in professional kitchens.

- Mid-Level Positions: Sous Chef, Pastry Chef, or Chef de Partie, taking on more complex tasks and managing specific sections of the kitchen.

- Senior-Level Positions: Executive Chef, Head Chef, or Chef de Cuisine, overseeing kitchen operations, managing staff, and ensuring compliance with quality standards and regulations.

- Specialization Areas: Pastry Chef, Saucier, Garde Manger, or Personal Chef. Specializing in these areas allows chefs to focus on specific types of cuisine or culinary techniques and enhance their expertise.

- Management Roles: Restaurant Manager, Food and Beverage Director, or Culinary Instructor. These positions involve overseeing food service operations, ensuring quality and safety, and managing budgets.

- Continued Education: Pursuing advanced certifications or degrees (e.g., Bachelor's in Culinary Arts or Hospitality Management) can lead to higher roles and increased salaries.

70.5 Tips for Success

To excel as a chef, consider the following strategies:

- Stay Updated: Continuously update your knowledge and skills through continuing education, professional development courses, and staying current with culinary trends and techniques.

- Develop Strong Culinary Skills: Enhance your proficiency with cooking techniques and kitchen tools through continuous practice and training.

- Embrace Safety: Always prioritize food safety and sanitation by following established protocols and staying informed about potential hazards.

- Build a Professional Network: Establish connections with other chefs, restaurateurs, and industry professionals to gain insights and opportunities.

- Seek Specialization: Consider pursuing additional certifications in specialized areas to advance your career and enhance your expertise.

- Provide Excellent Customer Service: Develop strong communication and interpersonal skills to build positive relationships with customers and ensure their satisfaction.

- Focus on Quality: Strive for high-quality food preparation and presentation in all dishes to build a strong reputation and ensure long-term success.

- Stay Creative: Continuously innovate and experiment with new recipes and culinary techniques to keep your menu fresh and exciting.

By following these tips, you can build a successful and fulfilling career as a chef, making a significant impact on the culinary world and providing exceptional dining experiences for your customers.

71. Hotel Manager

71.1 Overview of the Role

Hotel managers oversee the daily operations of hotels, ensuring that guests have a positive experience and that the establishment runs smoothly. They manage staff, handle budgets, maintain facilities, and develop marketing strategies. Hotel managers are responsible for ensuring high standards of service, addressing guest concerns, and maximizing the hotel's profitability.

71.2 Required Skills and Education

To become a successful hotel manager, a combination of management skills, education, and industry experience is essential. Key requirements include:

Technical Skills:

- Operations Management: Understanding of hotel operations, including front desk, housekeeping, food and beverage, and maintenance.

- Financial Acumen: Proficiency in budgeting, financial reporting, and cost control.

- Marketing: Skills in developing and implementing marketing strategies to attract and retain guests.

- Human Resources: Knowledge of recruitment, training, and employee relations.

- Technology: Familiarity with hotel management software and booking systems.

Educational Background:

- Education: A bachelor's degree in hospitality management, business administration, or a related field is typically required.

- Certifications: Obtaining certifications such as Certified Hotel Administrator (CHA) can enhance career prospects and demonstrate advanced expertise.

- Experience: Gaining hands-on experience through internships, management trainee programs, or working in various hotel departments is crucial for career development.

Soft Skills:

- Leadership: Strong leadership skills to manage and motivate staff.

- Communication: Effective communication with guests, staff, and stakeholders.

- Problem-Solving: Strong problem-solving skills to address guest complaints and operational challenges.

- Customer Service: Commitment to providing exceptional customer service and ensuring guest satisfaction.

- Time Management: Efficiently managing time to oversee multiple departments and tasks.

71.3 Typical Work Environment

Hotel managers work in various environments, including large hotels, boutique hotels, resorts, and inns. The work can be demanding and may involve long hours, including evenings, weekends, and holidays. Hotel managers often work in office settings but also spend significant time on the floor, interacting with guests and staff. The role can be high-pressure, especially during peak seasons or large events, and involves addressing guest concerns, managing staff, and ensuring smooth operations.

71.4 Career Path and Growth Opportunities

The career path for hotel managers offers numerous opportunities for advancement and specialization:

- Entry-Level Positions: Front Desk Manager, Housekeeping Manager, or Food and Beverage Manager, focusing on developing skills in specific hotel departments.

- Mid-Level Positions: Assistant Hotel Manager, Operations Manager, or Revenue Manager, taking on more responsibilities and overseeing multiple departments.

- Senior-Level Positions: General Manager, Regional Manager, or Director of Operations, overseeing hotel operations at a single property or across multiple locations.

- Specialization Areas: Resort Management, Boutique Hotel Management, or Conference and Event Management. Specializing in these areas allows managers to focus on specific types of properties or services.

- Executive Roles: Vice President of Operations, Chief Operating Officer (COO), or Chief Executive Officer (CEO) of a hotel chain or hospitality company. These positions involve strategic planning, overseeing multiple properties, and ensuring organizational success.

- Continued Education: Pursuing advanced certifications or degrees (e.g., Master's in Hospitality Management or Business Administration) can lead to higher roles and increased salaries.

71.5 Tips for Success

To excel as a hotel manager, consider the following strategies:

- Stay Updated: Continuously update your knowledge and skills through continuing education, professional development courses, and staying current with industry trends and best practices.

- Develop Strong Leadership Skills: Enhance your ability to lead and motivate staff through training and experience.

- Embrace Technology: Familiarize yourself with the latest hotel management software and systems to improve efficiency and guest satisfaction.

- Focus on Customer Service: Prioritize providing exceptional customer service and addressing guest concerns promptly and effectively.

- Build a Professional Network: Establish connections with other hotel managers, industry professionals, and hospitality organizations to gain insights and opportunities.

- Seek Specialization: Consider pursuing additional certifications or training in specialized areas to advance your career and enhance your expertise.

- Improve Financial Acumen: Develop strong financial management skills to effectively control costs and maximize profitability.

- Foster a Positive Work Environment: Create a supportive and positive work environment for staff to ensure high morale and productivity.

By following these tips, you can build a successful and fulfilling career as a hotel manager, making a significant impact on your establishment's success and providing exceptional experiences for your guests.

72. Event Planner

72.1 Overview of the Role

Event planners are professionals who coordinate and manage all aspects of events such as weddings, conferences, corporate meetings, and parties. They are responsible for planning, organizing, and executing events from conception to completion, ensuring that everything runs smoothly and meets the client's expectations. Event planners work closely with clients, vendors, and venues to create memorable and successful events.

72.2 Required Skills and Education

To become a successful event planner, a combination of organizational skills, creativity, and industry knowledge is essential. Key requirements include:

Technical Skills:

- Project Management: Ability to plan, organize, and manage all aspects of an event.

- Budgeting: Skills in creating and managing event budgets to ensure financial efficiency.

- Vendor Coordination: Experience in negotiating contracts and coordinating with vendors such as caterers, decorators, and entertainment providers.

- Logistics: Knowledge of event logistics, including transportation, accommodation, and scheduling.

- Marketing: Skills in promoting events and managing social media and other promotional activities.

Educational Background:

- Education: A bachelor's degree in event management, hospitality management, business administration, or a related field is typically preferred.

- Certifications: Obtaining certifications such as Certified Meeting Professional (CMP) or Certified Special Events Professional (CSEP) can enhance career prospects and demonstrate advanced expertise.

- Experience: Gaining hands-on experience through internships, volunteer work, or entry-level positions in event planning or related fields is crucial for career development.

Soft Skills:

- Attention to Detail: Precision in planning and executing every aspect of an event to ensure success.

- Communication: Effective communication with clients, vendors, and team members.

- Creativity: Innovative thinking to design unique and memorable events.

- Problem-Solving: Strong problem-solving skills to address issues that arise during event planning and execution.

- Time Management: Efficiently managing time to meet deadlines and ensure all event components are in place.

72.3 Typical Work Environment

Event planners work in various environments, including offices, event venues, and on-site locations for event setup and management. The work can be fast-paced and demanding, often involving long hours, including evenings and weekends, especially during the event season. Event planners spend a significant amount of time meeting with clients and vendors, conducting site visits, and coordinating logistics. The role can be high-pressure, requiring the ability to handle multiple tasks simultaneously and adapt to changing circumstances.

72.4 Career Path and Growth Opportunities

The career path for event planners offers numerous opportunities for specialization and advancement:

- Entry-Level Positions: Event Coordinator, Assistant Event Planner, or Meeting Coordinator, focusing on developing basic event planning skills and gaining practical experience.

- Mid-Level Positions: Event Planner, Conference Planner, or Wedding Planner, taking on more complex events and managing client relationships.

- Senior-Level Positions: Senior Event Planner, Event Manager, or Director of Events, overseeing multiple events, managing teams, and ensuring compliance with quality standards and client expectations.

- Specialization Areas: Corporate Event Planner, Wedding Planner, Festival Coordinator, or Non-Profit Event Planner. Specializing in these areas allows event planners to focus on specific types of events and enhance their expertise.

- Executive Roles: Vice President of Events, Chief Event Officer, or Senior Event Consultant. These positions involve strategic planning, overseeing event operations for large organizations, and ensuring the success of major events.

- Continued Education: Pursuing advanced certifications or degrees (e.g., Master's in Event Management or Business Administration) can lead to higher roles and increased salaries.

72.5 Tips for Success

To excel as an event planner, consider the following strategies:

- Stay Updated: Continuously update your knowledge and skills through continuing education, professional development courses, and staying current with industry trends and best practices.

- Develop Strong Organizational Skills: Enhance your ability to manage multiple tasks and details through effective project management techniques.

- Embrace Creativity: Continuously innovate and experiment with new ideas and themes to create unique and memorable events.

- Build a Professional Network: Establish connections with other event planners, vendors, and industry professionals to gain insights and opportunities.

- Seek Specialization: Consider pursuing additional certifications or training in specialized areas to advance your career and enhance your expertise.

- Improve Communication Skills: Develop strong communication and interpersonal skills to build positive relationships with clients, vendors, and team members.

- Focus on Customer Service: Prioritize providing exceptional customer service and addressing client concerns promptly and effectively.

- Stay Flexible: Be prepared to adapt to changing circumstances and handle unexpected challenges with grace and efficiency.

By following these tips, you can build a successful and fulfilling career as an event planner, making a significant impact on the events industry and creating memorable experiences for your clients and attendees.

73. Travel Agent

73.1 Overview of the Role

Travel agents are professionals who assist clients in planning, organizing, and booking their travel arrangements. This includes everything from flights and hotels to tours and car rentals. They provide valuable advice on destinations, travel regulations, and itineraries, ensuring that clients have a smooth and enjoyable travel experience. Travel agents often specialize in specific types of travel, such as corporate, leisure, or adventure travel.

73.2 Required Skills and Education

To become a successful travel agent, a combination of customer service skills, industry knowledge, and practical experience is essential. Key requirements include:

Technical Skills:

- Destination Knowledge: In-depth knowledge of various travel destinations, attractions, and cultural nuances.

- Booking Systems: Proficiency in using travel booking systems (GDS) like Amadeus, Sabre, or Travelport.

- Itinerary Planning: Skills in creating detailed and customized travel itineraries.

- Regulation Awareness: Understanding of travel regulations, visa requirements, and health advisories.

- Sales Skills: Ability to sell travel products and services effectively.

Educational Background:

- Education: A high school diploma or equivalent is typically required. Courses in geography, world history, and foreign languages are beneficial.

- Certifications: Obtaining certifications such as Certified Travel Associate (CTA) or Certified Travel Counselor (CTC) can enhance career prospects and demonstrate advanced expertise.

- Training: Hands-on training through internships or entry-level positions in travel agencies is crucial for gaining practical experience.

Soft Skills:

- Attention to Detail: Precision in planning and booking travel arrangements to ensure accuracy and client satisfaction.

- Communication: Effective communication with clients, suppliers, and team members.

- Problem-Solving: Strong problem-solving skills to address travel-related issues and provide solutions.

- Customer Service: Commitment to providing exceptional customer service and ensuring client satisfaction.

- Organizational Skills: Efficiently managing multiple travel arrangements and client requests simultaneously.

73.3 Typical Work Environment

Travel agents work in various environments, including travel agencies, corporate offices, and home offices. The work can involve long hours, especially during peak travel seasons or when dealing with urgent client requests. Travel agents spend significant time on the phone, responding to emails, and using booking systems to make travel arrangements. The role can be high-pressure, requiring the ability to handle multiple tasks simultaneously and adapt to changing client needs.

73.4 Career Path and Growth Opportunities

The career path for travel agents offers numerous opportunities for specialization and advancement:

- Entry-Level Positions: Travel Consultant, Travel Coordinator, or Junior Travel Agent, focusing on developing basic travel planning skills and gaining practical experience.

- Mid-Level Positions: Senior Travel Agent, Corporate Travel Agent, or Cruise Specialist, taking on more complex travel arrangements and managing client relationships.

- Senior-Level Positions: Travel Agency Manager, Travel Sales Manager, or Destination Specialist, overseeing travel operations, managing teams, and ensuring client satisfaction.

- Specialization Areas: Luxury Travel Advisor, Adventure Travel Specialist, Destination Wedding Planner, or Corporate Travel Manager. Specializing in these areas allows travel agents to focus on specific types of travel and enhance their expertise.

- Executive Roles: Vice President of Travel Services, Director of Travel Operations, or Chief Travel Officer. These positions involve strategic planning, overseeing travel services for large organizations, and ensuring the success of travel operations.

- Continued Education: Pursuing advanced certifications or degrees (e.g., Bachelor's in Tourism Management or Hospitality Management) can lead to higher roles and increased salaries.

73.5 Tips for Success

To excel as a travel agent, consider the following strategies:

- Stay Updated: Continuously update your knowledge and skills through continuing education, professional development courses, and staying current with industry trends and travel regulations.

- Develop Strong Customer Service Skills: Enhance your ability to provide exceptional service and address client concerns promptly and effectively.

- Embrace Technology: Familiarize yourself with the latest travel booking systems and online tools to improve efficiency and client satisfaction.

- Build a Professional Network: Establish connections with other travel agents, suppliers, and industry professionals to gain insights and opportunities.

- Seek Specialization: Consider pursuing additional certifications in specialized areas to advance your career and enhance your expertise.

- Improve Sales Skills: Develop strong sales techniques to effectively promote and sell travel products and services.

- Focus on Attention to Detail: Ensure accuracy in planning and booking travel arrangements to avoid mistakes and ensure client satisfaction.

- Stay Flexible: Be prepared to adapt to changing client needs and handle unexpected travel-related challenges with grace and efficiency.

By following these tips, you can build a successful and fulfilling career as a travel agent, making a significant impact on the travel industry and providing memorable travel experiences for your clients.

74. Customer Service Representative

74.1 Overview of the Role

Customer service representatives (CSRs) are the frontline of customer support, responsible for handling inquiries, resolving complaints, and providing information about products and services. They interact with customers through various channels, including phone, email, live chat, and in-person. CSRs play a critical role in ensuring customer satisfaction and maintaining the company's reputation by delivering efficient and effective service.

74.2 Required Skills and Education

To become a successful customer service representative, a combination of communication skills, problem-solving abilities, and industry knowledge is essential. Key requirements include:

Technical Skills:

- Communication Skills: Proficiency in verbal and written communication to interact effectively with customers.

- Computer Literacy: Ability to use customer service software, CRM systems, and office applications.

- Problem-Solving: Skills in identifying issues, troubleshooting problems, and providing solutions.

- Product Knowledge: Understanding of the company's products and services to provide accurate information and assistance.

- Multitasking: Ability to handle multiple customer interactions and tasks simultaneously.

Educational Background:

- Education: A high school diploma or equivalent is typically required. Some positions may prefer an associate's degree or higher, especially in business or communication.

- Training: On-the-job training is common, covering company policies, product knowledge, and customer service techniques.

- Certifications: Obtaining certifications such as Certified Customer Service Professional (CCSP) can enhance career prospects and demonstrate advanced expertise.

Soft Skills:

- Empathy: Ability to understand and relate to customers' needs and concerns.

- Patience: Maintaining composure and professionalism, especially when dealing with difficult customers.

- Attention to Detail: Precision in recording information and following procedures to ensure accuracy.

- Interpersonal Skills: Building rapport and positive relationships with customers.

- Time Management: Efficiently managing time to handle customer inquiries and tasks promptly.

74.3 Typical Work Environment

Customer service representatives work in various environments, including call centers, corporate offices, retail stores, and remote/home offices. The work can involve long hours, including evenings, weekends, and holidays, especially in industries with 24/7 customer support. CSRs spend significant time on the phone or computer, handling customer inquiries and resolving issues. The role can be high-pressure, requiring the ability to handle a high volume of interactions and adapt to changing customer needs.

74.4 Career Path and Growth Opportunities

The career path for customer service representatives offers numerous opportunities for specialization and advancement:

- Entry-Level Positions: Customer Service Representative, Help Desk Agent, or Call Center Agent, focusing on developing basic customer service skills and gaining practical experience.

- Mid-Level Positions: Senior Customer Service Representative, Customer Service Team Lead, or Technical Support Specialist, taking on more complex inquiries and managing junior staff.

- Senior-Level Positions: Customer Service Supervisor, Customer Service Manager, or Call Center Manager, overseeing customer service operations, managing teams, and ensuring service quality and efficiency.

- Specialization Areas: Technical Support, Client Relations, Account Management, or Sales Support. Specializing in these areas allows CSRs to focus on specific types of customer interactions and enhance their expertise.

- Executive Roles: Director of Customer Service, Vice President of Customer Experience, or Chief Customer Officer. These positions involve strategic planning, overseeing customer service strategies for large organizations, and ensuring the success of customer service operations.

- Continued Education: Pursuing advanced certifications or degrees (e.g., Bachelor's in Business Administration or Communication) can lead to higher roles and increased salaries.

74.5 Tips for Success

To excel as a customer service representative, consider the following strategies:

- Stay Updated: Continuously update your knowledge and skills through continuing education, professional development courses, and staying current with industry trends and best practices.

- Develop Strong Communication Skills: Enhance your ability to communicate clearly and effectively with customers through training and practice.

- Embrace Technology: Familiarize yourself with the latest customer service software and systems to improve efficiency and customer satisfaction.

- Build a Professional Network: Establish connections with other customer service professionals, industry experts, and organizations to gain insights and opportunities.

- Seek Specialization: Consider pursuing additional certifications or training in specialized areas to advance your career and enhance your expertise.

- Focus on Empathy: Prioritize understanding and addressing customers' needs and concerns to build positive relationships and ensure customer satisfaction.

- Improve Problem-Solving Skills: Develop strong problem-solving techniques to handle a wide range of customer issues effectively.

- Maintain a Positive Attitude: Stay positive and professional, even when dealing with difficult customers, to ensure a high level of service quality.

By following these tips, you can build a successful and fulfilling career as a customer service representative, making a significant impact on your company's reputation and providing exceptional service to your customers.

75. Barista

75.1 Overview of the Role

Baristas are skilled professionals who prepare and serve coffee and espresso-based beverages in coffee shops, cafes, and restaurants. They are responsible for creating high-quality drinks, providing excellent customer service, and maintaining a clean and inviting environment. Baristas often develop a deep understanding of coffee varieties, brewing methods, and presentation techniques to ensure customer satisfaction.

75.2 Required Skills and Education

To become a successful barista, a combination of technical skills, customer service abilities, and product knowledge is essential. Key requirements include:

Technical Skills:

- Coffee Preparation: Proficiency in brewing coffee and espresso drinks, including lattes, cappuccinos, and mochas.

- Espresso Machine Operation: Skills in operating and maintaining espresso machines and other coffee equipment.

- Milk Steaming and Frothing: Ability to steam and froth milk to the correct texture and temperature for various beverages.

- Coffee Knowledge: Understanding of coffee beans, roast profiles, and flavor characteristics.

- Cash Handling: Proficiency in handling cash, using point-of-sale (POS) systems, and managing transactions.

Educational Background:

- Education: A high school diploma or equivalent is typically required. Courses in hospitality or culinary arts can be beneficial.

- Training: On-the-job training is common, covering coffee preparation, equipment use, and customer service techniques.

- Certifications: Obtaining certifications such as the Specialty Coffee Association (SCA) Barista Certification can enhance career prospects and demonstrate advanced expertise.

Soft Skills:

- Customer Service: Commitment to providing exceptional customer service and building positive relationships with customers.

- Attention to Detail: Precision in preparing and presenting beverages to ensure consistency and quality.

- Communication: Effective communication with customers, team members, and management.

- Time Management: Efficiently managing time to prepare drinks quickly and accurately during busy periods.

- Teamwork: Ability to work collaboratively with other staff to maintain a smooth operation.

75.3 Typical Work Environment

Baristas work in various environments, including coffee shops, cafes, restaurants, and retail establishments. The work can be fast-paced and physically demanding, often involving standing for long periods, handling hot liquids, and working with sharp tools. Baristas typically work indoors in well-lit and comfortable settings, but the job can expose them to potential hazards such as burns and slips. Safety protocols and protective gear, such as aprons and non-slip shoes, are essential to minimize risks. Baristas often work part-time or full-time, with flexible hours that may include early mornings, evenings, weekends, and holidays.

75.4 Career Path and Growth Opportunities

The career path for baristas offers numerous opportunities for specialization and advancement:

- Entry-Level Positions: Barista Trainee or Junior Barista, focusing on developing basic coffee preparation skills and gaining practical experience.

- Mid-Level Positions: Senior Barista, Lead Barista, or Shift Supervisor, taking on more complex tasks, managing junior staff, and ensuring quality control.

- Senior-Level Positions: Head Barista, Coffee Shop Manager, or Store Manager, overseeing coffee shop operations, managing teams, and ensuring customer satisfaction.

- Specialization Areas: Coffee Roaster, Barista Trainer, or Coffee Quality Specialist. Specializing in these areas allows baristas to focus on specific aspects of coffee production and enhance their expertise.

- Entrepreneurial Roles: Coffee Shop Owner, Coffee Consultant, or Barista Competition Judge. These positions involve starting and running a coffee business, providing expert advice, or evaluating barista skills in competitions.

- Continued Education: Pursuing advanced certifications or degrees (e.g., Bachelor's in Hospitality Management or Culinary Arts) can lead to higher roles and increased salaries.

75.5 *Tips for Success*

To excel as a barista, consider the following strategies:

- Stay Updated: Continuously update your knowledge and skills through continuing education, professional development courses, and staying current with coffee trends and brewing techniques.

- Develop Strong Customer Service Skills: Enhance your ability to provide exceptional service and build positive relationships with customers through training and practice.

- Embrace Quality: Focus on preparing high-quality beverages with consistency and attention to detail to ensure customer satisfaction.

- Build a Professional Network: Establish connections with other baristas, coffee shop owners, and industry professionals to gain insights and opportunities.

- Seek Specialization: Consider pursuing additional certifications or training in specialized areas to advance your career and enhance your expertise.

- Improve Communication Skills: Develop strong communication and interpersonal skills to interact effectively with customers and team members.

- Focus on Efficiency: Enhance your time management and multitasking abilities to handle busy periods and ensure quick service.

- Stay Passionate: Cultivate a genuine passion for coffee and continuously seek to improve your skills and knowledge.

By following these tips, you can build a successful and fulfilling career as a barista, making a significant impact on the coffee industry and providing exceptional coffee experiences for your customers.

76. Sommelier

76.1 Overview of the Role

Sommeliers are wine experts responsible for all aspects of wine service, including selection, pairing, storage, and presentation. They work in fine dining restaurants, hotels, and wineries, advising customers on wine choices to enhance their dining experience. Sommeliers also manage wine inventories, conduct wine tastings, and stay updated with industry trends and new wine releases.

76.2 Required Skills and Education

To become a successful sommelier, a combination of wine knowledge, tasting skills, and customer service abilities is essential. Key requirements include:

Technical Skills:

- Wine Knowledge: Extensive understanding of different wine regions, grape varieties, and winemaking processes.

- Tasting Skills: Ability to identify and describe wine flavors, aromas, and textures.

- Wine Pairing: Expertise in pairing wines with various foods to enhance the dining experience.

- Inventory Management: Skills in managing wine inventories, including ordering, storing, and rotating stock.

- Presentation Skills: Proficiency in presenting and serving wine, including decanting and pouring techniques.

Educational Background:

- Education: A high school diploma or equivalent is typically required. Courses in hospitality, culinary arts, or business can be beneficial.

- Certifications: Obtaining certifications such as Certified Sommelier (CS), Advanced Sommelier, or Master Sommelier from the Court of Master Sommeliers can enhance career prospects and demonstrate advanced expertise.

- Training: Hands-on experience through internships, apprenticeships, or entry-level positions in the wine or hospitality industry is crucial for gaining practical skills.

Soft Skills:

- Attention to Detail: Precision in wine selection, pairing, and presentation to ensure high-quality service.

- Communication: Effective communication with customers, team members, and suppliers.

- Customer Service: Commitment to providing exceptional customer service and ensuring guest satisfaction.

- Sales Skills: Ability to promote and sell wines effectively to enhance the dining experience and increase revenue.

- Continuous Learning: A passion for wine and a commitment to ongoing education and staying current with industry trends.

76.3 Typical Work Environment

Sommeliers work in various environments, including fine dining restaurants, hotels, wineries, and wine retail stores. The work can be fast-paced and demanding, especially during peak dining hours. Sommeliers typically work indoors in well-lit and comfortable settings, but the role can involve standing for long periods, moving wine cases, and handling fragile bottles. Sommeliers often work evenings, weekends, and holidays to accommodate dining schedules and special events.

76.4 Career Path and Growth Opportunities

The career path for sommeliers offers numerous opportunities for specialization and advancement:

- Entry-Level Positions: Wine Steward, Junior Sommelier, or Wine Sales Associate, focusing on developing basic wine knowledge and gaining practical experience.

- Mid-Level Positions: Certified Sommelier, Wine Director, or Beverage Manager, taking on more complex tasks and managing wine programs.

- Senior-Level Positions: Advanced Sommelier, Master Sommelier, or Wine Consultant, overseeing wine operations, conducting high-level tastings, and advising on wine selections.

- Specialization Areas: Wine Educator, Wine Critic, Wine Importer, or Wine Writer. Specializing in these areas allows sommeliers to focus on specific aspects of the wine industry and enhance their expertise.

- Executive Roles: Director of Wine and Beverage Programs, Vice President of Wine Operations, or Chief Wine Officer. These positions involve strategic planning, overseeing wine programs for large organizations, and ensuring the success of wine operations.

- Continued Education: Pursuing advanced certifications or degrees (e.g., Master's in Wine Business or Oenology) can lead to higher roles and increased salaries.

76.5 Tips for Success

To excel as a sommelier, consider the following strategies:

- Stay Updated: Continuously update your knowledge and skills through continuing education, professional development courses, and staying current with wine industry trends and new releases.

- Develop Strong Tasting Skills: Enhance your ability to identify and describe wine flavors and aromas through regular tasting practice and training.

- Embrace Quality: Focus on providing high-quality wine service and presentation to ensure customer satisfaction.

- Build a Professional Network: Establish connections with other sommeliers, wine producers, and industry professionals to gain insights and opportunities.

- Seek Specialization: Consider pursuing additional certifications or training in specialized areas to advance your career and enhance your expertise.

- Improve Communication Skills: Develop strong communication and interpersonal skills to interact effectively with customers and team members.

- Focus on Sales: Enhance your sales techniques to effectively promote and sell wines, increasing revenue and customer satisfaction.

- Stay Passionate: Cultivate a genuine passion for wine and continuously seek to improve your skills and knowledge.

By following these tips, you can build a successful and fulfilling career as a sommelier, making a significant impact on the wine industry and providing exceptional wine experiences for your customers.

77. Casino Dealer

77.1 Overview of the Role

Casino dealers are responsible for operating table games such as blackjack, poker, roulette, and craps in casinos. They interact with players, enforce game rules, handle bets, and manage payouts. Casino dealers play a crucial role in ensuring a fair and enjoyable gaming experience for patrons while maintaining the integrity of the casino's operations.

77.2 Required Skills and Education

To become a successful casino dealer, a combination of technical skills, customer service abilities, and attention to detail is essential. Key requirements include:

Technical Skills:

- Game Knowledge: In-depth understanding of various casino games, including rules, procedures, and strategies.

- Mathematical Skills: Proficiency in basic math to calculate bets, payouts, and handle chips accurately.

- Manual Dexterity: Skills in handling cards, chips, and gaming equipment smoothly and efficiently.

- Regulation Awareness: Knowledge of gaming regulations and laws to ensure compliance and fair play.

Educational Background:

- Education: A high school diploma or equivalent is typically required. Courses in math and communication can be beneficial.

- Training: Completion of a dealer training program or attending a dealer school is often required to learn the specifics of casino games and dealing techniques.

- Certifications: Some states require casino dealers to obtain a gaming license or certification, which may involve background checks and training.

Soft Skills:

- Attention to Detail: Precision in managing bets, dealing cards, and enforcing game rules to ensure accuracy and fair play.

- Communication: Effective communication with players, supervisors, and team members.

- Customer Service: Commitment to providing exceptional customer service and ensuring a positive gaming experience.

- Patience: Maintaining composure and professionalism, especially in high-pressure situations.

- Problem-Solving: Ability to address disputes and resolve issues promptly and effectively.

77.3 Typical Work Environment

Casino dealers work in various environments, including land-based casinos, cruise ships, and online gaming platforms. The work can be fast-paced and demanding, often involving standing for long periods, handling chips and cards, and interacting with a diverse range of players. Casino dealers typically work indoors in well-lit and noisy settings, with shifts that may include evenings, weekends, and holidays to accommodate peak gaming times. The role can be high-pressure, requiring the ability to handle large sums of money and maintain concentration in a dynamic environment.

77.4 Career Path and Growth Opportunities

The career path for casino dealers offers numerous opportunities for specialization and advancement:

- Entry-Level Positions: Trainee Dealer, focusing on developing basic dealing skills and gaining practical experience in a casino setting.

- Mid-Level Positions: Experienced Dealer, taking on more complex games and managing larger tables.

- Senior-Level Positions: Pit Boss, Floor Supervisor, or Casino Manager, overseeing multiple tables, managing dealer teams, and ensuring compliance with gaming regulations and customer satisfaction.

- Specialization Areas: Poker Dealer, Blackjack Dealer, Roulette Dealer, or Craps Dealer. Specializing in these areas allows dealers to focus on specific games and enhance their expertise.

- Executive Roles: Director of Table Games, Vice President of Casino Operations, or Chief Gaming Officer. These positions involve strategic planning, overseeing gaming operations for large casinos or casino chains, and ensuring the success of casino operations.

- Continued Education: Pursuing advanced certifications or degrees (e.g., Bachelor's in Hospitality Management or Business Administration) can lead to higher roles and increased salaries.

77.5 Tips for Success

To excel as a casino dealer, consider the following strategies:

- Stay Updated: Continuously update your knowledge and skills through continuing education, professional development courses, and staying current with industry trends and gaming regulations.

- Develop Strong Technical Skills: Enhance your proficiency with dealing techniques and game rules through continuous practice and training.

- Embrace Quality: Focus on providing high-quality service and ensuring fair play to build a positive reputation and ensure customer satisfaction.

- Build a Professional Network: Establish connections with other dealers, casino managers, and industry professionals to gain insights and opportunities.

- Seek Specialization: Consider pursuing additional training or certifications in specialized games to advance your career and enhance your expertise.

- Improve Communication Skills: Develop strong communication and interpersonal skills to interact effectively with players and team members.

- Focus on Customer Service: Prioritize providing exceptional customer service and addressing player concerns promptly and effectively.

- Stay Professional: Maintain a high level of professionalism and composure, even in challenging situations, to ensure a positive gaming environment.

By following these tips, you can build a successful and fulfilling career as a casino dealer, making a significant impact on the gaming industry and providing enjoyable gaming experiences for your patrons.

78. Housekeeper

78.1 Overview of the Role

Housekeepers are responsible for maintaining cleanliness and orderliness in various environments, such as hotels, private residences, hospitals, and office buildings. Their duties include cleaning rooms, changing bed linens, replenishing supplies, and ensuring that all areas meet the establishment's cleanliness standards. Housekeepers play a crucial role in creating a comfortable and hygienic environment for guests, residents, and employees.

78.2 Required Skills and Education

To become a successful housekeeper, a combination of practical skills, attention to detail, and physical stamina is essential. Key requirements include:

Technical Skills:

- Cleaning Techniques: Proficiency in using cleaning tools and products to clean different surfaces effectively.

- Time Management: Ability to efficiently manage time to complete cleaning tasks within specified timeframes.

- Attention to Detail: Precision in cleaning tasks to ensure thoroughness and high standards of cleanliness.

- Basic Maintenance: Skills in performing minor repairs and maintenance tasks, such as changing light bulbs or unclogging drains.

- Inventory Management: Ability to manage cleaning supplies and request restocks when necessary.

Educational Background:

- Education: A high school diploma or equivalent is typically required. Basic education is sufficient for most housekeeping roles, but additional training can be beneficial.

- Training: On-the-job training is common, covering cleaning techniques, use of equipment, and safety procedures.

- Certifications: Obtaining certifications such as Certified Executive Housekeeper (CEH) or Registered Executive Housekeeper (REH) can enhance career prospects and demonstrate advanced expertise.

Soft Skills:

- Customer Service: Commitment to providing excellent service and ensuring guest or resident satisfaction.

- Communication: Effective communication with supervisors, team members, and guests.

- Dependability: Reliability and consistency in performing cleaning duties.

- Physical Stamina: Ability to perform physically demanding tasks, such as lifting, bending, and standing for long periods.

- Problem-Solving: Skills in identifying and addressing cleaning or maintenance issues promptly.

78.3 Typical Work Environment

Housekeepers work in various environments, including hotels, private homes, hospitals, and office buildings. The work can be physically demanding and may involve standing for long periods, lifting heavy objects, and using cleaning chemicals. Housekeepers typically work indoors, but some tasks may require outdoor work, such as cleaning windows or maintaining grounds. The role can involve early mornings, evenings, weekends, and holidays, depending on the establishment's needs. Housekeepers must adhere to safety protocols and use protective gear, such as gloves and masks, to minimize risks associated with cleaning chemicals and physical labor.

78.4 Career Path and Growth Opportunities

The career path for housekeepers offers numerous opportunities for specialization and advancement:

- Entry-Level Positions: Housekeeping Assistant or Room Attendant, focusing on developing basic cleaning skills and gaining practical experience.

- Mid-Level Positions: Senior Housekeeper, Housekeeping Supervisor, or Lead Housekeeper, taking on more responsibilities and managing junior staff.

- Senior-Level Positions: Executive Housekeeper, Housekeeping Manager, or Director of Housekeeping, overseeing housekeeping operations, managing teams, and ensuring compliance with cleanliness standards.

- Specialization Areas: Hospital Housekeeper, Hotel Housekeeper, Residential Housekeeper, or Office Cleaner. Specializing in these areas allows housekeepers to focus on specific environments and enhance their expertise.

- Management Roles: Facility Manager, Operations Manager, or Hospitality Manager. These positions involve overseeing cleaning and maintenance operations for larger establishments or multiple properties.

- Continued Education: Pursuing advanced certifications or degrees (e.g., Bachelor's in Hospitality Management or Facility Management) can lead to higher roles and increased salaries.

78.5 Tips for Success

To excel as a housekeeper, consider the following strategies:

- Stay Updated: Continuously update your knowledge and skills through continuing education, professional development courses, and staying current with cleaning techniques and industry standards.

- Develop Strong Cleaning Skills: Enhance your proficiency with cleaning tools and products through continuous practice and training.

- Embrace Quality: Focus on providing high-quality cleaning and maintenance services to ensure customer satisfaction.

- Build a Professional Network: Establish connections with other housekeepers, supervisors, and industry professionals to gain insights and opportunities.

- Seek Specialization: Consider pursuing additional certifications or training in specialized areas to advance your career and enhance your expertise.

- Improve Communication Skills: Develop strong communication and interpersonal skills to interact effectively with supervisors, team members, and guests.

- Focus on Efficiency: Enhance your time management and multitasking abilities to handle cleaning tasks quickly and accurately.

- Stay Professional: Maintain a high level of professionalism and reliability, even in challenging situations, to ensure a positive working environment.

By following these tips, you can build a successful and fulfilling career as a housekeeper, making a significant impact on the cleanliness and comfort of your workplace and providing exceptional service to your clients or guests.

Chapter 8 Review

Overview of Hospitality and Service Careers

In Chapter 8, we explored a variety of careers in the hospitality and service industries. These roles are essential in creating memorable experiences for guests and clients, ensuring high standards of service, and maintaining smooth operations in various settings such as hotels, restaurants, and event venues. Here's a summary of the key points covered for each role:

70. Chef

- Overview of the Role: Chefs oversee the preparation, cooking, and presentation of food in various establishments.

- Required Skills and Education: Culinary knowledge, recipe development, food safety, and a degree from a culinary school or related training.

- Typical Work Environment: Kitchens in restaurants, hotels, and other food service establishments; physically demanding and often high-pressure.

- Career Path and Growth Opportunities: From line cook to executive chef, with specializations in pastry, saucier, and other culinary areas.

- Tips for Success: Continuous learning, developing strong culinary skills, embracing food safety, building a professional network, and staying creative.

71. Hotel Manager

- Overview of the Role: Hotel managers oversee daily operations, ensuring guest satisfaction and efficient management of hotel staff.

- Required Skills and Education: Operations management, financial acumen, marketing, human resources, and a degree in hospitality management.

- Typical Work Environment: Hotels, resorts, and inns; demanding and often requiring long hours.

- Career Path and Growth Opportunities: From front desk manager to general manager, with specialization in resort or boutique hotel management.

- Tips for Success: Strong leadership, embracing technology, focusing on customer service, building a network, and fostering a positive work environment.

72. Event Planner

- Overview of the Role: Event planners coordinate and manage all aspects of events, ensuring successful execution from start to finish.

- Required Skills and Education: Project management, budgeting, vendor coordination, logistics, and a degree in event management.

- Typical Work Environment: Offices and on-site event locations; fast-paced and demanding.

- Career Path and Growth Opportunities: From event coordinator to senior event planner, with specialization in corporate, wedding, or festival planning.

- Tips for Success: Strong organizational skills, embracing creativity, building a network, improving communication skills, and staying flexible.

73. Travel Agent

- Overview of the Role: Travel agents assist clients in planning and booking travel arrangements, providing advice on destinations and travel regulations.

- Required Skills and Education: Destination knowledge, booking systems, itinerary planning, and a degree in tourism or related field.

- Typical Work Environment: Travel agencies, corporate offices, and home offices; can involve long hours, especially during peak travel seasons.

- Career Path and Growth Opportunities: From travel consultant to travel agency manager, with specialization in corporate or luxury travel.

- Tips for Success: Strong customer service skills, embracing technology, improving sales skills, and maintaining attention to detail.

74. Customer Service Representative

- Overview of the Role: CSRs handle customer inquiries, resolve complaints, and provide information about products and services.

- Required Skills and Education: Communication skills, computer literacy, problem-solving, and a high school diploma.

- Typical Work Environment: Call centers, corporate offices, and retail stores; often involves long hours and high-pressure situations.

- Career Path and Growth Opportunities: From junior CSR to customer service manager, with specialization in technical support or client relations.

- Tips for Success: Strong communication skills, embracing technology, focusing on empathy, and maintaining a positive attitude.

75. Barista

- Overview of the Role: Baristas prepare and serve coffee and espresso-based beverages in coffee shops and cafes.

- Required Skills and Education: Coffee preparation, espresso machine operation, milk steaming, and customer service.

- Typical Work Environment: Coffee shops, cafes, and restaurants; fast-paced and physically demanding.

- Career Path and Growth Opportunities: From junior barista to coffee shop manager, with specialization in coffee roasting or barista training.

- Tips for Success: Strong customer service skills, embracing quality, staying updated with coffee trends, and maintaining efficiency.

76. Sommelier

- Overview of the Role: Sommeliers are wine experts responsible for selecting, pairing, and presenting wines in fine dining establishments.

- Required Skills and Education: Wine knowledge, tasting skills, wine pairing, and certifications such as Certified Sommelier.

- Typical Work Environment: Fine dining restaurants, hotels, and wineries; demanding and often involving long hours.

- Career Path and Growth Opportunities: From junior sommelier to wine director, with specialization in wine education or consulting.

- Tips for Success: Continuous learning, strong tasting skills, focusing on sales, and maintaining a passion for wine.

77. Casino Dealer

- Overview of the Role: Casino dealers operate table games, manage bets, and interact with players in casinos.

- Required Skills and Education: Game knowledge, mathematical skills, manual dexterity, and dealer training.

- Typical Work Environment: Casinos, cruise ships, and online gaming platforms; fast-paced and high-pressure.

- Career Path and Growth Opportunities: From trainee dealer to casino manager, with specialization in specific games or casino operations.

- Tips for Success: Strong technical skills, embracing quality, focusing on customer service, and staying professional.

78. Housekeeper

- Overview of the Role: Housekeepers maintain cleanliness and orderliness in hotels, residences, and other establishments.

- Required Skills and Education: Cleaning techniques, time management, attention to detail, and a high school diploma.

- Typical Work Environment: Hotels, private homes, hospitals, and office buildings; physically demanding.

- Career Path and Growth Opportunities: From housekeeping assistant to director of housekeeping, with specialization in hospital or hotel housekeeping.

- Tips for Success: Strong cleaning skills, embracing quality, building a network, and maintaining efficiency.

79. Concierge

- Overview of the Role: Concierges assist guests by providing a wide range of personalized services and information.

- Required Skills and Education: Local knowledge, booking and reservations, problem-solving, and customer service.

- Typical Work Environment: Hotels, resorts, corporate offices, and residential buildings; service-oriented and often fast-paced.

- Career Path and Growth Opportunities: From junior concierge to director of concierge services, with specialization in corporate or residential concierge.

- Tips for Success: Strong customer service skills, staying updated, improving communication skills, and maintaining discretion.

Key Takeaways

- Continuous Learning: Staying updated with industry trends, technological advancements, and service standards is crucial across all hospitality and service careers.

- Networking: Building a professional network through industry events, online forums, and professional associations can provide valuable opportunities and insights.

- Customer Service: Providing exceptional customer service and addressing guest needs promptly is fundamental to success in hospitality and service careers.

- Attention to Detail: Ensuring accuracy and quality in all tasks is essential for maintaining high standards and customer satisfaction.

- Professionalism: Maintaining a high level of professionalism and composure, even in challenging situations, is key to building a positive reputation and ensuring long-term success.

By understanding the roles, required skills, typical work environments, career paths, and tips for success, you can make informed decisions about pursuing a career in the hospitality and service fields covered in this chapter. Whether you are just starting out or looking to advance your career, this guide provides the essential information to help you succeed.

Chapter 9: Retail and Sales Careers

80. Retail Manager

80.1 Overview of the Role

Retail managers oversee the day-to-day operations of retail stores, ensuring that sales targets are met, staff are effectively managed, and customers have a positive shopping experience. They are responsible for managing inventory, merchandising, staffing, customer service, and sales strategies. Retail managers play a crucial role in driving the store's success and profitability.

80.2 Required Skills and Education

To become a successful retail manager, a combination of leadership skills, business acumen, and retail knowledge is essential. Key requirements include:

Technical Skills:

- Sales and Marketing: Understanding of sales techniques and marketing strategies to drive store traffic and sales.

- Inventory Management: Skills in managing stock levels, ordering products, and minimizing shrinkage.

- Merchandising: Ability to create appealing store layouts and displays that attract customers.

- Financial Acumen: Proficiency in budgeting, financial reporting, and cost control.

- Technology: Familiarity with retail management software and point-of-sale (POS) systems.

Educational Background:

- Education: A high school diploma or equivalent is typically required. A bachelor's degree in business administration, retail management, or a related field is often preferred.

- Certifications: Obtaining certifications such as Certified Retail Management Professional (CRMP) can enhance career prospects and demonstrate advanced expertise.

- Training: On-the-job training and management trainee programs are common, covering store operations, sales techniques, and management skills.

Soft Skills:

- Leadership: Strong leadership skills to manage and motivate staff.

- Communication: Effective verbal and written communication skills to interact with customers, staff, and suppliers.

- Customer Service: Commitment to providing exceptional customer service and ensuring customer satisfaction.

- Problem-Solving: Ability to address and resolve issues promptly and effectively.

- Time Management: Efficiently managing time to balance multiple responsibilities and tasks.

80.3 Typical Work Environment

Retail managers work in various retail settings, including department stores, specialty shops, supermarkets, and boutiques.

The work can be demanding and often involves long hours, including evenings, weekends, and holidays, especially during peak shopping seasons. Retail managers spend significant time on the sales floor, interacting with customers and staff, but also work in office settings for administrative tasks. The role requires standing for long periods, handling merchandise, and managing a fast-paced environment.

80.4 Career Path and Growth Opportunities

The career path for retail managers offers numerous opportunities for specialization and advancement:

- Entry-Level Positions: Sales Associate, Cashier, or Assistant Manager, focusing on developing basic retail skills and gaining practical experience.

- Mid-Level Positions: Store Manager, Department Manager, or Inventory Manager, taking on more responsibilities and managing specific areas of the store.

- Senior-Level Positions: Regional Manager, District Manager, or General Manager, overseeing multiple stores or large retail operations.

- Specialization Areas: Visual Merchandiser, Loss Prevention Manager, or Buyer. Specializing in these areas allows retail managers to focus on specific aspects of retail operations and enhance their expertise.

- Executive Roles: Director of Retail Operations, Vice President of Sales, or Chief Retail Officer. These positions involve strategic planning, overseeing retail operations for large organizations, and ensuring the success of retail strategies.

- Continued Education: Pursuing advanced certifications or degrees (e.g., MBA in Retail Management or Business Administration) can lead to higher roles and increased salaries.

80.5 Tips for Success

To excel as a retail manager, consider the following strategies:

- Stay Updated: Continuously update your knowledge of retail trends, consumer behavior, and industry developments through continuing education and professional development courses.

- Develop Strong Leadership Skills: Enhance your ability to lead and motivate staff through training and experience.

- Embrace Technology: Familiarize yourself with the latest retail management software and systems to improve efficiency and sales performance.

- Focus on Customer Service: Prioritize providing exceptional customer service and addressing customer concerns promptly and effectively.

- Build a Professional Network: Establish connections with other retail managers, industry professionals, and suppliers to gain insights and opportunities.

- Seek Specialization: Consider pursuing additional certifications or training in specialized areas to advance your career and enhance your expertise.

- Improve Financial Acumen: Develop strong financial management skills to effectively control costs and maximize profitability.

- Foster a Positive Work Environment: Create a supportive and positive work environment for staff to ensure high morale and productivity.

By following these tips, you can build a successful and fulfilling career as a retail manager, making a significant impact on your store's success and providing exceptional shopping experiences for your customers.

81. Sales Representative

81.1 Overview of the Role

Sales representatives are responsible for selling products or services to customers. They interact with potential and existing clients, understand their needs, and provide solutions that meet those needs. Sales representatives often work in various industries, including retail, pharmaceuticals, technology, and manufacturing. Their primary goal is to drive sales, build customer relationships, and achieve sales targets.

81.2 Required Skills and Education

To become a successful sales representative, a combination of interpersonal skills, sales techniques, and industry knowledge is essential. Key requirements include:

Technical Skills:

- Sales Techniques: Proficiency in various sales techniques, including consultative selling, upselling, and cross-selling.

- Product Knowledge: In-depth understanding of the products or services being sold.

- CRM Systems: Familiarity with customer relationship management (CRM) software to manage client interactions and track sales.

- Market Analysis: Ability to analyze market trends and competitor activities to identify sales opportunities.

Educational Background:

- Education: A high school diploma or equivalent is typically required. A bachelor's degree in business, marketing, or a related field is often preferred.

- Certifications: Obtaining certifications such as Certified Professional Sales Person (CPSP) can enhance career prospects and demonstrate advanced expertise.

- Training: On-the-job training and sales training programs are common, covering sales techniques, product knowledge, and CRM systems.

Soft Skills:

- Communication: Effective verbal and written communication skills to interact with clients and present products persuasively.

- Customer Service: Commitment to providing exceptional customer service and building long-term relationships with clients.

- Negotiation: Strong negotiation skills to close deals and achieve favorable terms.

- Problem-Solving: Ability to identify customer needs and provide appropriate solutions.

- Time Management: Efficiently managing time to handle multiple client interactions and sales tasks.

81.3 Typical Work Environment

Sales representatives work in various environments, depending on the industry and type of products or services they sell. Common work environments include offices, retail stores, and on the road, visiting clients and attending trade shows. The role can be demanding, often involving long hours and travel to meet with clients. Sales representatives must be adaptable and able to work in a fast-paced environment. They may also work remotely, using technology to communicate with clients and manage sales activities.

81.4 Career Path and Growth Opportunities

The career path for sales representatives offers numerous opportunities for specialization and advancement:

- Entry-Level Positions: Junior Sales Representative or Sales Associate, focusing on developing basic sales skills and gaining practical experience.

- Mid-Level Positions: Senior Sales Representative, Account Manager, or Territory Manager, taking on more complex sales tasks and managing larger client portfolios.

- Senior-Level Positions: Sales Manager, Regional Sales Manager, or National Sales Manager, overseeing sales teams, developing sales strategies, and ensuring sales targets are met.

- Specialization Areas: Technical Sales Representative, Pharmaceutical Sales Representative, or Real Estate Agent. Specializing in these areas allows sales representatives to focus on specific industries and enhance their expertise.

- Executive Roles: Director of Sales, Vice President of Sales, or Chief Sales Officer. These positions involve strategic planning, overseeing sales operations for large organizations, and ensuring the success of sales strategies.

- Continued Education: Pursuing advanced certifications or degrees (e.g., MBA in Sales Management or Marketing) can lead to higher roles and increased salaries.

81.5 Tips for Success

To excel as a sales representative, consider the following strategies:

- Stay Updated: Continuously update your knowledge of sales techniques, industry trends, and product developments through continuing education and professional development courses.

- Develop Strong Communication Skills: Enhance your ability to communicate clearly and persuasively with clients through training and practice.

- Embrace Technology: Familiarize yourself with the latest CRM systems and sales tools to improve efficiency and client management.

- Focus on Customer Service: Prioritize providing exceptional customer service and building long-term relationships with clients.

- Build a Professional Network: Establish connections with other sales professionals, industry experts, and clients to gain insights and opportunities.

- Seek Specialization: Consider pursuing additional certifications or training in specialized areas to advance your career and enhance your expertise.

- Improve Negotiation Skills: Develop strong negotiation techniques to close deals effectively and achieve favorable terms for both parties.

- Set and Achieve Goals: Set clear sales goals and develop strategies to achieve them, tracking progress and adjusting as needed.

By following these tips, you can build a successful and fulfilling career as a sales representative, making a significant impact on your organization's success and providing valuable solutions to your clients.

82. Real Estate Agent

82.1 Overview of the Role

Real estate agents are professionals who assist clients in buying, selling, and renting properties. They guide clients through the entire process, from property listing to closing the deal. Real estate agents conduct market research, provide property valuations, negotiate deals, and ensure that all legal requirements are met. They play a crucial role in helping clients find their ideal homes or investment properties.

82.2 Required Skills and Education

To become a successful real estate agent, a combination of market knowledge, negotiation skills, and customer service abilities is essential. Key requirements include:

Technical Skills:

- Market Analysis: Ability to analyze market trends, property values, and economic factors affecting real estate.

- Negotiation Skills: Proficiency in negotiating purchase agreements, contracts, and closing terms.

- Legal Knowledge: Understanding of real estate laws, regulations, and contracts to ensure compliance.

- Marketing: Skills in marketing properties through various channels, including online listings, social media, and open houses.

- Technology: Familiarity with real estate software, CRM systems, and digital marketing tools.

Educational Background:

- Education: A high school diploma or equivalent is typically required. Some states may require college coursework in real estate or related fields.

- Licensure: Obtaining a real estate license is mandatory in all states, which involves completing pre-licensing courses and passing a state exam.

- Certifications: Pursuing additional certifications such as Certified Residential Specialist (CRS) or Accredited Buyer's Representative (ABR) can enhance career prospects and demonstrate advanced expertise.

- Training: On-the-job training through internships or mentorship programs is valuable for gaining practical experience.

Soft Skills:

- Communication: Effective verbal and written communication skills to interact with clients, attorneys, and other real estate professionals.

- Customer Service: Commitment to providing exceptional service and building long-term relationships with clients.

- Attention to Detail: Precision in preparing contracts, listings, and other documents to avoid errors.

- Problem-Solving: Ability to address and resolve issues that may arise during property transactions.

- Time Management: Efficiently managing time to handle multiple clients and property listings.

82.3 Typical Work Environment

Real estate agents work in various environments, including real estate offices, client properties, and their own homes. The job involves significant travel to show properties, meet with clients, and attend closings. Real estate agents often work irregular hours, including evenings and weekends, to accommodate client schedules. The role can be high-pressure, requiring the ability to handle multiple tasks and deadlines simultaneously. Real estate agents must be adaptable and prepared to work in a dynamic and competitive market.

82.4 Career Path and Growth Opportunities

The career path for real estate agents offers numerous opportunities for specialization and advancement:

- Entry-Level Positions: Junior Real Estate Agent or Real Estate Assistant, focusing on developing basic skills and gaining practical experience in property transactions.

- Mid-Level Positions: Senior Real Estate Agent, Buyer's Agent, or Seller's Agent, taking on more complex transactions and managing larger client portfolios.

- Senior-Level Positions: Real Estate Broker, Real Estate Office Manager, or Team Leader, overseeing agents, managing office operations, and ensuring compliance with regulations.

- Specialization Areas: Commercial Real Estate Agent, Luxury Real Estate Specialist, Property Manager, or Real Estate Investor. Specializing in these areas allows agents to focus on specific market segments and enhance their expertise.

- Executive Roles: Director of Real Estate Operations, Vice President of Real Estate, or Chief Real Estate Officer. These positions involve strategic planning, overseeing real estate operations for large firms, and ensuring the success of real estate transactions.

- Continued Education: Pursuing advanced certifications or degrees (e.g., Master's in Real Estate or Business Administration) can lead to higher roles and increased salaries.

82.5 Tips for Success

To excel as a real estate agent, consider the following strategies:

- Stay Updated: Continuously update your knowledge of market trends, property values, and legal requirements through continuing education and professional development courses.

- Develop Strong Communication Skills: Enhance your ability to communicate clearly and persuasively with clients, attorneys, and other real estate professionals.

- Embrace Technology: Familiarize yourself with the latest real estate software, CRM systems, and digital marketing tools to improve efficiency and client management.

- Focus on Customer Service: Prioritize providing exceptional customer service and building long-term relationships with clients.

- Build a Professional Network: Establish connections with other real estate agents, industry professionals, and potential clients to gain insights and opportunities.

- Seek Specialization: Consider pursuing additional certifications or training in specialized areas to advance your career and enhance your expertise.

- Improve Negotiation Skills: Develop strong negotiation techniques to close deals effectively and achieve favorable terms for your clients.

- Stay Organized: Maintain detailed records and manage your time efficiently to handle multiple clients and property listings simultaneously.

By following these tips, you can build a successful and fulfilling career as a real estate agent, making a significant impact on the real estate market and providing valuable services to your clients.

83. Merchandiser

83.1 Overview of the Role

Merchandisers are responsible for ensuring that products are displayed in a way that maximizes sales. They work closely with retail stores and suppliers to manage product placement, inventory levels, and promotional displays. Merchandisers analyze sales data, forecast trends, and develop strategies to improve product visibility and sales performance.

83.2 Required Skills and Education

To become a successful merchandiser, a combination of analytical skills, creativity, and industry knowledge is essential. Key requirements include:

Technical Skills:

- Data Analysis: Proficiency in analyzing sales data, market trends, and customer behavior to make informed decisions.

- Inventory Management: Skills in managing stock levels, ordering products, and ensuring optimal inventory turnover.

- Visual Merchandising: Ability to create appealing product displays that attract customers and drive sales.

- Marketing: Understanding of marketing principles and strategies to promote products effectively.

- Technology: Familiarity with merchandising software, POS systems, and other retail technology tools.

Educational Background:

- Education: A high school diploma or equivalent is typically required. A bachelor's degree in business, marketing, or a related field is often preferred.

- Certifications: Obtaining certifications such as Certified Merchandising Specialist (CMS) can enhance career prospects and demonstrate advanced expertise.

- Training: On-the-job training and merchandising courses are common, covering inventory management, data analysis, and visual merchandising techniques.

Soft Skills:

- Attention to Detail: Precision in creating product displays and managing inventory to ensure accuracy and effectiveness.

- Communication: Effective verbal and written communication skills to interact with store managers, suppliers, and team members.

- Creativity: Innovative thinking to develop unique and eye-catching product displays.

- Problem-Solving: Ability to address and resolve issues related to product placement, inventory, and sales performance.

- Time Management: Efficiently managing time to handle multiple tasks and meet deadlines.

83.3 Typical Work Environment

Merchandisers work in various environments, including retail stores, corporate offices, and distribution centers. The work can be physically demanding, involving standing for long periods, moving products, and setting up displays. Merchandisers often travel between different store locations to implement merchandising plans and check on product placements. The role requires flexibility, as work hours may include early mornings, evenings, and weekends to meet merchandising schedules and promotional deadlines.

83.4 Career Path and Growth Opportunities

The career path for merchandisers offers numerous opportunities for specialization and advancement:

- Entry-Level Positions: Merchandising Assistant or Junior Merchandiser, focusing on developing basic merchandising skills and gaining practical experience.

- Mid-Level Positions: Merchandiser, Visual Merchandiser, or Inventory Planner, taking on more complex merchandising tasks and managing larger product categories.

- Senior-Level Positions: Senior Merchandiser, Merchandising Manager, or Category Manager, overseeing merchandising strategies, managing teams, and ensuring sales targets are met.

- Specialization Areas: E-commerce Merchandiser, Product Developer, or Retail Buyer. Specializing in these areas allows merchandisers to focus on specific market segments and enhance their expertise.

- Executive Roles: Director of Merchandising, Vice President of Merchandising, or Chief Merchandising Officer. These positions involve strategic planning, overseeing merchandising operations for large retailers, and ensuring the success of merchandising strategies.

- Continued Education: Pursuing advanced certifications or degrees (e.g., MBA in Retail Management or Marketing) can lead to higher roles and increased salaries.

83.5 Tips for Success

To excel as a merchandiser, consider the following strategies:

- Stay Updated: Continuously update your knowledge of market trends, consumer behavior, and merchandising techniques through continuing education and professional development courses.

- Develop Strong Analytical Skills: Enhance your ability to analyze sales data and market trends to make informed merchandising decisions.

- Embrace Creativity: Continuously innovate and experiment with new product displays and promotional strategies to attract customers.

- Build a Professional Network: Establish connections with other merchandisers, retail managers, and industry professionals to gain insights and opportunities.

- Seek Specialization: Consider pursuing additional certifications or training in specialized areas to advance your career and enhance your expertise.

- Improve Communication Skills: Develop strong communication and interpersonal skills to interact effectively with store managers, suppliers, and team members.

- Focus on Attention to Detail: Ensure accuracy in managing inventory, creating displays, and implementing merchandising plans to avoid mistakes and ensure effectiveness.

- Stay Organized: Maintain detailed records and manage your time efficiently to handle multiple tasks and meet deadlines.

By following these tips, you can build a successful and fulfilling career as a merchandiser, making a significant impact on the retail industry and driving sales performance for your organization.

84. Telemarketer

84.1 Overview of the Role

Telemarketers are responsible for contacting potential customers via phone to promote products or services, generate leads, or conduct market research. They aim to persuade customers to make purchases, set appointments, or participate in surveys. Telemarketers play a crucial role in a company's sales and marketing efforts, often working from scripts to ensure consistent messaging.

84.2 Required Skills and Education

To become a successful telemarketer, a combination of communication skills, persistence, and sales techniques is essential. Key requirements include:

Technical Skills:

- Sales Techniques: Proficiency in various sales techniques, including cold calling, upselling, and cross-selling.

- CRM Systems: Familiarity with customer relationship management (CRM) software to manage client interactions and track sales.

- Script Adherence: Ability to follow sales scripts while personalizing conversations to engage customers.

- Data Entry: Skills in accurately recording customer information and updating databases.

Educational Background:

- Education: A high school diploma or equivalent is typically required. Some positions may prefer candidates with postsecondary education in business or marketing.

- Certifications: While not always required, obtaining certifications such as Certified Professional Sales Person (CPSP) can enhance career prospects and demonstrate advanced expertise.

- Training: On-the-job training is common, covering product knowledge, sales techniques, and CRM systems.

Soft Skills:

- Communication: Effective verbal communication skills to engage customers and convey information clearly.

- Customer Service: Commitment to providing excellent customer service and addressing customer inquiries or concerns.

- Persistence: Determination and resilience to handle rejection and continue making calls.

- Problem-Solving: Ability to address customer objections and provide solutions to meet their needs.

- Time Management: Efficiently managing time to handle multiple calls and follow-up tasks.

84.3 Typical Work Environment

Telemarketers typically work in call centers, corporate offices, or remotely from home. The work environment can be fast-paced and high-pressure, involving long hours of phone communication. Telemarketers usually work in a structured setting with individual workstations and access to telecommunication technology and CRM systems. The role requires sitting for extended periods, handling repetitive tasks, and maintaining a high level of concentration. Work hours may include evenings and weekends to reach potential customers during their available times.

84.4 Career Path and Growth Opportunities

The career path for telemarketers offers numerous opportunities for specialization and advancement:

- Entry-Level Positions: Junior Telemarketer or Telemarketing Assistant, focusing on developing basic sales skills and gaining practical experience.

- Mid-Level Positions: Senior Telemarketer, Lead Generator, or Telemarketing Supervisor, taking on more complex sales tasks and managing junior staff.

- Senior-Level Positions: Telemarketing Manager, Sales Manager, or Account Manager, overseeing telemarketing operations, managing teams, and ensuring sales targets are met.

- Specialization Areas: Inside Sales Representative, Customer Success Manager, or Business Development Representative. Specializing in these areas allows telemarketers to focus on specific sales functions and enhance their expertise.

- Executive Roles: Director of Sales, Vice President of Sales, or Chief Sales Officer. These positions involve strategic planning, overseeing sales operations for large organizations, and ensuring the success of sales strategies.

- Continued Education: Pursuing advanced certifications or degrees (e.g., MBA in Sales Management or Marketing) can lead to higher roles and increased salaries.

84.5 Tips for Success

To excel as a telemarketer, consider the following strategies:

- Stay Updated: Continuously update your knowledge of sales techniques, industry trends, and product developments through continuing education and professional development courses.

- Develop Strong Communication Skills: Enhance your ability to communicate clearly and persuasively with customers through training and practice.

- Embrace Technology: Familiarize yourself with the latest CRM systems and telemarketing tools to improve efficiency and client management.

- Focus on Customer Service: Prioritize providing excellent customer service and addressing customer concerns promptly and effectively.

- Build a Professional Network: Establish connections with other telemarketers, sales professionals, and industry experts to gain insights and opportunities.

- Seek Specialization: Consider pursuing additional certifications or training in specialized areas to advance your career and enhance your expertise.

- Improve Persistence: Develop resilience and determination to handle rejection and maintain a positive attitude.

- Set and Achieve Goals: Set clear sales goals and develop strategies to achieve them, tracking progress and adjusting as needed.

By following these tips, you can build a successful and fulfilling career as a telemarketer, making a significant impact on your organization's sales efforts and providing valuable services to your customers.

85. Store Clerk

85.1 Overview of the Role

Store clerks are responsible for assisting customers, managing inventory, handling cash transactions, and maintaining the cleanliness and organization of the store. They play a vital role in ensuring a positive shopping experience for customers by providing excellent service and keeping the store well-stocked and orderly.

85.2 Required Skills and Education

To become a successful store clerk, a combination of customer service skills, basic retail knowledge, and attention to detail is essential. Key requirements include:

Technical Skills:

- Cash Handling: Proficiency in managing cash transactions, using cash registers, and handling credit/debit card transactions.

- Inventory Management: Skills in stocking shelves, managing inventory levels, and conducting stock checks.

- Point-of-Sale (POS) Systems: Familiarity with POS systems for processing sales and managing customer transactions.

- Basic Math: Ability to perform basic arithmetic for handling cash and making change.

Educational Background:

- Education: A high school diploma or equivalent is typically required. Some positions may prefer candidates with additional coursework in business or retail management.

- Certifications: While not mandatory, certifications in customer service or retail operations can enhance career prospects and demonstrate advanced expertise.

- Training: On-the-job training is common, covering store procedures, cash handling, and customer service techniques.

Soft Skills:

- Customer Service: Strong customer service skills to assist customers, answer questions, and provide a positive shopping experience.

- Communication: Effective verbal communication skills to interact with customers and team members.

- Attention to Detail: Precision in managing inventory, handling transactions, and maintaining store organization.

- Reliability: Dependability and consistency in performing duties and adhering to schedules.

- Problem-Solving: Ability to address customer concerns and resolve issues promptly.

85.3 Typical Work Environment

Store clerks work in various retail environments, including grocery stores, convenience stores, department stores, and specialty shops. The work can be physically demanding, involving standing for long periods, lifting and moving products, and performing repetitive tasks. Store clerks typically work indoors, but some tasks may require outdoor work, such as assisting with curbside pickup or managing outdoor displays. The role may involve working irregular hours, including evenings, weekends, and holidays, to accommodate store hours and customer needs.

85.4 *Career Path and Growth Opportunities*

The career path for store clerks offers numerous opportunities for specialization and advancement:

- Entry-Level Positions: Junior Store Clerk or Cashier, focusing on developing basic retail skills and gaining practical experience.

- Mid-Level Positions: Senior Store Clerk, Inventory Specialist, or Department Lead, taking on more responsibilities and managing specific store areas.

- Senior-Level Positions: Store Supervisor, Assistant Store Manager, or Store Manager, overseeing store operations, managing staff, and ensuring customer satisfaction.

- Specialization Areas: Inventory Control Specialist, Visual Merchandiser, or Customer Service Representative. Specializing in these areas allows store clerks to focus on specific functions and enhance their expertise.

- Executive Roles: District Manager, Regional Manager, or Director of Retail Operations. These positions involve strategic planning, overseeing multiple store locations, and ensuring the success of retail operations.

- Continued Education: Pursuing advanced certifications or degrees (e.g., Bachelor's in Retail Management or Business Administration) can lead to higher roles and increased salaries.

85.5 Tips for Success

To excel as a store clerk, consider the following strategies:

- Stay Updated: Continuously update your knowledge of retail trends, customer service techniques, and store procedures through continuing education and professional development courses.

- Develop Strong Customer Service Skills: Enhance your ability to provide excellent service and address customer concerns through training and practice.

- Embrace Technology: Familiarize yourself with the latest POS systems and retail technology to improve efficiency and customer satisfaction.

- Focus on Attention to Detail: Ensure accuracy in handling transactions, managing inventory, and maintaining store organization to avoid mistakes and ensure smooth operations.

- Build a Professional Network: Establish connections with other store clerks, retail managers, and industry professionals to gain insights and opportunities.

- Seek Specialization: Consider pursuing additional certifications or training in specialized areas to advance your career and enhance your expertise.

- Improve Communication Skills: Develop strong communication and interpersonal skills to interact effectively with customers and team members.

- Stay Reliable: Maintain a high level of reliability and consistency in performing duties and adhering to schedules to build trust and ensure operational efficiency.

By following these tips, you can build a successful and fulfilling career as a store clerk, making a significant impact on the retail industry and providing exceptional service to your customers.

86. Car Salesperson

86.1 Overview of the Role

Car salespeople are responsible for selling new and used vehicles to customers. They assist customers in selecting the right vehicle based on their needs and budget, arrange test drives, negotiate prices, and help with financing options. Car salespeople play a crucial role in the automotive sales industry by providing excellent customer service and meeting sales targets.

86.2 Required Skills and Education

To become a successful car salesperson, a combination of sales techniques, automotive knowledge, and customer service skills is essential. Key requirements include:

Technical Skills:

- Sales Techniques: Proficiency in various sales techniques, including negotiation, upselling, and closing deals.

- Automotive Knowledge: Understanding of different vehicle models, features, and specifications to provide accurate information to customers.

- Financing Options: Knowledge of financing options, loan terms, and credit approval processes.

- CRM Systems: Familiarity with customer relationship management (CRM) software to manage client interactions and track sales.

Educational Background:

- Education: A high school diploma or equivalent is typically required. Some positions may prefer candidates with postsecondary education in business, marketing, or a related field.

- Certifications: While not always required, obtaining certifications such as Certified Professional Sales Person (CPSP) or Automotive Sales Certification can enhance career prospects and demonstrate advanced expertise.

- Training: On-the-job training and sales training programs are common, covering automotive knowledge, sales techniques, and customer service skills.

Soft Skills:

- Communication: Effective verbal communication skills to interact with customers and present vehicle information persuasively.

- Customer Service: Commitment to providing excellent customer service and building long-term relationships with customers.

- Negotiation: Strong negotiation skills to close deals and achieve favorable terms for both the dealership and the customer.

- Problem-Solving: Ability to address customer objections and provide solutions to meet their needs.

- Time Management: Efficiently managing time to handle multiple customer interactions and sales tasks.

86.3 Typical Work Environment

Car salespeople typically work in automotive dealerships, where they spend a significant amount of time interacting with customers, both in person and over the phone. The work environment can be fast-paced and competitive, involving long hours, including evenings and weekends, to accommodate customer schedules. Car salespeople may spend time outdoors on the dealership lot, showing vehicles to customers and arranging test drives. The role requires adaptability, as sales targets and customer needs can change frequently.

86.4 Career Path and Growth Opportunities

The career path for car salespeople offers numerous opportunities for specialization and advancement:

- Entry-Level Positions: Junior Salesperson or Sales Trainee, focusing on developing basic sales skills and gaining practical experience in automotive sales.

- Mid-Level Positions: Senior Salesperson, Finance and Insurance (F&I) Manager, or Sales Team Lead, taking on more complex sales tasks and managing larger client portfolios.

- Senior-Level Positions: Sales Manager, General Sales Manager, or Dealership Manager, overseeing sales operations, managing teams, and ensuring sales targets are met.

- Specialization Areas: Fleet Sales Specialist, Certified Pre-Owned Sales Specialist, or Internet Sales Manager. Specializing in these areas allows car salespeople to focus on specific market segments and enhance their expertise.

- Executive Roles: Director of Sales, Vice President of Sales, or Chief Sales Officer. These positions involve strategic planning, overseeing sales operations for large dealerships or dealership groups, and ensuring the success of sales strategies.

- Continued Education: Pursuing advanced certifications or degrees (e.g., MBA in Sales Management or Marketing) can lead to higher roles and increased salaries.

86.5 Tips for Success

To excel as a car salesperson, consider the following strategies:

- Stay Updated: Continuously update your knowledge of automotive trends, vehicle models, and financing options through continuing education and professional development courses.

- Develop Strong Communication Skills: Enhance your ability to communicate clearly and persuasively with customers through training and practice.

- Embrace Technology: Familiarize yourself with the latest CRM systems and automotive sales tools to improve efficiency and client management.

- Focus on Customer Service: Prioritize providing excellent customer service and building long-term relationships with customers.

- Build a Professional Network: Establish connections with other sales professionals, industry experts, and potential customers to gain insights and opportunities.

- Seek Specialization: Consider pursuing additional certifications or training in specialized areas to advance your career and enhance your expertise.

- Improve Negotiation Skills: Develop strong negotiation techniques to close deals effectively and achieve favorable terms for your customers and the dealership.

- Set and Achieve Goals: Set clear sales goals and develop strategies to achieve them, tracking progress and adjusting as needed.

By following these tips, you can build a successful and fulfilling career as a car salesperson, making a significant impact on the automotive sales industry and providing valuable services to your customers.

87. Real Estate Broker

87.1 Overview of the Role

Real estate brokers are licensed professionals who oversee real estate transactions between buyers and sellers. They manage their own brokerage or work under a brokerage firm, ensuring compliance with legal requirements and providing expert advice to clients. Brokers facilitate the buying, selling, and leasing of properties, negotiate contracts, and supervise the activities of real estate agents.

87.2 Required Skills and Education

To become a successful real estate broker, a combination of industry knowledge, negotiation skills, and leadership abilities is essential. Key requirements include:

Technical Skills:

- Market Analysis: Ability to analyze market trends, property values, and economic factors affecting real estate.

- Legal Knowledge: Understanding of real estate laws, regulations, contracts, and ethical standards to ensure compliance.

- Negotiation Skills: Proficiency in negotiating purchase agreements, leases, and closing terms.

- Financial Acumen: Skills in managing brokerage finances, including budgeting, forecasting, and financial reporting.

- Technology: Familiarity with real estate software, CRM systems, and digital marketing tools.

Educational Background:

- Education: A high school diploma or equivalent is typically required. A bachelor's degree in real estate, business administration, or a related field is often preferred.

- Licensure: Obtaining a real estate broker's license is mandatory, which involves completing advanced coursework and passing a state licensing exam.

- Certifications: Pursuing additional certifications such as Certified Real Estate Broker (CRB) can enhance career prospects and demonstrate advanced expertise.

- Training: Practical experience as a real estate agent is often required before becoming a broker.

Soft Skills:

- Leadership: Strong leadership skills to manage and mentor real estate agents and staff.

- Communication: Effective verbal and written communication skills to interact with clients, agents, and other real estate professionals.

- Customer Service: Commitment to providing exceptional service and building long-term relationships with clients.

- Attention to Detail: Precision in preparing contracts, listings, and other documents to avoid errors.

- Problem-Solving: Ability to address and resolve issues that may arise during property transactions.

87.3 Typical Work Environment

Real estate brokers work in various environments, including real estate offices, client properties, and their own homes. The job involves significant travel to show properties, meet with clients, and attend closings. Brokers often work irregular hours, including evenings and weekends, to accommodate client schedules and market demands. The role requires adaptability, as market conditions and client needs can change frequently.

87.4 Career Path and Growth Opportunities

The career path for real estate brokers offers numerous opportunities for specialization and advancement:

- Entry-Level Positions: Junior Broker or Real Estate Agent, focusing on developing basic skills and gaining practical experience in property transactions.

- Mid-Level Positions: Senior Broker, Brokerage Manager, or Team Leader, taking on more complex transactions and managing larger client portfolios.

- Senior-Level Positions: Managing Broker, Regional Manager, or Real Estate Office Manager, overseeing brokerage operations, managing teams, and ensuring compliance with regulations.

- Specialization Areas: Commercial Real Estate Broker, Luxury Real Estate Specialist, Property Manager, or Real Estate Investor. Specializing in these areas allows brokers to focus on specific market segments and enhance their expertise.

- Executive Roles: Director of Real Estate Operations, Vice President of Real Estate, or Chief Real Estate Officer. These positions involve strategic planning, overseeing real estate operations for large firms, and ensuring the success of real estate transactions.

- Continued Education: Pursuing advanced certifications or degrees (e.g., Master's in Real Estate or Business Administration) can lead to higher roles and increased salaries.

87.5 Tips for Success

To excel as a real estate broker, consider the following strategies:

- Stay Updated: Continuously update your knowledge of market trends, property values, and legal requirements through continuing education and professional development courses.

- Develop Strong Leadership Skills: Enhance your ability to lead and mentor real estate agents through training and experience.

- Embrace Technology: Familiarize yourself with the latest real estate software, CRM systems, and digital marketing tools to improve efficiency and client management.

- Focus on Customer Service: Prioritize providing exceptional customer service and building long-term relationships with clients.

- Build a Professional Network: Establish connections with other real estate professionals, industry experts, and potential clients to gain insights and opportunities.

- Seek Specialization: Consider pursuing additional certifications or training in specialized areas to advance your career and enhance your expertise.

- Improve Negotiation Skills: Develop strong negotiation techniques to close deals effectively and achieve favorable terms for your clients.

- Stay Organized: Maintain detailed records and manage your time efficiently to handle multiple clients and property transactions simultaneously.

By following these tips, you can build a successful and fulfilling career as a real estate broker, making a significant impact on the real estate market and providing valuable services to your clients.

88. Product Manager

88.1 Overview of the Role

Product managers are responsible for overseeing the development and lifecycle of a product from conception to launch. They work closely with cross-functional teams, including engineering, marketing, sales, and customer support, to ensure the product meets market needs and business objectives. Product managers play a crucial role in defining product strategy, gathering and prioritizing requirements, and delivering innovative solutions to customers.

88.2 Required Skills and Education

To become a successful product manager, a combination of strategic thinking, technical knowledge, and leadership abilities is essential. Key requirements include:

Technical Skills:

- Product Development: Knowledge of product development processes, including Agile and Scrum methodologies.

- Market Analysis: Ability to analyze market trends, customer needs, and competitive landscapes.

- Data-Driven Decision Making: Proficiency in using data and analytics to inform product decisions and measure success.

- Project Management: Skills in managing timelines, budgets, and resources to deliver products on time and within scope.

- Technical Acumen: Understanding of the technical aspects of the product to effectively communicate with engineering teams.

Educational Background:

- Education: A bachelor's degree in business administration, marketing, engineering, or a related field is typically required. A master's degree, such as an MBA, is often preferred.

- Certifications: Obtaining certifications such as Certified Scrum Product Owner (CSPO) or Product Management Certification can enhance career prospects and demonstrate advanced expertise.

- Training: Hands-on experience in product management, project management, or related roles is valuable for gaining practical skills.

Soft Skills:

- Leadership: Strong leadership skills to inspire and guide cross-functional teams.

- Communication: Effective verbal and written communication skills to interact with stakeholders, team members, and customers.

- Problem-Solving: Ability to address and resolve challenges that arise during product development.

- Customer Focus: Commitment to understanding and meeting customer needs.

- Strategic Thinking: Ability to think strategically and align product initiatives with business goals.

88.3 Typical Work Environment

Product managers work in various environments, including corporate offices, remote settings, and collaborative workspaces. The role involves frequent interaction with cross-functional teams, requiring excellent communication and collaboration skills. Product managers often juggle multiple projects and deadlines, making time management crucial. The work environment can be fast-paced and dynamic, with the need to adapt to changing market conditions and customer feedback.

88.4 Career Path and Growth Opportunities

The career path for product managers offers numerous opportunities for specialization and advancement:

- Entry-Level Positions: Associate Product Manager or Junior Product Manager, focusing on developing basic product management skills and gaining practical experience.

- Mid-Level Positions: Product Manager, Senior Product Manager, or Technical Product Manager, taking on more complex products and larger projects.

- Senior-Level Positions: Director of Product Management, VP of Product, or Chief Product Officer, overseeing product strategy, managing teams, and ensuring alignment with business objectives.

- Specialization Areas: Product Marketing Manager, Product Operations Manager, or UX/UI Product Manager. Specializing in these areas allows product managers to focus on specific functions and enhance their expertise.

- Executive Roles: Chief Product Officer or Head of Product. These positions involve strategic planning, overseeing product development for large organizations, and ensuring the success of product initiatives.

- Continued Education: Pursuing advanced certifications or degrees (e.g., MBA) can lead to higher roles and increased salaries.

88.5 Tips for Success

To excel as a product manager, consider the following strategies:

- Stay Updated: Continuously update your knowledge of market trends, customer needs, and product management techniques through continuing education and professional development courses.

- Develop Strong Leadership Skills: Enhance your ability to lead and inspire cross-functional teams through training and experience.

- Embrace Technology: Familiarize yourself with the latest product management tools and software to improve efficiency and collaboration.

- Focus on Customer Needs: Prioritize understanding and meeting customer needs through research, feedback, and user testing.

- Build a Professional Network: Establish connections with other product managers, industry experts, and potential customers to gain insights and opportunities.

- Seek Specialization: Consider pursuing additional certifications or training in specialized areas to advance your career and enhance your expertise.

- Improve Communication Skills: Develop strong communication and interpersonal skills to interact effectively with stakeholders, team members, and customers.

- Stay Agile: Embrace Agile methodologies and be prepared to adapt to changing market conditions and customer feedback.

By following these tips, you can build a successful and fulfilling career as a product manager, making a significant impact on product development and delivering innovative solutions to customers.

89. Market Research Analyst

89.1 Overview of the Role

Market research analysts are responsible for gathering and analyzing data on consumers and market conditions to help companies understand what products or services are in demand. They use various methods to collect data, such as surveys, interviews, focus groups, and analyzing statistical data. Market research analysts help companies understand their target markets, identify trends, and make informed business decisions.

89.2 Required Skills and Education

To become a successful market research analyst, a combination of analytical skills, technical knowledge, and attention to detail is essential. Key requirements include:

Technical Skills:

- Data Analysis: Proficiency in statistical analysis and data interpretation using tools like SPSS, SAS, R, or Excel.

- Survey Design: Skills in designing surveys and questionnaires to collect relevant data.

- Research Methods: Understanding of qualitative and quantitative research methods.

- Reporting: Ability to create detailed reports and presentations to communicate findings effectively.

- Software Proficiency: Familiarity with database management and data visualization tools, such as Tableau or Power BI.

Educational Background:

- Education: A bachelor's degree in marketing, business administration, statistics, or a related field is typically required. A master's degree can be advantageous.

- Certifications: Obtaining certifications such as Professional Researcher Certification (PRC) can enhance career prospects and demonstrate advanced expertise.

- Training: Hands-on experience through internships or entry-level positions in market research or related fields is valuable for gaining practical skills.

Soft Skills:

- Analytical Thinking: Strong analytical skills to interpret complex data and identify trends.

- Attention to Detail: Precision in data collection, analysis, and reporting to ensure accuracy.

- Communication: Effective verbal and written communication skills to present findings to stakeholders.

- Problem-Solving: Ability to address research challenges and provide actionable insights.

- Time Management: Efficiently managing time to handle multiple research projects and meet deadlines.

89.3 Typical Work Environment

Market research analysts work in various environments, including corporate offices, research firms, and consulting agencies. The role often involves a mix of desk work, analyzing data, and fieldwork, such as conducting surveys and interviews. Market research analysts typically work regular business hours, but may occasionally work evenings or weekends to meet project deadlines or conduct research. The work environment can be fast-paced and requires adaptability to handle changing research needs and priorities.

89.4 Career Path and Growth Opportunities

The career path for market research analysts offers numerous opportunities for specialization and advancement:

- Entry-Level Positions: Market Research Assistant or Junior Market Research Analyst, focusing on developing basic research skills and gaining practical experience.

- Mid-Level Positions: Market Research Analyst, Senior Market Research Analyst, or Data Analyst, taking on more complex research projects and managing larger datasets.

- Senior-Level Positions: Market Research Manager, Research Director, or Head of Market Research, overseeing research projects, managing teams, and ensuring research quality and relevance.

- Specialization Areas: Consumer Insights Analyst, Competitive Intelligence Analyst, or Data Scientist. Specializing in these areas allows market research analysts to focus on specific research functions and enhance their expertise.

- Executive Roles: Vice President of Market Research, Chief Marketing Officer (CMO), or Chief Data Officer. These positions involve strategic planning, overseeing research operations for large organizations, and ensuring the success of market research initiatives.

- Continued Education: Pursuing advanced certifications or degrees (e.g., MBA, Master's in Market Research, or Data Science) can lead to higher roles and increased salaries.

89.5 Tips for Success

To excel as a market research analyst, consider the following strategies:

- Stay Updated: Continuously update your knowledge of market research techniques, industry trends, and data analysis tools through continuing education and professional development courses.

- Develop Strong Analytical Skills: Enhance your ability to analyze data and interpret complex information to provide actionable insights.

- Embrace Technology: Familiarize yourself with the latest data analysis and visualization tools to improve efficiency and reporting.

- Focus on Communication: Develop strong communication skills to present research findings effectively to stakeholders and team members.

- Build a Professional Network: Establish connections with other market research professionals, industry experts, and potential clients to gain insights and opportunities.

- Seek Specialization: Consider pursuing additional certifications or training in specialized areas to advance your career and enhance your expertise.

- Improve Problem-Solving Skills: Develop strong problem-solving techniques to address research challenges and provide valuable insights.

- Stay Detail-Oriented: Maintain a high level of attention to detail in all aspects of research to ensure accuracy and reliability of data.

By following these tips, you can build a successful and fulfilling career as a market research analyst, making a significant impact on business decision-making and providing valuable insights to drive market success.

Chapter 9 Review

Overview of Retail and Sales Careers

In Chapter 9, we explored various careers in the retail and sales sectors. These roles are essential for driving business growth, managing customer relationships, and ensuring product availability. Here's a summary of the key points covered for each role:

80. Retail Manager

- Overview of the Role: Overseeing store operations, managing staff, and ensuring customer satisfaction.

- Required Skills and Education: Leadership, sales and marketing, inventory management, a degree in business or retail management preferred.

- Typical Work Environment: Retail stores, department stores, supermarkets; often involves long hours and managing teams.

- Career Path and Growth Opportunities: From Sales Associate to Store Manager, with further advancement to Regional or District Manager.

- Tips for Success: Stay updated with retail trends, develop strong leadership skills, embrace technology, focus on customer service, and build a professional network.

81. Sales Representative

- Overview of the Role: Selling products or services to customers, generating leads, and achieving sales targets.

- Required Skills and Education: Sales techniques, product knowledge, CRM systems, a degree in business or marketing preferred.

- Typical Work Environment: Offices, retail stores, on the road; often involves irregular hours and travel.

- Career Path and Growth Opportunities: From Junior Sales Representative to Senior Sales Manager, with specialization in technical sales or business development.

- Tips for Success: Stay updated, develop strong communication skills, embrace technology, focus on customer service, and build a professional network.

82. Real Estate Agent

- Overview of the Role: Assisting clients in buying, selling, and renting properties, providing market insights.

- Required Skills and Education: Market analysis, negotiation skills, real estate laws, a real estate license.

- Typical Work Environment: Real estate offices, client properties; involves significant travel and irregular hours.

- Career Path and Growth Opportunities: From Junior Real Estate Agent to Broker or Real Estate Office Manager, specializing in commercial or luxury real estate.

- Tips for Success: Stay updated, develop strong communication skills, embrace technology, focus on customer service, and build a professional network.

83. Merchandiser

- Overview of the Role: Managing product placement, inventory, and promotional displays to maximize sales.

- Required Skills and Education: Data analysis, inventory management, visual merchandising, a degree in business or marketing preferred.

- Typical Work Environment: Retail stores, corporate offices; involves travel between locations and physical tasks.

- Career Path and Growth Opportunities: From Merchandising Assistant to Category Manager or Director of Merchandising.

- Tips for Success: Stay updated, develop strong analytical skills, embrace creativity, focus on attention to detail, and build a professional network.

84. Telemarketer

- Overview of the Role: Contacting potential customers via phone to promote products or services, generate leads.

- Required Skills and Education: Sales techniques, CRM systems, communication skills, high school diploma.

- Typical Work Environment: Call centers, corporate offices, remote work; involves long hours of phone communication.

- Career Path and Growth Opportunities: From Junior Telemarketer to Sales Manager or Account Manager, specializing in inside sales or customer success.

- Tips for Success: Stay updated, develop strong communication skills, embrace technology, focus on customer service, and build persistence.

85. Store Clerk

- Overview of the Role: Assisting customers, managing inventory, handling transactions, and maintaining store organization.

- Required Skills and Education: Customer service, cash handling, inventory management, high school diploma.

- Typical Work Environment: Retail stores, grocery stores, convenience stores; involves standing for long periods and physical tasks.

- Career Path and Growth Opportunities: From Junior Store Clerk to Store Manager or Inventory Control Specialist.

- Tips for Success: Stay updated, develop strong customer service skills, embrace technology, focus on attention to detail, and stay reliable.

86. Car Salesperson

- Overview of the Role: Selling new and used vehicles, assisting customers in selecting and financing cars.

- Required Skills and Education: Sales techniques, automotive knowledge, negotiation skills, high school diploma.

- Typical Work Environment: Automotive dealerships; involves significant customer interaction and irregular hours.

- Career Path and Growth Opportunities: From Junior Salesperson to Sales Manager or Dealership Manager.

- Tips for Success: Stay updated, develop strong communication skills, embrace technology, focus on customer service, and improve negotiation skills.

87. Real Estate Broker

- Overview of the Role: Overseeing real estate transactions, managing agents, ensuring legal compliance.

- Required Skills and Education: Market analysis, legal knowledge, leadership, real estate broker's license.

- Typical Work Environment: Real estate offices, client properties; involves significant travel and irregular hours.

- Career Path and Growth Opportunities: From Junior Broker to Managing Broker or Chief Real Estate Officer.

- Tips for Success: Stay updated, develop strong leadership skills, embrace technology, focus on customer service, and improve negotiation skills.

88. Product Manager

- Overview of the Role: Overseeing product development, defining strategy, managing cross-functional teams.

- Required Skills and Education: Product development, market analysis, project management, bachelor's degree in business or related field.

- Typical Work Environment: Corporate offices, remote settings; involves collaboration with various departments.

- Career Path and Growth Opportunities: From Associate Product Manager to Chief Product Officer.

- Tips for Success: Stay updated, develop strong leadership skills, embrace technology, focus on customer needs, and build a professional network.

89. Market Research Analyst

- Overview of the Role: Gathering and analyzing data to help companies understand market conditions and customer preferences.

- Required Skills and Education: Data analysis, research methods, reporting, bachelor's degree in marketing or related field.

- Typical Work Environment: Corporate offices, research firms; involves desk work and fieldwork.

- Career Path and Growth Opportunities: From Market Research Assistant to Head of Market Research.

- Tips for Success: Stay updated, develop strong analytical skills, embrace technology, focus on communication, and build a professional network.

Key Takeaways

- Continuous Learning: Staying updated with industry trends, technological advancements, and best practices is crucial across all retail and sales careers.

- Customer Service: Providing exceptional customer service and addressing customer needs promptly is fundamental to success in retail and sales roles.

- Analytical Skills: Strong analytical skills are essential for roles that involve data analysis, market research, and inventory management.

- Communication and Negotiation: Effective communication and negotiation skills are key to building relationships, closing deals, and managing teams.

- Professional Networking: Building a professional network through industry events, online forums, and professional associations can provide valuable opportunities and insights.

By understanding the roles, required skills, typical work environments, career paths, and tips for success, you can make informed decisions about pursuing a career in the retail and sales fields covered in this chapter. Whether you are just starting out or looking to advance your career, this guide provides the essential information to help you succeed.

Chapter 10: Public Service and Government Careers

90. Police Officer

90.1 Overview of the Role

Police officers are responsible for maintaining public order, enforcing laws, preventing and investigating crimes, and protecting citizens and property. They patrol assigned areas, respond to emergency calls, conduct investigations, and apprehend suspects. Police officers also engage with the community to build trust and improve public safety.

90.2 Required Skills and Education

To become a successful police officer, a combination of physical fitness, law enforcement knowledge, and interpersonal skills is essential. Key requirements include:

Technical Skills:

- Law Enforcement Knowledge: Understanding of laws, regulations, and law enforcement procedures.

- Firearms Proficiency: Ability to safely and effectively use firearms and other law enforcement equipment.

- First Aid: Basic knowledge of first aid and emergency medical procedures.

- Report Writing: Skills in writing clear and detailed incident reports and legal documents.

Educational Background:

- Education: A high school diploma or equivalent is typically required. Some departments may prefer candidates with an associate's or bachelor's degree in criminal justice or a related field.

- Training: Completion of a police academy training program is mandatory, covering law enforcement techniques, physical fitness, firearms training, and legal education.

- Certifications: Obtaining certifications in areas such as first aid, CPR, and specialized law enforcement training can enhance career prospects and demonstrate advanced expertise.

Soft Skills:

- Communication: Effective verbal and written communication skills to interact with the public, colleagues, and other law enforcement agencies.

- Problem-Solving: Ability to assess situations quickly and make sound decisions under pressure.

- Empathy: Understanding and addressing the needs and concerns of the community.

- Physical Fitness: Maintaining a high level of physical fitness to handle the physical demands of the job.

- Integrity: Upholding ethical standards and demonstrating honesty and integrity in all actions.

90.3 Typical Work Environment

Police officers work in various environments, including urban, suburban, and rural areas. The job involves a mix of indoor and outdoor work, often in challenging and potentially dangerous conditions. Officers may work in patrol cars, on foot, or on bicycles, and they frequently interact with the public. The role requires shift work, including nights, weekends, and holidays, to ensure round-the-clock public safety. Police officers must be prepared to handle stressful situations and respond to emergencies at any time.

90.4 Career Path and Growth Opportunities

The career path for police officers offers numerous opportunities for specialization and advancement:

- Entry-Level Positions: Patrol Officer or Police Officer, focusing on basic law enforcement duties and gaining practical experience.

- Mid-Level Positions: Detective, Sergeant, or K-9 Officer, taking on more specialized roles and responsibilities.

- Senior-Level Positions: Lieutenant, Captain, or Chief of Police, overseeing police operations, managing teams, and ensuring departmental goals are met.

- Specialization Areas: SWAT Team Member, Narcotics Officer, Traffic Enforcement Officer, or Community Policing Officer. Specializing in these areas allows officers to focus on specific aspects of law enforcement and enhance their expertise.

- Executive Roles: Chief of Police, Police Commissioner, or Director of Public Safety. These positions involve strategic planning, overseeing police operations for large departments, and ensuring the success of law enforcement initiatives.

- Continued Education: Pursuing advanced degrees or certifications in criminal justice, public administration, or law enforcement leadership can lead to higher roles and increased salaries.

90.5 Tips for Success

To excel as a police officer, consider the following strategies:

- Stay Updated: Continuously update your knowledge of laws, regulations, and law enforcement techniques through continuing education and professional development courses.

- Develop Strong Communication Skills: Enhance your ability to communicate effectively with the public, colleagues, and other law enforcement agencies.

- Embrace Physical Fitness: Maintain a high level of physical fitness to handle the physical demands of the job and ensure personal safety.

- Focus on Community Engagement: Build positive relationships with the community through outreach programs and proactive policing strategies.

- Build a Professional Network: Establish connections with other law enforcement professionals, industry experts, and community leaders to gain insights and opportunities.

- Seek Specialization: Consider pursuing additional certifications or training in specialized areas to advance your career and enhance your expertise.

- Improve Problem-Solving Skills: Develop strong problem-solving techniques to assess situations quickly and make sound decisions under pressure.

- Uphold Integrity: Demonstrate honesty, integrity, and ethical behavior in all actions to build trust and respect within the community.

By following these tips, you can build a successful and fulfilling career as a police officer, making a significant impact on public safety and providing valuable services to your community.

91. Firefighter

91.1 Overview of the Role

Firefighters are responsible for responding to emergency situations, including fires, accidents, natural disasters, and hazardous material incidents. They work to protect lives and property by extinguishing fires, rescuing individuals in danger, providing emergency medical care, and conducting fire prevention and education programs. Firefighters also perform routine maintenance of firefighting equipment and participate in training exercises to stay prepared for emergencies.

91.2 Required Skills and Education

To become a successful firefighter, a combination of physical fitness, technical skills, and the ability to work under pressure is essential. Key requirements include:

Technical Skills:

- Firefighting Techniques: Proficiency in using firefighting equipment, such as hoses, ladders, and fire extinguishers.

- Emergency Medical Care: Knowledge of basic first aid and CPR, with many firefighters also being certified EMTs or paramedics.

- Hazardous Material Handling: Skills in managing and mitigating hazardous materials incidents.

- Rescue Operations: Ability to conduct search and rescue operations in various environments.

- Fire Prevention: Understanding of fire prevention techniques and building codes.

Educational Background:

- Education: A high school diploma or equivalent is typically required. Some positions may prefer candidates with postsecondary education in fire science or emergency management.

- Training: Completion of a fire academy training program is mandatory, covering firefighting techniques, physical fitness, emergency medical care, and hazardous materials handling.

- Certifications: Obtaining certifications such as Firefighter I and II, EMT, or paramedic can enhance career prospects and demonstrate advanced expertise.

Soft Skills:

- Communication: Effective verbal and written communication skills to interact with the public, colleagues, and other emergency responders.

- Problem-Solving: Ability to assess situations quickly and make sound decisions under pressure.

- Physical Fitness: Maintaining a high level of physical fitness to handle the demanding physical tasks of the job.

- Teamwork: Strong teamwork skills to work effectively with other firefighters and emergency responders.

- Courage and Resilience: Demonstrating bravery and the ability to remain calm in dangerous and high-stress situations.

91.3 Typical Work Environment

Firefighters work in various environments, including urban, suburban, and rural areas. The job involves a mix of indoor and outdoor work, often in hazardous and potentially life-threatening conditions. Firefighters typically work in fire stations, but they spend much of their time responding to emergencies and conducting community outreach. The role requires shift work, including nights, weekends, and holidays, with many firefighters working 24-hour shifts followed by several days off. Firefighters must be prepared to respond to emergencies at any time and handle physically demanding tasks.

91.4 Career Path and Growth Opportunities

The career path for firefighters offers numerous opportunities for specialization and advancement:

- Entry-Level Positions: Firefighter or Firefighter/EMT, focusing on developing basic firefighting skills and gaining practical experience.

- Mid-Level Positions: Fire Engineer, Fire Lieutenant, or Fire Inspector, taking on more specialized roles and responsibilities.

- Senior-Level Positions: Fire Captain, Battalion Chief, or Fire Marshal, overseeing firefighting operations, managing teams, and ensuring departmental goals are met.

- Specialization Areas: Hazardous Materials Technician, Fire Investigator, Wildland Firefighter, or Fire Prevention Officer. Specializing in these areas allows firefighters to focus on specific aspects of firefighting and enhance their expertise.

- Executive Roles: Fire Chief, Deputy Fire Chief, or Director of Emergency Services. These positions involve strategic planning, overseeing fire department operations for large municipalities, and ensuring the success of firefighting and emergency response initiatives.

- Continued Education: Pursuing advanced degrees or certifications in fire science, emergency management, or public administration can lead to higher roles and increased salaries.

91.5 Tips for Success

To excel as a firefighter, consider the following strategies:

- Stay Updated: Continuously update your knowledge of firefighting techniques, emergency medical care, and hazardous materials handling through continuing education and professional development courses.

- Develop Strong Physical Fitness: Maintain a high level of physical fitness to handle the demanding physical tasks of the job and ensure personal safety.

- Focus on Teamwork: Build strong teamwork skills to work effectively with other firefighters and emergency responders.

- Embrace Training: Participate in regular training exercises and drills to stay prepared for emergencies and enhance your skills.

- Build a Professional Network: Establish connections with other firefighters, emergency responders, and industry experts to gain insights and opportunities.

- Seek Specialization: Consider pursuing additional certifications or training in specialized areas to advance your career and enhance your expertise.

- Improve Problem-Solving Skills: Develop strong problem-solving techniques to assess situations quickly and make sound decisions under pressure.

- Engage with the Community: Participate in fire prevention and education programs to build positive relationships with the community and promote fire safety.

By following these tips, you can build a successful and fulfilling career as a firefighter, making a significant impact on public safety and providing valuable services to your community.

92. Public Administrator

92.1 Overview of the Role

Public administrators manage and oversee public agencies, programs, and policies at the local, state, or federal levels. They work to implement and evaluate public policies, manage budgets, and ensure that public services are delivered effectively and efficiently. Public administrators play a crucial role in shaping public policy, managing government resources, and improving community services.

92.2 Required Skills and Education

To become a successful public administrator, a combination of leadership skills, policy knowledge, and analytical abilities is essential. Key requirements include:

Technical Skills:

- Policy Analysis: Proficiency in analyzing and evaluating public policies and their impact on communities.

- Budget Management: Skills in managing budgets, financial reporting, and allocating resources efficiently.

- Project Management: Ability to manage projects, set goals, and meet deadlines.

- Data Analysis: Proficiency in using data to inform decision-making and measure program effectiveness.

- Legal Knowledge: Understanding of government regulations, laws, and ethical standards.

Educational Background:

- Education: A bachelor's degree in public administration, political science, or a related field is typically required. A master's degree in public administration (MPA) or public policy (MPP) is often preferred.

- Certifications: Obtaining certifications such as Certified Public Manager (CPM) can enhance career prospects and demonstrate advanced expertise.

- Training: Practical experience through internships or entry-level positions in government or public service is valuable for gaining practical skills.

Soft Skills:

- Leadership: Strong leadership skills to manage teams and guide public programs.

- Communication: Effective verbal and written communication skills to interact with stakeholders, government officials, and the public.

- Problem-Solving: Ability to address and resolve complex issues related to public policy and administration.

- Analytical Thinking: Strong analytical skills to interpret data and make informed decisions.

- Integrity: Upholding ethical standards and demonstrating honesty and integrity in all actions.

92.3 Typical Work Environment

Public administrators work in various environments, including government offices, non-profit organizations, and public agencies. The job often involves a mix of desk work, attending meetings, and fieldwork. Public administrators typically work regular business hours, but may occasionally work evenings or weekends to meet project deadlines or attend community events. The role requires adaptability to handle changing policies, regulations, and community needs.

92.4 Career Path and Growth Opportunities

The career path for public administrators offers numerous opportunities for specialization and advancement:

- Entry-Level Positions: Administrative Assistant, Policy Analyst, or Program Coordinator, focusing on developing basic skills and gaining practical experience.

- Mid-Level Positions: Public Administrator, Budget Analyst, or Program Manager, taking on more complex projects and managing larger teams.

- Senior-Level Positions: Director of Public Administration, City Manager, or Chief Administrative Officer, overseeing public programs, managing departments, and ensuring compliance with regulations.

- Specialization Areas: Urban Planner, Health Services Administrator, or Emergency Management Director. Specializing in these areas allows public administrators to focus on specific functions and enhance their expertise.

- Executive Roles: City Manager, County Administrator, or State Agency Director. These positions involve strategic planning, overseeing public administration operations for large jurisdictions, and ensuring the success of public policies and programs.

- Continued Education: Pursuing advanced certifications or degrees (e.g., MPA, MPP, or Doctor of Public Administration) can lead to higher roles and increased salaries.

92.5 Tips for Success

To excel as a public administrator, consider the following strategies:

- Stay Updated: Continuously update your knowledge of public policy, regulations, and best practices through continuing education and professional development courses.

- Develop Strong Leadership Skills: Enhance your ability to lead and inspire teams through training and experience.

- Embrace Technology: Familiarize yourself with the latest data analysis and project management tools to improve efficiency and decision-making.

- Focus on Communication: Develop strong communication skills to present information effectively to stakeholders, government officials, and the public.

- Build a Professional Network: Establish connections with other public administrators, industry experts, and community leaders to gain insights and opportunities.

- Seek Specialization: Consider pursuing additional certifications or training in specialized areas to advance your career and enhance your expertise.

- Improve Analytical Skills: Develop strong analytical techniques to interpret data and make informed decisions.

- Uphold Integrity: Demonstrate honesty, integrity, and ethical behavior in all actions to build trust and respect within the community.

By following these tips, you can build a successful and fulfilling career as a public administrator, making a significant impact on public policy and improving services for your community.

93. Social Worker

93.1 Overview of the Role

Social workers are dedicated professionals who help individuals, families, and communities cope with challenges and improve their well-being. They provide support through counseling, advocacy, and connecting clients with resources and services. Social workers address a wide range of issues, including mental health, child welfare, substance abuse, and housing.

93.2 Required Skills and Education

To become a successful social worker, a combination of empathy, problem-solving skills, and specialized knowledge is essential. Key requirements include:

Technical Skills:

- Case Management: Proficiency in assessing client needs, developing treatment plans, and coordinating services.

- Counseling: Skills in providing therapeutic support to individuals and families.

- Crisis Intervention: Ability to handle emergencies and provide immediate support to clients in distress.

- Advocacy: Knowledge of social justice issues and the ability to advocate for clients' rights and needs.

- Record Keeping: Competence in maintaining accurate and confidential client records.

Educational Background:

- Education: A bachelor's degree in social work (BSW) is typically required for entry-level positions. A master's degree in social work (MSW) is often necessary for clinical positions and advanced roles.

- Licensure: Obtaining a social work license is mandatory in most states, which involves completing supervised clinical experience and passing a licensing exam.

- Certifications: Pursuing additional certifications, such as Certified Social Worker in Health Care (C-SWHC) or Licensed Clinical Social Worker (LCSW), can enhance career prospects and demonstrate advanced expertise.

Soft Skills:

- Empathy: Strong ability to understand and share the feelings of clients.

- Communication: Effective verbal and written communication skills to interact with clients, families, and other professionals.

- Problem-Solving: Ability to develop practical solutions to help clients overcome challenges.

- Patience: Patience and perseverance to work with clients who may have complex and long-term issues.

- Cultural Competence: Understanding and respecting cultural differences to provide appropriate services to diverse populations.

93.3 Typical Work Environment

Social workers work in various environments, including schools, hospitals, mental health clinics, child welfare agencies, and non-profit organizations. The job involves a mix of office work, client visits, and community outreach. Social workers often handle high caseloads and may work irregular hours, including evenings and weekends, to meet client needs. The role can be emotionally demanding, requiring resilience and self-care to prevent burnout.

93.4 Career Path and Growth Opportunities

The career path for social workers offers numerous opportunities for specialization and advancement:

- Entry-Level Positions: Case Worker, Social Work Assistant, or Child Welfare Worker, focusing on developing basic skills and gaining practical experience.

- Mid-Level Positions: Clinical Social Worker, School Social Worker, or Mental Health Counselor, taking on more complex cases and providing specialized services.

- Senior-Level Positions: Senior Social Worker, Program Director, or Clinical Supervisor, overseeing social work programs, managing teams, and ensuring compliance with regulations.

- Specialization Areas: Substance Abuse Counselor, Medical Social Worker, or Gerontological Social Worker. Specializing in these areas allows social workers to focus on specific client populations and enhance their expertise.

- Executive Roles: Director of Social Services, Chief Social Worker, or Executive Director of a non-profit organization. These positions involve strategic planning, overseeing social work operations for large agencies, and ensuring the success of social work initiatives.

- Continued Education: Pursuing advanced certifications or degrees (e.g., Doctor of Social Work or PhD in Social Work) can lead to higher roles and increased salaries.

93.5 Tips for Success

To excel as a social worker, consider the following strategies:

- Stay Updated: Continuously update your knowledge of social work practices, mental health issues, and community resources through continuing education and professional development courses.

- Develop Strong Empathy: Enhance your ability to understand and share the feelings of clients through training and practice.

- Embrace Self-Care: Prioritize self-care and seek support to prevent burnout and maintain personal well-being.

- Focus on Communication: Develop strong communication skills to interact effectively with clients, families, and other professionals.

- Build a Professional Network: Establish connections with other social workers, industry experts, and community leaders to gain insights and opportunities.

- Seek Specialization: Consider pursuing additional certifications or training in specialized areas to advance your career and enhance your expertise.

- Improve Problem-Solving Skills: Develop strong problem-solving techniques to address client challenges and develop practical solutions.

- Engage in Advocacy: Advocate for clients' rights and needs, and work towards social justice and systemic change.

By following these tips, you can build a successful and fulfilling career as a social worker, making a significant impact on the well-being of individuals and communities.

94. Urban Planner

94.1 Overview of the Role

Urban planners are responsible for developing plans and programs for the use of land and the physical design of urban environments. They work to create sustainable, functional, and aesthetically pleasing communities by addressing issues such as zoning, transportation, housing, and environmental sustainability. Urban planners collaborate with government officials, developers, and the public to ensure that development meets the needs of the community while complying with regulations and policies.

94.2 Required Skills and Education

To become a successful urban planner, a combination of technical knowledge, analytical skills, and creativity is essential. Key requirements include:

Technical Skills:

- Land Use Planning: Proficiency in analyzing and developing plans for land use, zoning, and urban design.

- GIS and Mapping: Skills in using Geographic Information Systems (GIS) and other mapping tools to analyze spatial data and create maps.

- Regulatory Knowledge: Understanding of zoning laws, building codes, and environmental regulations.

- Project Management: Ability to manage projects, set goals, and meet deadlines.

- Data Analysis: Proficiency in using data to inform planning decisions and measure the impact of development projects.

Educational Background:

- Education: A bachelor's degree in urban planning, geography, architecture, or a related field is typically required. A master's degree in urban planning (MUP) or a related field is often preferred.

- Certifications: Obtaining certifications such as American Institute of Certified Planners (AICP) can enhance career prospects and demonstrate advanced expertise.

- Training: Practical experience through internships or entry-level positions in urban planning or related fields is valuable for gaining practical skills.

Soft Skills:

- Communication: Effective verbal and written communication skills to interact with government officials, developers, and the public.

- Problem-Solving: Ability to address and resolve complex issues related to urban development and land use.

- Analytical Thinking: Strong analytical skills to interpret data and make informed decisions.

- Creativity: Innovative thinking to develop sustainable and aesthetically pleasing urban designs.

- Collaboration: Strong teamwork skills to work effectively with various stakeholders.

94.3 Typical Work Environment

Urban planners work in various environments, including government offices, planning firms, and non-profit organizations. The job involves a mix of desk work, attending meetings, and fieldwork, such as site visits and public hearings. Urban planners typically work regular business hours, but may occasionally work evenings or weekends to attend community meetings or public forums. The role requires adaptability to handle changing regulations, community needs, and project requirements.

94.4 Career Path and Growth Opportunities

The career path for urban planners offers numerous opportunities for specialization and advancement:

- Entry-Level Positions: Planning Assistant, Junior Urban Planner, or Zoning Technician, focusing on developing basic skills and gaining practical experience.

- Mid-Level Positions: Urban Planner, Senior Planner, or Transportation Planner, taking on more complex projects and managing larger initiatives.

- Senior-Level Positions: Principal Planner, Planning Manager, or Urban Planning Director, overseeing planning operations, managing teams, and ensuring compliance with regulations.

- Specialization Areas: Environmental Planner, Transportation Planner, Housing Planner, or Community Development Planner. Specializing in these areas allows urban planners to focus on specific aspects of urban development and enhance their expertise.

- Executive Roles: Director of Planning, Chief Planner, or Planning Commissioner. These positions involve strategic planning, overseeing planning operations for large jurisdictions, and ensuring the success of urban development initiatives.

- Continued Education: Pursuing advanced certifications or degrees (e.g., Doctor of Urban Planning or PhD in Urban Studies) can lead to higher roles and increased salaries.

94.5 Tips for Success

To excel as an urban planner, consider the following strategies:

- Stay Updated: Continuously update your knowledge of urban planning practices, regulations, and best practices through continuing education and professional development courses.

- Develop Strong Analytical Skills: Enhance your ability to analyze data and interpret complex information to inform planning decisions.

- Embrace Technology: Familiarize yourself with the latest GIS tools, mapping software, and data analysis techniques to improve efficiency and accuracy.

- Focus on Communication: Develop strong communication skills to present information effectively to stakeholders, government officials, and the public.

- Build a Professional Network: Establish connections with other urban planners, industry experts, and community leaders to gain insights and opportunities.

- Seek Specialization: Consider pursuing additional certifications or training in specialized areas to advance your career and enhance your expertise.

- Improve Problem-Solving Skills: Develop strong problem-solving techniques to address and resolve complex urban development issues.

- Engage with the Community: Participate in public forums and community meetings to understand the needs and concerns of the community and incorporate their input into planning decisions.

By following these tips, you can build a successful and fulfilling career as an urban planner, making a significant impact on the development and sustainability of urban environments and improving the quality of life for communities.

95. Diplomat

95.1 Overview of the Role

Diplomats represent their country's government abroad, working to maintain and strengthen international relations. They engage in negotiations, promote their nation's interests, protect citizens abroad, and facilitate international cooperation on various issues such as trade, security, and human rights. Diplomats serve in embassies, consulates, and international organizations, acting as a vital link between their home country and the host nation.

95.2 Required Skills and Education

To become a successful diplomat, a combination of diplomatic skills, cultural awareness, and specialized knowledge is essential. Key requirements include:

Technical Skills:

- Negotiation Skills: Proficiency in negotiating agreements and resolving conflicts between nations.

- Foreign Languages: Ability to speak one or more foreign languages fluently.

- International Law and Relations: Understanding of international law, treaties, and diplomatic protocols.

- Policy Analysis: Skills in analyzing foreign policy issues and their implications.

- Communication: Strong verbal and written communication skills for drafting reports, speeches, and diplomatic correspondence.

Educational Background:

- Education: A bachelor's degree in international relations, political science, law, or a related field is typically required. A master's degree in international affairs, public policy, or a related field is often preferred.

- Certifications: Obtaining certifications such as Certified International Negotiator (CIN) can enhance career prospects and demonstrate advanced expertise.

- Training: Diplomatic training programs provided by government agencies, such as the Foreign Service Institute (FSI), are crucial for gaining practical skills.

Soft Skills:

- Cultural Sensitivity: Strong cultural awareness and sensitivity to understand and respect different customs and traditions.

- Problem-Solving: Ability to address and resolve complex international issues and conflicts.

- Adaptability: Flexibility to adapt to different cultural environments and work conditions.

- Integrity: Upholding ethical standards and demonstrating honesty and integrity in all actions.

- Interpersonal Skills: Ability to build and maintain relationships with foreign officials, colleagues, and local communities.

95.3 Typical Work Environment

Diplomats work in various environments, including embassies, consulates, and international organizations. The job involves significant travel, long hours, and the need to attend numerous meetings, events, and negotiations. Diplomats often work under high-pressure conditions, dealing with sensitive and complex issues. They must be prepared to relocate frequently, sometimes to regions with challenging living conditions or political instability. The role requires adaptability, resilience, and the ability to work effectively in diverse cultural settings.

95.4 Career Path and Growth Opportunities

The career path for diplomats offers numerous opportunities for specialization and advancement:

- Entry-Level Positions: Junior Foreign Service Officer or Attaché, focusing on developing basic diplomatic skills and gaining practical experience.

- Mid-Level Positions: Foreign Service Officer, Consul, or Political Officer, taking on more complex assignments and responsibilities.

- Senior-Level Positions: Ambassador, Deputy Chief of Mission, or Consul General, overseeing diplomatic missions, managing teams, and representing the country at the highest levels.

- Specialization Areas: Trade Negotiator, Human Rights Officer, or Intelligence Liaison. Specializing in these areas allows diplomats to focus on specific issues and enhance their expertise.

- Executive Roles: Undersecretary for Foreign Affairs, Director-General of Foreign Services, or Chief Diplomatic Advisor. These positions involve strategic planning, overseeing foreign service operations, and ensuring the success of diplomatic initiatives.

- Continued Education: Pursuing advanced degrees or certifications in international relations, diplomacy, or related fields can lead to higher roles and increased responsibilities.

95.5 Tips for Success

To excel as a diplomat, consider the following strategies:

- Stay Updated: Continuously update your knowledge of international relations, foreign policy issues, and diplomatic practices through continuing education and professional development courses.

- Develop Strong Negotiation Skills: Enhance your ability to negotiate agreements and resolve conflicts through training and practice.

- Embrace Cultural Sensitivity: Develop strong cultural awareness and sensitivity to effectively navigate different cultural environments.

- Build a Professional Network: Establish connections with other diplomats, foreign officials, and international organizations to gain insights and opportunities.

- Seek Specialization: Consider pursuing additional certifications or training in specialized areas to advance your career and enhance your expertise.

- Improve Communication Skills: Develop strong communication and interpersonal skills to interact effectively with foreign officials, colleagues, and local communities.

- Stay Adaptable: Be prepared to adapt to different cultural environments, work conditions, and political situations.

- Uphold Integrity: Demonstrate honesty, integrity, and ethical behavior in all actions to build trust and respect in international relations.

By following these tips, you can build a successful and fulfilling career as a diplomat, making a significant impact on international relations and promoting your country's interests abroad.

96. Customs Officer

96.1 Overview of the Role

Customs officers are responsible for enforcing laws and regulations related to the import and export of goods. They inspect cargo, luggage, and individuals entering and leaving a country to prevent illegal goods, such as drugs and weapons, from crossing borders. Customs officers also ensure that proper duties and taxes are paid on imported goods and work to facilitate legitimate trade and travel.

96.2 Required Skills and Education

To become a successful customs officer, a combination of law enforcement skills, attention to detail, and knowledge of customs regulations is essential. Key requirements include:

Technical Skills:

- Inspection Skills: Proficiency in conducting thorough inspections of cargo, luggage, and individuals.

- Regulatory Knowledge: Understanding of customs laws, regulations, and procedures.

- Detection Technology: Skills in using technology and tools, such as X-ray machines and drug-sniffing dogs, to detect illegal goods.

- Data Analysis: Ability to analyze documentation and data related to imports and exports.

- Report Writing: Competence in writing clear and detailed reports on inspections and enforcement actions.

Educational Background:

- Education: A high school diploma or equivalent is typically required. Some positions may prefer candidates with a degree in criminal justice, international trade, or a related field.

- Training: Completion of a customs officer training program is mandatory, covering customs laws, inspection techniques, and law enforcement procedures.

- Certifications: Obtaining certifications in areas such as hazardous materials handling or anti-terrorism can enhance career prospects and demonstrate advanced expertise.

Soft Skills:

- Attention to Detail: Precision in conducting inspections and reviewing documentation to ensure compliance with regulations.

- Communication: Effective verbal and written communication skills to interact with travelers, importers, and other law enforcement agencies.

- Problem-Solving: Ability to address and resolve issues related to customs enforcement and border security.

- Integrity: Upholding ethical standards and demonstrating honesty and integrity in all actions.

- Interpersonal Skills: Ability to interact professionally with the public and maintain composure in potentially confrontational situations.

96.3 Typical Work Environment

Customs officers work in various environments, including airports, seaports, border crossings, and international mail facilities. The job involves a mix of indoor and outdoor work, often in challenging and potentially hazardous conditions. Customs officers typically work in shifts, including nights, weekends, and holidays, to ensure 24/7 border security. The role requires standing for long periods, handling heavy luggage or cargo, and being prepared to respond to emergencies or security threats at any time.

96.4 Career Path and Growth Opportunities

The career path for customs officers offers numerous opportunities for specialization and advancement:

- Entry-Level Positions: Customs Trainee or Junior Customs Officer, focusing on developing basic skills and gaining practical experience.

- Mid-Level Positions: Customs Officer, Senior Customs Officer, or Cargo Inspector, taking on more complex inspections and enforcement responsibilities.

- Senior-Level Positions: Supervisory Customs Officer, Customs Manager, or Border Security Specialist, overseeing customs operations, managing teams, and ensuring compliance with regulations.

- Specialization Areas: Hazardous Materials Specialist, Anti-Smuggling Unit, or Trade Compliance Officer. Specializing in these areas allows customs officers to focus on specific aspects of customs enforcement and enhance their expertise.

- Executive Roles: Director of Customs Operations, Chief Customs Officer, or Head of Border Security. These positions involve strategic planning, overseeing customs operations for large regions or the entire country, and ensuring the success of customs enforcement initiatives.

- Continued Education: Pursuing advanced certifications or degrees (e.g., Master's in International Trade or Public Administration) can lead to higher roles and increased salaries.

96.5 Tips for Success

To excel as a customs officer, consider the following strategies:

- Stay Updated: Continuously update your knowledge of customs regulations, enforcement techniques, and international trade practices through continuing education and professional development courses.

- Develop Strong Attention to Detail: Enhance your ability to conduct thorough inspections and review documentation accurately to ensure compliance with regulations.

- Embrace Technology: Familiarize yourself with the latest detection technology and tools to improve efficiency and effectiveness in inspections.

- Focus on Communication: Develop strong communication skills to interact effectively with travelers, importers, and other law enforcement agencies.

- Build a Professional Network: Establish connections with other customs officers, law enforcement professionals, and industry experts to gain insights and opportunities.

- Seek Specialization: Consider pursuing additional certifications or training in specialized areas to advance your career and enhance your expertise.

- Improve Problem-Solving Skills: Develop strong problem-solving techniques to address and resolve issues related to customs enforcement and border security.

- Uphold Integrity: Demonstrate honesty, integrity, and ethical behavior in all actions to build trust and respect within the community and among colleagues.

By following these tips, you can build a successful and fulfilling career as a customs officer, making a significant impact on border security and facilitating legitimate trade and travel.

97. Correctional Officer

97.1 Overview of the Role

Correctional officers are responsible for overseeing individuals who have been arrested and are awaiting trial or who have been sentenced to serve time in a jail or prison. Their primary duties include maintaining security and order within the facility, supervising inmates, enforcing rules and regulations, preventing disturbances, and ensuring the safety of both inmates and staff.

97.2 Required Skills and Education

To become a successful correctional officer, a combination of law enforcement skills, physical fitness, and interpersonal abilities is essential. Key requirements include:

Technical Skills:

- Security Management: Proficiency in maintaining security and order within correctional facilities.

- Surveillance: Skills in monitoring inmate behavior and identifying potential security threats.

- Crisis Management: Ability to handle emergencies, including riots, escapes, and medical incidents.

- Report Writing: Competence in writing clear and detailed reports on incidents and daily activities.

- Basic First Aid: Knowledge of basic first aid and emergency medical procedures.

Educational Background:

- Education: A high school diploma or equivalent is typically required. Some positions may prefer candidates with postsecondary education in criminal justice or a related field.

- Training: Completion of a correctional officer training program is mandatory, covering security procedures, self-defense, firearms training, and legal education.

- Certifications: Obtaining certifications in areas such as CPR, first aid, or advanced correctional practices can enhance career prospects and demonstrate advanced expertise.

Soft Skills:

- Communication: Effective verbal and written communication skills to interact with inmates, colleagues, and other law enforcement agencies.

- Problem-Solving: Ability to address and resolve conflicts and issues within the correctional facility.

- Physical Fitness: Maintaining a high level of physical fitness to handle the physical demands of the job.

- Patience and Resilience: Patience and resilience to work in a challenging and potentially hostile environment.

- Integrity: Upholding ethical standards and demonstrating honesty and integrity in all actions.

97.3 Typical Work Environment

Correctional officers work in various environments, including local jails, state and federal prisons, and juvenile detention centers. The job involves a mix of indoor and outdoor work, often in challenging and potentially dangerous conditions. Correctional officers typically work in shifts, including nights, weekends, and holidays, to ensure 24/7 facility security. The role requires standing for long periods, handling confrontational situations, and being prepared to respond to emergencies at any time.

97.4 Career Path and Growth Opportunities

The career path for correctional officers offers numerous opportunities for specialization and advancement:

- Entry-Level Positions: Correctional Officer Trainee or Junior Correctional Officer, focusing on developing basic skills and gaining practical experience.

- Mid-Level Positions: Correctional Officer, Senior Correctional Officer, or Correctional Sergeant, taking on more complex supervisory and enforcement responsibilities.

- Senior-Level Positions: Correctional Lieutenant, Correctional Captain, or Facility Manager, overseeing correctional operations, managing teams, and ensuring compliance with regulations.

- Specialization Areas: K-9 Unit Officer, Tactical Response Team Member, or Correctional Counselor. Specializing in these areas allows correctional officers to focus on specific aspects of corrections and enhance their expertise.

- Executive Roles: Warden, Assistant Warden, or Director of Corrections. These positions involve strategic planning, overseeing correctional facility operations, and ensuring the success of correctional initiatives.

- Continued Education: Pursuing advanced certifications or degrees (e.g., Bachelor's in Criminal Justice or Master's in Public Administration) can lead to higher roles and increased salaries.

97.5 Tips for Success

To excel as a correctional officer, consider the following strategies:

- Stay Updated: Continuously update your knowledge of correctional practices, security procedures, and legal regulations through continuing education and professional development courses.

- Develop Strong Communication Skills: Enhance your ability to communicate effectively with inmates, colleagues, and other law enforcement agencies.

- Embrace Physical Fitness: Maintain a high level of physical fitness to handle the demanding physical tasks of the job and ensure personal safety.

- Focus on Crisis Management: Develop strong crisis management skills to handle emergencies and prevent disturbances within the facility.

- Build a Professional Network: Establish connections with other correctional officers, law enforcement professionals, and industry experts to gain insights and opportunities.

- Seek Specialization: Consider pursuing additional certifications or training in specialized areas to advance your career and enhance your expertise.

- Improve Problem-Solving Skills: Develop strong problem-solving techniques to address and resolve conflicts and issues within the correctional facility.

- Uphold Integrity: Demonstrate honesty, integrity, and ethical behavior in all actions to build trust and respect within the correctional facility and among colleagues.

By following these tips, you can build a successful and fulfilling career as a correctional officer, making a significant impact on the safety and security of correctional facilities and providing valuable services to the community.

98. Policy Analyst

98.1 Overview of the Role

Policy analysts research, evaluate, and develop policies and programs to address public issues. They work for government agencies, think tanks, non-profit organizations, and private firms to provide insights and recommendations on policy decisions. Their work involves analyzing data, reviewing legislation, consulting with stakeholders, and preparing reports to influence policy-making processes.

98.2 Required Skills and Education

To become a successful policy analyst, a combination of analytical skills, research abilities, and communication expertise is essential. Key requirements include:

Technical Skills:

- Research Skills: Proficiency in conducting thorough research using various methodologies and sources.

- Data Analysis: Skills in analyzing statistical data and economic models to inform policy recommendations.

- Policy Evaluation: Ability to assess the effectiveness and impact of existing policies and programs.

- Report Writing: Competence in writing clear, concise, and well-structured reports and policy briefs.

- Legislative Knowledge: Understanding of legislative processes and government regulations.

Educational Background:

- Education: A bachelor's degree in political science, public policy, economics, or a related field is typically required. A master's degree in public policy (MPP), public administration (MPA), or a related field is often preferred.

- Certifications: Obtaining certifications such as Certified Policy Analyst (CPA) can enhance career prospects and demonstrate advanced expertise.

- Training: Practical experience through internships or entry-level positions in policy analysis or related fields is valuable for gaining practical skills.

Soft Skills:

- Analytical Thinking: Strong analytical skills to interpret complex data and make informed policy recommendations.

- Communication: Effective verbal and written communication skills to present findings and recommendations to stakeholders and decision-makers.

- Problem-Solving: Ability to develop practical solutions to address public policy issues.

- Attention to Detail: Precision in conducting research, analyzing data, and preparing reports to ensure accuracy and reliability.

- Collaboration: Strong teamwork skills to work effectively with colleagues, stakeholders, and other professionals.

98.3 Typical Work Environment

Policy analysts work in various environments, including government offices, research institutes, non-profit organizations, and private firms. The job involves a mix of desk work, attending meetings, and conducting field research. Policy analysts typically work regular business hours, but may occasionally work evenings or weekends to meet project deadlines or attend public forums. The role requires adaptability to handle changing policy priorities, stakeholder needs, and legislative developments.

98.4 Career Path and Growth Opportunities

The career path for policy analysts offers numerous opportunities for specialization and advancement:

- Entry-Level Positions: Policy Research Assistant, Junior Policy Analyst, or Legislative Aide, focusing on developing basic skills and gaining practical experience.

- Mid-Level Positions: Policy Analyst, Senior Policy Analyst, or Program Evaluator, taking on more complex research projects and providing strategic recommendations.

- Senior-Level Positions: Policy Advisor, Policy Director, or Chief Policy Analyst, overseeing policy analysis operations, managing teams, and influencing policy decisions at higher levels.

- Specialization Areas: Health Policy Analyst, Environmental Policy Analyst, Education Policy Analyst, or Economic Policy Analyst. Specializing in these areas allows policy analysts to focus on specific policy issues and enhance their expertise.

- Executive Roles: Director of Policy Research, Vice President of Policy, or Chief Policy Officer. These positions involve strategic planning, overseeing policy research operations, and ensuring the success of policy initiatives.

- Continued Education: Pursuing advanced certifications or degrees (e.g., PhD in Public Policy or Economics) can lead to higher roles and increased responsibilities.

98.5 Tips for Success

To excel as a policy analyst, consider the following strategies:

- Stay Updated: Continuously update your knowledge of policy issues, legislative developments, and research methodologies through continuing education and professional development courses.

- Develop Strong Analytical Skills: Enhance your ability to analyze data and interpret complex information to inform policy recommendations.

- Embrace Technology: Familiarize yourself with the latest data analysis tools and software to improve efficiency and accuracy in research.

- Focus on Communication: Develop strong communication skills to present findings and recommendations effectively to stakeholders and decision-makers.

- Build a Professional Network: Establish connections with other policy analysts, industry experts, and government officials to gain insights and opportunities.

- Seek Specialization: Consider pursuing additional certifications or training in specialized policy areas to advance your career and enhance your expertise.

- Improve Problem-Solving Skills: Develop strong problem-solving techniques to address public policy issues and develop practical solutions.

- Engage with Stakeholders: Participate in public forums, community meetings, and stakeholder consultations to understand diverse perspectives and incorporate them into policy recommendations.

By following these tips, you can build a successful and fulfilling career as a policy analyst, making a significant impact on public policy and contributing to the development of effective and equitable solutions for societal issues.

99. Intelligence Analyst

99.1 Overview of the Role

Intelligence analysts gather, analyze, and interpret information to provide insights and recommendations on security threats, geopolitical developments, and other critical issues. They work for government agencies, military organizations, private security firms, and multinational corporations. Their tasks include data analysis, monitoring communication channels, reviewing intelligence reports, and preparing briefings to support decision-making processes.

99.2 Required Skills and Education

A successful intelligence analyst needs a combination of technical skills, analytical capabilities, and strong communication abilities. Key requirements include:

Technical Skills:

- Data Analysis: Proficiency in analyzing diverse data sources, including signals, human intelligence, and open-source information.

- Cybersecurity Knowledge: Understanding of cybersecurity principles and threats.

- Geopolitical Awareness: In-depth knowledge of international relations and global political landscapes.

- Report Writing: Competence in writing detailed, accurate, and insightful intelligence reports and briefs.

- Language Skills: Fluency in foreign languages can be an asset for analyzing non-English sources.

Educational Background:

- Education: A bachelor's degree in intelligence studies, international relations, political science, or a related field is typically required. Advanced degrees or specialized training in intelligence analysis or security studies are often preferred.

- Certifications: Certifications such as Certified Intelligence Analyst (CIA) or training from recognized intelligence institutions can enhance career prospects.

- Training: Practical experience through internships, military service, or entry-level intelligence roles is valuable for gaining practical skills.

Soft Skills:

- Analytical Thinking: Strong analytical skills to interpret complex data and provide actionable intelligence.

- Communication: Effective verbal and written communication skills to present findings and recommendations clearly.

- Attention to Detail: Precision in analyzing data and preparing reports to ensure accuracy and reliability.

- Problem-Solving: Ability to develop practical solutions to security and intelligence challenges.

- Teamwork: Strong collaboration skills to work effectively with colleagues and other stakeholders.

99.3 Typical Work Environment

Intelligence analysts work in a variety of settings, including government offices, military bases, corporate security departments, and intelligence agencies. The job involves a mix of desk work, data analysis, and attending briefings or meetings. Intelligence analysts typically work regular business hours, but may occasionally work evenings, weekends, or be on-call to respond to urgent situations. The role requires adaptability to handle changing security threats, intelligence priorities, and technological advancements.

99.4 Career Path and Growth Opportunities

The career path for intelligence analysts offers numerous opportunities for specialization and advancement:

- Entry-Level Positions: Intelligence Research Assistant, Junior Analyst, or Intelligence Officer, focusing on developing basic skills and gaining practical experience.

- Mid-Level Positions: Intelligence Analyst, Senior Intelligence Analyst, or Security Consultant, taking on more complex analysis projects and providing strategic recommendations.

- Senior-Level Positions: Intelligence Director, Chief Intelligence Officer, or National Security Advisor, overseeing intelligence operations, managing teams, and influencing high-level security decisions.

- Specialization Areas: Cyber Intelligence Analyst, Counterterrorism Analyst, Geospatial Intelligence Analyst, or Financial Intelligence Analyst. Specializing in these areas allows intelligence analysts to focus on specific threats and enhance their expertise.

- Executive Roles: Director of National Intelligence, Chief Security Officer, or Vice President of Intelligence Operations. These positions involve strategic planning, overseeing intelligence functions, and ensuring the success of intelligence initiatives.

- Continued Education: Pursuing advanced certifications or degrees (e.g., master's in intelligence studies or cybersecurity) can lead to higher roles and increased responsibilities.

99.5 Tips for Success

To excel as an intelligence analyst, consider the following strategies:

- Stay Updated: Continuously update your knowledge of security threats, geopolitical developments, and intelligence methodologies through continuing education and professional development courses.

- Develop Strong Analytical Skills: Enhance your ability to analyze diverse data sources and interpret complex information to provide actionable intelligence.

- Embrace Technology: Familiarize yourself with the latest intelligence analysis tools and software to improve efficiency and accuracy in your work.

- Focus on Communication: Develop strong communication skills to present findings and recommendations effectively to stakeholders and decision-makers.

- Build a Professional Network: Establish connections with other intelligence professionals, industry experts, and government officials to gain insights and opportunities.

- Seek Specialization: Consider pursuing additional certifications or training in specialized intelligence areas to advance your career and enhance your expertise.

- Improve Problem-Solving Skills: Develop strong problem-solving techniques to address security and intelligence challenges and develop practical solutions.

- Engage with Stakeholders: Participate in briefings, security forums, and inter-agency collaborations to understand diverse perspectives and incorporate them into your analysis.

By following these tips, you can build a successful and fulfilling career as an intelligence analyst, making a significant impact on national security and contributing to the safety and well-being of society.

100. Legislative Assistant

100.1 Overview of the Role

Legislative assistants support legislators by conducting research, drafting bills, and managing communication with constituents and stakeholders. They work in government offices, particularly within legislative bodies such as Congress or state legislatures. Their responsibilities include tracking legislation, preparing briefing materials, attending committee meetings, and liaising with other legislative staff and agencies.

100.2 Required Skills and Education

A successful legislative assistant requires a combination of research skills, legislative knowledge, and communication abilities. Key requirements include:

Technical Skills:

- Research Skills: Proficiency in conducting thorough research on legislative issues, policies, and constituent concerns.

- Legislative Knowledge: Understanding of legislative processes, procedures, and parliamentary rules.

- Drafting Skills: Ability to draft bills, amendments, and legislative summaries.

- Data Analysis: Skills in analyzing data to inform policy decisions and legislative strategies.

- Technology Proficiency: Familiarity with legislative tracking software and office productivity tools.

Educational Background:

- Education: A bachelor's degree in political science, public administration, law, or a related field is typically required. Advanced degrees in law (JD) or public policy (MPP) can be advantageous.

- Certifications: Legislative internships or certifications in legislative studies can enhance career prospects.

- Training: Practical experience through internships or entry-level positions in legislative offices is valuable for gaining practical skills.

Soft Skills:

- Analytical Thinking: Strong analytical skills to interpret complex information and develop legislative strategies.

- Communication: Effective verbal and written communication skills to draft legislation and communicate with constituents and stakeholders.

- Attention to Detail: Precision in drafting legislation, conducting research, and preparing reports to ensure accuracy and reliability.

- Organizational Skills: Ability to manage multiple tasks, prioritize effectively, and meet deadlines in a fast-paced environment.

- Collaboration: Strong teamwork skills to work effectively with legislators, colleagues, and other stakeholders.

100.3 Typical Work Environment

Legislative assistants work primarily in government offices, including the offices of legislators and legislative committees. The job involves a mix of desk work, attending legislative sessions, and meeting with constituents and stakeholders. Legislative assistants typically work long hours, especially when the legislature is in session, and may work evenings or weekends to meet deadlines and support legislative activities. The role requires adaptability to handle changing legislative priorities and respond to the needs of legislators and constituents.

100.4 Career Path and Growth Opportunities

The career path for legislative assistants offers numerous opportunities for advancement and specialization:

- Entry-Level Positions: Legislative Intern, Legislative Aide, or Junior Legislative Assistant, focusing on developing basic skills and gaining practical experience.

- Mid-Level Positions: Legislative Assistant, Senior Legislative Assistant, or Policy Advisor, taking on more complex legislative projects and providing strategic support to legislators.

- Senior-Level Positions: Chief of Staff, Legislative Director, or Senior Policy Advisor, overseeing legislative operations, managing teams, and influencing high-level legislative decisions.

- Specialization Areas: Health Policy Advisor, Environmental Policy Advisor, Education Policy Advisor, or Economic Policy

Advisor. Specializing in these areas allows legislative assistants to focus on specific policy issues and enhance their expertise.

- Executive Roles: Director of Legislative Affairs, Vice President of Government Relations, or Chief Legislative Officer. These positions involve strategic planning, overseeing legislative functions, and ensuring the success of legislative initiatives.

- Continued Education: Pursuing advanced degrees or certifications (e.g., JD, MPP) can lead to higher roles and increased responsibilities.

100.5 Tips for Success

To excel as a legislative assistant, consider the following strategies:

- Stay Informed: Continuously update your knowledge of legislative issues, policy developments, and parliamentary procedures through continuing education and professional development courses.

- Develop Strong Analytical Skills: Enhance your ability to analyze legislative issues and develop effective legislative strategies.

- Embrace Technology: Familiarize yourself with the latest legislative tracking tools and office productivity software to improve efficiency and accuracy in your work.

- Focus on Communication: Develop strong communication skills to draft legislation, write reports, and communicate effectively with constituents and stakeholders.

- Build a Professional Network: Establish connections with other legislative staff, policymakers, and industry experts to gain insights and opportunities.

- Seek Specialization: Consider pursuing additional certifications or training in specialized policy areas to advance your career and enhance your expertise.

- Improve Organizational Skills: Develop strong organizational techniques to manage multiple tasks, prioritize effectively, and meet tight deadlines.

- Engage with Constituents: Participate in community meetings, public forums, and stakeholder consultations to understand diverse perspectives and incorporate them into legislative strategies.

By following these tips, you can build a successful and fulfilling career as a legislative assistant, making a significant impact on the legislative process and contributing to the development of effective policies and laws.

Chapter 11: Emerging and Future Careers

101. Artificial Intelligence Specialist

101.1 Overview of the Role

Artificial Intelligence (AI) Specialists develop and implement AI solutions to solve complex problems. They design algorithms, create machine learning models, and integrate AI into various applications. AI Specialists work in a range of industries, including healthcare, finance, and technology, making their expertise highly valuable and versatile.

101.2 Required Skills and Education

A successful AI Specialist requires a blend of technical skills, advanced education, and strong problem-solving abilities. Key requirements include:

Technical Skills:

- Programming Proficiency: Expertise in languages like Python, R, Java, and C++.

- Machine Learning: In-depth knowledge of algorithms, neural networks, deep learning, and natural language processing.

- Data Analysis: Ability to manipulate and analyze large datasets.

- Mathematics: Strong understanding of linear algebra, calculus, probability, and statistics.

- Software Development: Familiarity with development tools and practices.

Educational Background:

- Education: A bachelor's degree in Computer Science, Engineering, Mathematics, or a related field is typically required. Advanced degrees (Master's or Ph.D.) in AI, Machine Learning, or a related discipline are highly beneficial.

- Certifications: Certifications like Google AI Certification or Microsoft Certified: Azure AI Engineer Associate can enhance career prospects.

- Training: Practical experience through internships or projects in AI is crucial for developing practical skills.

Soft Skills:

- Analytical Thinking: Ability to analyze complex problems and develop innovative AI solutions.

- Communication: Effective verbal and written communication skills to explain AI concepts and collaborate with teams.

- Attention to Detail: Precision in designing algorithms and models to ensure accuracy and reliability.

- Organizational Skills: Ability to manage multiple projects, prioritize effectively, and meet deadlines.

- Collaboration: Strong teamwork skills to work effectively with data scientists, engineers, and domain experts.

101.3 Typical Work Environment

AI Specialists typically work in tech companies, research institutions, corporate IT departments, startups, and consulting firms. The job involves a combination of desk work, coding, and collaborative meetings. AI Specialists often work long hours, especially when developing and testing new models. Remote work is increasingly common in this field.

101.4 Career Path and Growth Opportunities

The career path for AI Specialists offers numerous opportunities for advancement and specialization:

- Entry-Level Positions: AI Research Assistant, Machine Learning Engineer, or Data Scientist, focusing on developing foundational skills and gaining practical experience.

- Mid-Level Positions: AI Developer, AI Solutions Architect, or AI Consultant, handling more complex AI projects and providing strategic AI solutions.

- Senior-Level Positions: AI Project Manager, AI Research Scientist, or Chief AI Officer, overseeing AI initiatives, managing teams, and influencing high-level AI strategies.

- Specialization Areas: Natural Language Processing Specialist, Computer Vision Engineer, or Robotics AI Specialist. Specializing in these areas allows AI Specialists to focus on specific AI technologies and enhance their expertise.

- Executive Roles: Director of AI, Vice President of AI, or Chief AI Officer. These positions involve strategic planning, overseeing AI functions, and ensuring the success of AI initiatives.

- Continued Education: Pursuing advanced degrees or certifications can lead to higher roles and increased responsibilities.

101.5 Tips for Success

To excel as an AI Specialist, consider the following strategies:

- Stay Updated: Continuously update your knowledge of AI trends, research, and technologies through continuing education and professional development courses.

- Enhance Analytical Skills: Develop your ability to analyze complex problems and create innovative AI solutions.

- Leverage Technology: Familiarize yourself with the latest AI tools and software to improve efficiency and accuracy in your work.

- Improve Communication: Develop strong communication skills to explain AI concepts and collaborate effectively with teams.

- Network: Establish connections with other AI professionals, researchers, and industry experts to gain insights and opportunities.

- Specialize: Consider pursuing additional certifications or training in specialized AI areas to advance your career and enhance your expertise.

- Organize Effectively: Develop strong organizational techniques to manage multiple projects, prioritize tasks, and meet deadlines.

- Engage in Practical Projects: Participate in AI competitions, hackathons, and open-source projects to gain hands-on experience and build a strong portfolio.

By following these tips, you can build a successful and fulfilling career as an AI Specialist, making a significant impact on the advancement of artificial intelligence and its applications across various industries.

102. E-Commerce Entrepreneur

102.1 Overview of the Role

E-Commerce Entrepreneurs are business owners who sell products or services online. They identify market opportunities, develop business plans, create or source products, and manage online stores. Responsibilities include managing inventory, overseeing logistics, handling customer service, and executing marketing strategies to drive traffic and sales. E-Commerce Entrepreneurs often work across various platforms, such as their own websites, marketplaces like Amazon, or social media.

102.2 Required Skills and Education

A successful E-Commerce Entrepreneur needs a mix of business acumen, technical skills, and marketing knowledge. Key requirements include:

Technical Skills:

- Digital Marketing: Proficiency in SEO, social media marketing, email marketing, and content marketing.

- E-Commerce Platforms: Knowledge of platforms like Shopify, WooCommerce, Amazon, and eBay.

- Web Development: Basic understanding of web design, user experience (UX), and coding (HTML, CSS).

- Analytics: Skills in using tools like Google Analytics to track and analyze website performance and customer behavior.

- Payment Systems: Familiarity with online payment gateways and financial management software.

Educational Background:

- Education: A degree in Business Administration, Marketing, or a related field can be helpful, though not always necessary. Many successful E-Commerce Entrepreneurs are self-taught or have learned through practical experience.

- Certifications: Certifications in digital marketing, e-commerce, or related fields can be beneficial.

- Training: Practical experience through internships, previous business ventures, or online courses in e-commerce can be valuable.

Soft Skills:

- Entrepreneurial Mindset: Creativity, innovation, and a willingness to take risks.

- Communication: Strong verbal and written communication skills to engage with customers and partners.

- Customer Service: Ability to handle customer inquiries and issues efficiently and professionally.

- Problem-Solving: Strong problem-solving skills to navigate the challenges of running an online business.

- Adaptability: Flexibility to adapt to changing market trends and consumer behaviors.

- Time Management: Ability to manage multiple aspects of the business and prioritize tasks effectively.

102.3 Typical Work Environment

E-Commerce Entrepreneurs often work from home or small offices, with a significant amount of time spent on computers and mobile devices. Their work involves managing websites, coordinating with suppliers, handling customer service, and analyzing sales data. The role requires long hours, especially during peak sales periods or when launching new products. E-Commerce Entrepreneurs must be adaptable and prepared to handle various tasks, from technical issues to marketing strategies.

102.4 Career Path and Growth Opportunities

The career path for E-Commerce Entrepreneurs offers numerous opportunities for growth and diversification:

- Start-Up Phase: Launching an online store, building a brand, and gaining initial customers. This phase focuses on developing a viable business model and scaling operations.

- Growth Phase: Expanding product lines, increasing market reach, and optimizing operations. This phase may involve hiring additional staff or outsourcing tasks.

- Maturity Phase: Establishing a strong market presence, optimizing profit margins, and possibly expanding into new markets or verticals.

- Diversification: Adding multiple revenue streams, such as launching additional online stores, exploring international markets, or developing complementary products and services.

- Exit Opportunities: Selling the business to larger companies or investors, or transitioning into advisory or mentoring roles for other entrepreneurs.

102.5 Tips for Success

To excel as an E-Commerce Entrepreneur, consider the following strategies:

- Stay Informed: Keep up with the latest e-commerce trends, technologies, and consumer behaviors through continuing education and industry news.

- Focus on Customer Experience: Ensure your website is user-friendly, offer excellent customer service, and engage with your customers to build loyalty.

- Leverage Data: Use analytics to track performance, understand customer preferences, and make data-driven decisions.

- Optimize Marketing Efforts: Utilize various digital marketing strategies to drive traffic and increase conversions. Experiment with different tactics to find what works best for your business.

- Network: Build relationships with other entrepreneurs, suppliers, and industry experts to gain insights and support.

- Adapt Quickly: Be prepared to pivot your business model or strategies in response to market changes and new opportunities.

- Automate: Use tools and software to automate repetitive tasks, such as inventory management, order processing, and customer communication, to save time and increase efficiency.

- Maintain Work-Life Balance: Manage your time effectively to avoid burnout and ensure long-term sustainability of your business.

By following these tips, you can build a successful and sustainable e-commerce business, capitalizing on the growing trend of online shopping and making a significant impact in the digital marketplace.

Conclusion

103. Finding Your Perfect Career

103.1 Reflecting on Your Interests and Skills

Understanding Yourself:

The journey to finding your perfect career starts with self-reflection. Take time to understand your interests, strengths, and values. Consider what activities make you lose track of time, what subjects you naturally excel in, and what kind of work environment you thrive in. Here are a few steps to guide your reflection:

1. Self-Assessment Tools:

- Personality Tests: Utilize tools like the Myers-Briggs Type Indicator (MBTI) or the Big Five Personality Test to gain insights into your personality traits and how they align with various careers.

- Skill Inventories: Make a list of your skills, both hard (technical) and soft (interpersonal). Identify which skills you enjoy using the most.

- Interest Inventories: Use resources like the Strong Interest Inventory to match your interests with potential career paths.

2. Personal Reflection:

- Journal Your Thoughts: Spend time journaling about your experiences, achievements, and moments of fulfillment. What patterns emerge?

- Seek Feedback: Ask friends, family, and colleagues for their perspective on your strengths and potential career fits.

3. Identify Core Values:

- Prioritize What Matters: Reflect on what is most important to you in a job (e.g., work-life balance, salary, job security, creativity, helping others).

- Align Values with Careers: Ensure that potential career choices align with your core values for long-term satisfaction.

103.2 Exploring Different Career Paths

Research and Exploration:

Once you have a clear understanding of your interests and skills, the next step is to explore different career paths. This involves researching various industries, roles, and the day-to-day responsibilities they entail.

1. Industry Research:

- Read Industry Reports: Access reports from reputable sources like the Bureau of Labor Statistics or industry-specific publications to understand job outlooks, growth trends, and salary ranges.

- Join Professional Associations: Many industries have professional associations that offer resources, networking opportunities, and industry insights.

2. Informational Interviews:

- Connect with Professionals: Reach out to individuals working in roles you're interested in. Conduct informational interviews to learn about their career paths, job responsibilities, and industry challenges.

- Prepare Questions: Ask about their daily tasks, career progression, required skills, and any advice they have for someone entering the field.

3. Job Shadowing:

- Observe Firsthand: Spend a day or more shadowing professionals in your field of interest to gain firsthand experience and a realistic understanding of the job.

4. Online Resources:

- Career Websites: Utilize websites like LinkedIn, Glassdoor, and Indeed to research job descriptions, company reviews, and career advice.

- Educational Platforms: Explore online courses, webinars, and workshops related to your areas of interest on platforms like Coursera, Udemy, and LinkedIn Learning.

103.3 Making Informed Career Decisions

Decision-Making Process:

Armed with self-knowledge and industry research, it's time to make informed career decisions. This step involves evaluating your options, considering practical factors, and planning your next steps.

1. Evaluate Options:

   - Create a Pros and Cons List: For each potential career path, list the pros and cons based on your research and personal preferences.

   - Consider Long-Term Goals: Think about where you want to be in 5, 10, and 20 years. Which career paths align with your long-term aspirations?

2. Practical Considerations:

   - Educational Requirements: Assess the education and training needed for each career. Determine if you are willing and able to meet these requirements.

   - Financial Implications: Consider the financial aspects, including potential student debt, starting salaries, and future earning potential.

3. Seek Guidance:

   - Mentorship: Find a mentor in your chosen field who can provide guidance, support, and insight as you navigate your career path.

   - Career Counseling: Utilize career counseling services available through educational institutions, professional associations, or private career coaches.

4. Plan Your Steps:

   - Set SMART Goals: Define Specific, Measurable, Achievable, Relevant, and Time-bound goals to guide your career journey.

- Create an Action Plan: Develop a detailed action plan outlining the steps you need to take, from further education to gaining relevant experience.

103.4 Embracing Lifelong Learning and Growth

Continuous Development:

In today's rapidly evolving job market, embracing lifelong learning and growth is crucial for career success. Commit to continuous improvement and adaptability to stay relevant and fulfilled in your career.

1. Ongoing Education:

- Formal Education: Consider pursuing advanced degrees, certifications, or professional development courses to enhance your knowledge and skills.

- Informal Learning: Engage in self-directed learning through books, online courses, podcasts, and industry publications.

2. Skill Enhancement:

- Stay Updated: Keep up with industry trends, technological advancements, and new methodologies relevant to your field.

- Develop New Skills: Identify emerging skills in your industry and proactively work on acquiring them through training and practice.

3. Networking and Professional Development:

 - Expand Your Network: Attend industry conferences, workshops, and networking events to connect with professionals and stay informed about opportunities.

 - Join Professional Organizations: Participate in professional organizations to gain access to resources, mentorship, and career development programs.

4. Adaptability and Resilience:

 - Embrace Change: Be open to change and willing to pivot when necessary. The ability to adapt to new situations and challenges is a valuable asset.

 - Build Resilience: Develop resilience by maintaining a positive attitude, managing stress effectively, and learning from setbacks.

Conclusion

Finding your perfect career is a journey that requires self-reflection, exploration, informed decision-making, and a commitment to lifelong learning. By following these steps, you can navigate the complex landscape of job opportunities and build a fulfilling and successful career that aligns with your passions and strengths. Remember, the path to career satisfaction is not always linear, but with dedication and a proactive approach, you can achieve your professional goals and continue to grow and thrive in your chosen field.

Resources

104. Essential Resources for Career Development

104.1 Recommended Books and Guides

Building a Strong Foundation:

Books and guides can provide valuable insights, strategies, and inspiration for career development. Here are some essential reads to help you navigate various stages of your career journey:

1. Career Planning and Exploration:

 - What Color is Your Parachute? by Richard N. Bolles: A classic guide offering practical advice on job searching, career planning, and self-discovery.

 - Designing Your Life by Bill Burnett and Dave Evans: This book applies design thinking principles to career and life planning, encouraging creativity and flexibility.

2. Skill Development and Professional Growth:

 - Atomic Habits by James Clear: Learn how to build good habits and break bad ones to improve your personal and professional life.

 - The 7 Habits of Highly Effective People by Stephen R. Covey: A timeless guide to personal and professional effectiveness, focusing on key habits for success.

3. Networking and Building Relationships:

- Never Eat Alone by Keith Ferrazzi: A comprehensive guide on networking and building meaningful professional relationships.

- The Art of Networking by Dave Delaney: Practical tips and strategies for effective networking in various settings.

4. Job Search and Interviewing:

- The Job Search Solution by Tony Beshara: Step-by-step advice on finding and securing a job, from resume writing to interviewing.

- Cracking the Coding Interview by Gayle Laakmann McDowell: A must-read for aspiring software engineers, providing insights into technical interviews.

5. Leadership and Management:

- Leaders Eat Last by Simon Sinek: A guide to building strong leadership skills and fostering a positive work environment.

- The Lean Startup by Eric Ries: Essential reading for aspiring entrepreneurs, focusing on innovative and efficient business practices.

104.2 Online Courses and Certifications

Expanding Your Knowledge:

Online courses and certifications are excellent ways to acquire new skills, enhance your knowledge, and stay competitive in the job market. Here are some top platforms and courses:

1. General Learning Platforms:

- Coursera: Offers a wide range of courses and specializations from top universities and companies. Popular courses include Introduction to Data Science and Project Management Principles.

- edX: Provides access to courses from universities like MIT and Harvard. Consider MicroMasters programs for in-depth learning.

- Udemy: Features a vast selection of courses on various topics, from technical skills to personal development. Look for Python for Everybody and The Complete Digital Marketing Course.

2. Technical and IT Skills:

- LinkedIn Learning: Offers courses on software development, IT infrastructure, and data science. Recommended courses include Learning Python and AWS Certified Solutions Architect.

- Pluralsight: Focuses on technology and creative skills, with courses like CompTIA Security+ and Machine Learning for Developers.

3. Professional Certifications:

- Project Management Institute (PMI): Provides certifications like Project Management Professional (PMP) and Certified Associate in Project Management (CAPM).

- Scrum.org: Offers certifications for Scrum practices, including Professional Scrum Master (PSM) and Professional Scrum Product Owner (PSPO).

4. Industry-Specific Training:

- HubSpot Academy: Ideal for marketing professionals, offering certifications in Inbound Marketing and Content Marketing.

- Cisco Networking Academy: Provides networking and IT courses, including CCNA and Cybersecurity.

104.3 Professional Associations and Networks

Building Connections:

Joining professional associations and networks can significantly enhance your career development by providing access to resources, networking opportunities, and industry-specific insights.

1. General Professional Associations:

- American Management Association (AMA): Offers professional development, leadership training, and networking opportunities.

- National Association for the Advancement of Colored People (NAACP): Provides resources and advocacy for career advancement, especially for minorities.

2. Industry-Specific Associations:

- American Marketing Association (AMA): Offers marketing resources, certification programs, and networking events for marketing professionals.

- Society for Human Resource Management (SHRM): Provides HR certifications, professional development resources, and networking opportunities for HR professionals.

3. Networking Groups:

- LinkedIn Groups: Join relevant groups in your industry to connect with professionals, participate in discussions, and stay updated on industry trends.

- Meetup: Find local groups and events related to your field to expand your network and meet like-minded professionals.

4. Mentorship Programs:

- Score: Provides free business mentoring and educational workshops for entrepreneurs and small business owners.

- MentorNet: Connects students and early-career professionals with mentors in STEM fields.

104.4 Job Search Websites and Tools

Navigating the Job Market:

Job search websites and tools are crucial for finding job opportunities, researching companies, and preparing for interviews. Here are some essential resources:

1. Job Search Engines:

- Indeed: One of the largest job search engines, aggregating listings from various sources and offering company reviews and salary information.

- LinkedIn Jobs: Utilize LinkedIn's job search feature to find opportunities, apply directly, and leverage your professional network.

2. Company Research Tools:

- Glassdoor: Provides company reviews, salary reports, and interview insights from current and former employees.

- Vault: Offers in-depth company profiles, industry guides, and career advice.

3. Resume and Cover Letter Tools:

- Canva: Create professional-looking resumes and cover letters using customizable templates and design tools.

- Zety: Offers resume-building tools and cover letter templates with guidance on content and formatting.

4. Interview Preparation:

- Big Interview: An interview training platform offering practice questions, mock interviews, and expert advice.

- Interviewing.io: Provides mock technical interviews with engineers from top companies and feedback to improve your performance.

Conclusion

Utilizing the right resources is essential for effective career development. From books and guides to online courses, professional associations, and job search tools, the resources outlined in this section will help you gain knowledge, build skills, and connect with professionals in your field. By leveraging these resources, you can navigate your career journey with confidence and achieve your professional goals.

Appendices

105. Glossary of Career Terms

A comprehensive glossary can be an invaluable resource for readers, helping them to understand key terms, industry jargon, and technical concepts related to careers and job searching. This section will provide clear and concise definitions to ensure readers have a solid grasp of important terminology.

105.1 Definitions of Key Terms A to Z

Understanding key career-related terms is essential for navigating the job market effectively. Here is an A to Z glossary of fundamental career terms:

A

- Apprenticeship: A system of training a new generation of practitioners in a trade or profession through on-the-job training and often accompanying study.

- Assessment Center: A process involving multiple evaluation techniques (such as simulations, exercises, and tests) used to assess candidates' competencies and suitability for a specific job.

B

- Benchmarking: The process of comparing one's business processes and performance metrics to industry bests or best practices from other industries.

- Benefits: Non-wage compensation provided to employees in addition to their normal wages or salaries (e.g., health insurance, retirement plans, and paid time off).

C

- Career Development: The lifelong process of managing learning, work, leisure, and transitions in order to move toward a personally determined and evolving preferred future.

- Compensation: The total payment and benefits that an employee receives for their work, including salary, bonuses, and benefits.

D

- Downsizing: The process of reducing the number of employees within a company, typically to cut costs or streamline operations.

- Diversity: The inclusion of different types of people (such as people of different races, cultures, genders, etc.) in a group or organization.

E

- Entrepreneur: An individual who creates and operates a new business, taking on financial risks in the hope of profit.

- Equity: Ownership interest in a company, often in the form of stock or shares.

F

- Freelancing: Working on a self-employed basis, often for multiple clients, rather than being employed by a single organization.

- Full-Time Employment: A form of employment where an employee works a minimum number of hours defined as full-time by their employer, typically around 40 hours per week.

G

- Gig Economy: A labor market characterized by the prevalence of short-term contracts or freelance work as opposed to permanent jobs.

- Glass Ceiling: An unofficial barrier to advancement in a profession, especially affecting women and members of minorities.

H

- Human Resources (HR): The department within a business responsible for recruiting, managing, and directing employees.

- Hybrid Work: A flexible working model where employees split their time between working remotely and working in the office.

I

- Internship: A period of work experience offered by an organization for a limited period of time, often used by students or recent graduates to gain practical experience.

- Innovation: The process of translating an idea or invention into a good or service that creates value or for which customers will pay.

J

- Job Analysis: The process of studying a job to determine its tasks, responsibilities, and the skills and qualifications needed to perform it.

- Job Satisfaction: The extent to which an employee feels fulfilled and content with their job.

K

- Key Performance Indicator (KPI): A measurable value that demonstrates how effectively an organization is achieving key business objectives.

- Knowledge Management: The process of capturing, distributing, and effectively using knowledge within an organization.

L

- Leadership: The action of leading a group of people or an organization, involving the ability to influence and guide individuals or teams.

- Lateral Move: A job change that involves a move to a position with similar responsibilities and salary within the same organization.

M

- Mentorship: A professional relationship in which an experienced person (mentor) provides guidance, support, and advice to a less experienced person (mentee).

- Mobility: The ability of employees to move within an organization or between jobs and locations.

N

- Networking: The process of interacting with others to exchange information and develop professional or social contacts.

- Non-Disclosure Agreement (NDA): A legal contract between two or more parties that outlines confidential material, knowledge, or information that the parties wish to share with one another for certain purposes, but wish to restrict access to or by third parties.

O

- Onboarding: The process of integrating a new employee into an organization and its culture, and providing them with the tools and information they need to become productive members of the team.

- Outsourcing: The business practice of hiring a third party to perform services or create goods that were traditionally performed in-house by the company's own employees.

P

- Performance Appraisal: The regular review of an employee's job performance and overall contribution to a company.

- Professional Development: The process of improving and increasing capabilities through access to education and training opportunities in the workplace, through outside organizations, or through watching others perform the job.

Q

- Quality Assurance (QA): The maintenance of a desired level of quality in a service or product, especially by means of attention to every stage of the process of delivery or production.

- Quantitative Analysis: The process of using mathematical and statistical modeling, measurement, and research to understand behavior.

R

- Recruitment: The process of finding and hiring the best-qualified candidate for a job opening, in a timely and cost-effective manner.

- Retention: The ability of an organization to keep its employees and reduce turnover.

S

- Succession Planning: The process of identifying and developing new leaders who can replace old leaders when they leave, retire, or die.

- Sustainability: The ability to maintain or improve certain processes or states indefinitely, often relating to environmental, social, and economic dimensions.

T

- Talent Management: The strategy of attracting, developing, retaining, and utilizing people with the required skills and aptitudes to meet current and future business needs.

- Telecommuting: The practice of working from a remote location outside of the traditional office setting, often from home, using the internet, email, and telephone.

U

- Upskilling: The process of teaching employees new skills to enhance their current job performance or prepare them for a new role within the organization.

- Unemployment Rate: The percentage of the total labor force that is unemployed but actively seeking employment and willing to work.

V

- Virtual Team: A group of individuals who work together from different geographic locations and rely on communication technology such as email, instant messaging, and video or voice conferencing services.

- Vocational Training: Education that prepares individuals for specific trades, crafts, and careers at various levels, focusing on practical applications of skills learned.

W

- Work-Life Balance: The equilibrium between personal life and career work, ensuring adequate time for both professional and personal activities.

- Workforce Diversity: The inclusion of a variety of individuals from different backgrounds and demographics in the workplace.

X

- X-Factor: An exceptional talent or quality that makes someone stand out from the crowd, often leading to success in their career.

- Xenophobia: A fear or hatred of that which is perceived to be foreign or strange, which can affect workplace dynamics and inclusivity.

Y

- Yield Ratio: A measure of the effectiveness of a recruitment process, calculated by dividing the number of hires by the number of applicants.

- Yellow-Dog Contract: An agreement between an employer and an employee in which the employee agrees, as a condition of employment, not to join or remain a member of a labor union.

Z

- Zero-Based Budgeting (ZBB): A budgeting method where all expenses must be justified for each new period, starting from a "zero base" rather than using previous budgets as a reference.

- Zoom Fatigue: The feeling of tiredness, worry, or burnout associated with overuse of virtual platforms for communication.

Conclusion

This glossary of career terms A to Z provides a comprehensive reference for readers to understand key concepts and terminology essential for navigating their career paths. Familiarity with these terms will enhance readers' knowledge, improve their communication skills, and equip them with the language needed to succeed in professional environments.

105.2 Common Industry Jargon A to Z

Understanding industry-specific jargon is crucial for effective communication and success in any field. Here is an A to Z glossary of common industry jargon across various industries:

A

- Agile (Technology): A methodology for software development that emphasizes iterative progress, collaboration, and flexibility.

- AR (Marketing): Stands for "Augmented Reality," which is the technology that superimposes digital content onto the real world through devices like smartphones or AR glasses.

B

- Bandwidth (IT): The amount of data that can be transmitted over an internet connection in a given amount of time.

- Burn Rate (Finance): The rate at which a company is spending its capital before it starts generating its own income.

C

- CAC (Marketing): Stands for "Customer Acquisition Cost," which is the cost associated with acquiring a new customer.

- Crowdsourcing (Business): Obtaining input or information from a large number of people, typically via the internet.

D

- Disruptive Innovation (Business): Innovations that significantly alter the way businesses or entire industries operate.

- DevOps (Technology): A set of practices that combines software development (Dev) and IT operations (Ops) to shorten the development lifecycle.

E

- EOD (Business): Stands for "End of Day," often used to set deadlines or expectations for tasks to be completed by the close of business hours.

- EPC (Energy): Stands for "Engineering, Procurement, and Construction," a common form of contracting arrangement in the construction industry.

F

- Freemium (Business): A business model that offers basic services for free while charging a premium for advanced features or services.

- FYI (Business): Stands for "For Your Information," used in communications to share information without requiring action.

G

- Gamification (Marketing): The application of game-design elements and game principles in non-game contexts to engage users.

- GDP (Economics): Stands for "Gross Domestic Product," which is the total value of goods produced and services provided in a country during one year.

H

- HRIS (Human Resources): Stands for "Human Resources Information System," a software solution for managing HR functions.

- Hackathon (Technology): An event where programmers and others involved in software development collaborate intensively on software projects.

I

- IPO (Finance): Stands for "Initial Public Offering," the process by which a private company offers shares to the public for the first time.

- IoT (Technology): Stands for "Internet of Things," which refers to the network of physical devices connected to the internet, collecting and sharing data.

J

- JIT (Manufacturing): Stands for "Just-In-Time," an inventory management system that aims to increase efficiency and decrease waste by receiving goods only as they are needed.

- Jobber (Retail): A merchant who buys in bulk from manufacturers and sells to retailers or other merchants.

K

- KPI (Business): Stands for "Key Performance Indicator," a measurable value that indicates how effectively a company is achieving its key business objectives.

- Kanban (Manufacturing/Project Management): A scheduling system for lean and just-in-time production.

L

- Lean (Manufacturing): A systematic method for waste minimization within a manufacturing system without sacrificing productivity.

- Liquidity (Finance): The availability of liquid assets to a market or company.

M

- MVP (Technology/Startups): Stands for "Minimum Viable Product," the most basic version of a product that can be released to start the learning process as quickly as possible.

- Market Penetration (Marketing): The extent to which a product is recognized and bought by customers in a particular market.

N

- NDA (Legal): Stands for "Non-Disclosure Agreement," a legally binding contract establishing a confidential relationship between parties.

- Net Promoter Score (NPS) (Marketing): A metric that measures the loyalty of customers to a company, based on their likelihood to recommend it.

O

- Outsourcing (Business): The practice of having certain job functions done outside a company instead of having an in-house department handle them.

- OEM (Manufacturing): Stands for "Original Equipment Manufacturer," a company whose goods are used as components in the products of another company.

P

- Pivot (Startups): A significant change in strategy to ensure the viability and growth of a startup.

- PMO (Project Management): Stands for "Project Management Office," a group or department within a business that defines and maintains standards for project management.

Q

- QC (Manufacturing): Stands for "Quality Control," the process of ensuring that products meet the required standards of quality.

- Quant (Finance): Short for "Quantitative Analyst," a professional who uses mathematical models to analyze financial and risk management problems.

R

- ROI (Finance/Marketing): Stands for "Return on Investment," a measure used to evaluate the efficiency of an investment.

- Run Rate (Finance): The financial performance of a company based on using current financial information as a predictor of future performance.

S

- SaaS (Technology): Stands for "Software as a Service," a software distribution model in which applications are hosted by a vendor or service provider and made available to customers over a network.

- SWOT Analysis (Business): A strategic planning technique used to identify Strengths, Weaknesses, Opportunities, and Threats.

T

- TCO (Finance): Stands for "Total Cost of Ownership," a financial estimate intended to help buyers and owners determine the direct and indirect costs of a product or system.

- Turnkey (Business): A product or service that is designed, supplied, built, or installed fully complete and ready to operate.

U

- UI (Technology): Stands for "User Interface," the space where interactions between humans and machines occur.

- USP (Marketing): Stands for "Unique Selling Proposition," the factor that differentiates a product from its competitors.

V

- Venture Capital (Finance): A type of private equity and a form of financing that investors provide to startup companies and small businesses that are believed to have long-term growth potential.

- Viral Marketing (Marketing): A strategy that encourages individuals to share a marketing message with others, creating the potential for exponential growth in the message's exposure and influence.

W

- Workflow (Business): The sequence of processes through which a piece of work passes from initiation to completion.

- Win-Win (Negotiation): A situation or outcome where all parties benefit or gain something of value.

X

- XML (Technology): Stands for "eXtensible Markup Language," a markup language that defines a set of rules for encoding documents in a format that is both human-readable and machine-readable.

- XP (Technology): Stands for "Extreme Programming," a software development methodology intended to improve software quality and responsiveness to changing customer requirements.

Y

- Yield (Finance): The income return on an investment, such as the interest or dividends received from holding a particular security.

- Year over Year (YoY) (Finance): A method of evaluating two or more measured events to compare the results at one period with those of a comparable period on an annualized basis.

Z

- Zero-Based Budgeting (Finance): A budgeting method where all expenses must be justified for each new period, starting from a "zero base" rather than using previous budgets as a reference.

- Zero Defects (Manufacturing): A philosophy that emphasizes the idea of doing things right the first time, with a focus on preventing defects in the manufacturing process.

Conclusion

This glossary of common industry jargon A to Z provides a comprehensive reference for readers to understand the specialized language used across various fields. Familiarity with these terms will enhance readers' professional communication, enable them to better navigate their industries, and contribute to their overall career success.

105.3 Technical Terms and Concepts A to Z

Understanding technical terms and concepts is essential for navigating various industries and professions. Here is an A to Z glossary of important technical terms and concepts:

A

- API (Application Programming Interface): A set of rules that allows different software entities to communicate with each other.

- Algorithm: A step-by-step procedure for solving a problem or accomplishing a task, often used in computer programming.

B

- Big Data: Large and complex data sets that traditional data-processing software cannot manage effectively, often requiring advanced analytics.

- Blockchain: A decentralized digital ledger that records transactions across many computers in a way that ensures security and transparency.

C

- Cloud Computing: The delivery of computing services (including storage, processing, and software) over the internet ("the cloud").

- Cryptography: The practice of securing information by transforming it into a format that is unreadable to unauthorized users.

D

- Database: An organized collection of data, generally stored and accessed electronically from a computer system.

- Data Mining: The process of discovering patterns and knowledge from large amounts of data, often using machine learning and statistical methods.

E

- Encryption: The process of converting information or data into a code to prevent unauthorized access.

- Ethernet: A family of networking technologies used for local area networks (LANs), enabling devices to communicate over a common medium.

F

- Firewall: A network security device that monitors and filters incoming and outgoing network traffic based on predetermined security rules.

- Firmware: A specific class of computer software that provides low-level control for a device's specific hardware.

G

- GIS (Geographic Information System): A system designed to capture, store, manipulate, analyze, manage, and present spatial or geographic data.

- GUI (Graphical User Interface): A type of user interface that allows users to interact with electronic devices using graphical icons and visual indicators.

H

- HTML (HyperText Markup Language): The standard language for creating web pages and web applications.

- Hypervisor: A software layer that enables the virtualization of hardware, allowing multiple operating systems to run on a single physical machine.

I

- IoT (Internet of Things): A network of physical devices connected to the internet, collecting and sharing data.

- IP Address (Internet Protocol Address): A numerical label assigned to each device connected to a computer network that uses the Internet Protocol for communication.

J

- Java: A high-level programming language used to create applications for web, mobile, and desktop platforms.

- JSON (JavaScript Object Notation): A lightweight data-interchange format that is easy for humans to read and write, and easy for machines to parse and generate.

K

- Kernel: The core part of an operating system, managing system resources and communication between hardware and software.

- Key Pair: A pair of cryptographic keys used in public key encryption and digital signatures, consisting of a public key and a private key.

L

- Latency: The delay before a transfer of data begins following an instruction for its transfer.

- Load Balancer: A device or software that distributes network or application traffic across multiple servers to ensure no single server becomes overwhelmed.

M

- Machine Learning: A branch of artificial intelligence that involves the development of algorithms that allow computers to learn from and make predictions based on data.

- Microservices: An architectural style that structures an application as a collection of small, loosely coupled services, each implementing a business capability.

N

- Nanotechnology: The science, engineering, and application of materials and devices with structures on the nanometer scale (one billionth of a meter).

- Neural Network: A series of algorithms that attempt to recognize underlying relationships in a set of data through a process that mimics the way the human brain operates.

O

- Open Source: Software for which the original source code is made freely available and may be redistributed and modified.

- Operating System (OS): System software that manages computer hardware, software resources, and provides common services for computer programs.

P

- Protocol: A set of rules or procedures for transmitting data between electronic devices, such as computers.

- Python: A high-level programming language known for its readability and versatility, often used for web development, data analysis, and automation.

Q

- Quantum Computing: A type of computing that leverages the principles of quantum mechanics to perform calculations much faster than traditional computers.

- Query: A request for data or information from a database, usually written in a query language like SQL.

R

- RAID (Redundant Array of Independent Disks): A data storage virtualization technology that combines multiple physical disk drive components into one or more logical units for redundancy and performance improvement.

- RAM (Random Access Memory): A type of computer memory that can be accessed randomly, used for storing working data and machine code.

S

- SEO (Search Engine Optimization): The process of optimizing web content to rank higher in search engine results.

- SSL (Secure Sockets Layer): A standard security technology for establishing an encrypted link between a server and a client.

T

- TCP/IP (Transmission Control Protocol/Internet Protocol): The suite of communication protocols used to interconnect network devices on the internet.

- Tokenization: The process of converting sensitive data into non-sensitive tokens that can be used in a database or internal system without bringing it into scope.

U

- URL (Uniform Resource Locator): The address of a web page on the internet.

- UX (User Experience): The overall experience of a person using a product, especially in terms of how easy or pleasing it is to use.

V

- Virtualization: The creation of a virtual version of something, such as a server, a storage device, or network resources.

- VPN (Virtual Private Network): A service that allows users to connect to the internet via a server run by a VPN provider, ensuring online privacy and security.

W

- WAN (Wide Area Network): A telecommunications network that extends over a large geographic area for the primary purpose of computer networking.

- Webhook: A method of augmenting or altering the behavior of a web page or web application with custom callbacks.

X

- XaaS (Anything as a Service): A collective term referring to the delivery of anything as a service, often via cloud computing, encompassing many products, tools, and technologies.

- XAML (eXtensible Application Markup Language): A declarative XML-based language used to initialize structured values and objects in Windows applications.

Y

- Yottabyte: A unit of data equal to one septillion (10^{24}) bytes, or 1,000 zettabytes.

- Yield Management: A variable pricing strategy based on understanding, anticipating, and influencing consumer behavior to maximize revenue or profits from a fixed, perishable resource.

Z

- Zero-Day Exploit: A cyber attack that occurs on the same day a weakness is discovered in software, before the developer has time to create a patch to fix the vulnerability.

- Zigbee: A specification for a suite of high-level communication protocols using low-power digital radios for personal area networks.

Conclusion

This glossary of technical terms and concepts A to Z provides readers with a comprehensive reference to understand the specialized language used across various technical fields. Familiarity with these terms will enhance readers' technical literacy, improve their communication skills, and equip them with the knowledge needed to succeed in their respective industries.

About the Author

HowExpert publishes quick 'how to' guides on all topics from A to Z by everyday experts. Visit HowExpert.com to learn more.

About the Publisher

Byungjoon "BJ" Min / 민병준 is a Korean American author, publisher, entrepreneur, and founder of HowExpert. He started off as a once broke convenience store clerk to eventually becoming a fulltime internet marketer and finding his niche in publishing. The mission of HowExpert is to discover, empower, and maximize everyday people's talents to ultimately make a positive impact in the world for all topics from A to Z. Visit BJMin.com and HowExpert.com to learn more. John 14:6

Recommended Resources

- HowExpert.com – How To Guides on All Topics from A to Z by Everyday Experts.
- HowExpert.com/free – Free HowExpert Email Newsletter.
- HowExpert.com/books – HowExpert Books
- HowExpert.com/courses – HowExpert Courses
- HowExpert.com/clothing – HowExpert Clothing
- HowExpert.com/membership – HowExpert Membership Site
- HowExpert.com/affiliates – HowExpert Affiliate Program
- HowExpert.com/jobs – HowExpert Jobs
- HowExpert.com/writers – Write About Your #1 Passion/Knowledge/Expertise & Become a HowExpert Author.
- HowExpert.com/resources – Additional HowExpert Recommended Resources
- YouTube.com/HowExpert – Subscribe to HowExpert YouTube.
- Instagram.com/HowExpert – Follow HowExpert on Instagram.
- Facebook.com/HowExpert – Follow HowExpert on Facebook.
- TikTok.com/@HowExpert – Follow HowExpert on TikTok.

Printed in Great Britain
by Amazon

61130314R00302